T0374878

THE

PUBLICATIONS

OF THE

SURTEES SOCIETY

VOL. CC

THE

PUBLICATIONS

OF THE

SURTEES SOCIETY

ESTABLISHED IN THE YEAR
M.DCCC.XXXIV

VOL. CC
FOR THE YEAR M.CM.LXXXIX

At a COUNCIL MEETING of the SURTEES SOCIETY, held on 3 June 1991, it was ORDERED —

"That the edition of James Raine the elder's memoir of his childhood and other family materials prepared by his great-grand-daughter, Mrs Angela Marsden, should be printed in the year of the bicentenary of his birth, as the volume of the Society's publications for 1989."

A.J.Piper, *Secretary*
The Prior's Kitchen
The College
Durham

A RAINE MISCELLANY

EDITED
BY

ANGELA MARSDEN

TYPESET FROM DISC BY
ROGER BOOTH ASSOCIATES, NEWCASTLE UPON TYNE

PRINTED FOR THE SOCIETY BY
ATHENÆUM PRESS LIMITED, NEWCASTLE UPON TYNE
1991

CONTENTS

ACKNOWLEDGEMENTS

I wish to thank Durham County Library for permission to print the letters of James Raine to Edward Blore, and the York City Archives for permission to print the memoir by Margaret Hunt and the letters of Thomas Peacock.

I should also like to thank the staff of the Ripon Branch of North Yorkshire County Library for their unfailing help, and many others who have patiently answered my queries. I am indebted to Mr A. J. Piper for general guidance, as well as additional information for footnotes.

I remember with gratitude the support and encouragement of my late husband.

The memoir of James Raine, my great-grandfather, was passed down to me by my father, Angelo Raine of York, rector of All Saints' Pavement, honorary archivist to the City for many years, and author of *Mediaeval York*. This volume is dedicated to his memory.

EDITING

The memoir by James Raine which forms part 1 of this volume has required extensive editing. All the original material has been used but its order has been considerably rearranged. Page numbers in square brackets show where the text is to be found in the original manuscript. This practice is also adopted in part 3 of the volume. From time to time in the memoir Raine apologised for wandering from his subject. The editing has rendered such remarks unnecessary and they have been omitted.

On his death, Raine's memoir passed to his son James who added occasional notes, usually on facing pages which had been left blank. These have been placed in Addita to be found at the end of the Memoir, together with material by Raine senior. A very few almost illegible scribbles in blue ink were added to his grandfather's memoir by Angelo Raine in extreme old age; these have not been included.

Throughout the volume, additions by the editor have been placed in square brackets.

Principal Sources used for Notes.

DNB: *Dictionary of National Biography*

George, Dorothy, *England in Transition*, (1931)

Hughes, H. D., *A History of Durham Cathedral Library*, (1925)

Neuberg, Victor E., *Popular Education in Eighteenth Century England*, (1971)

Ornsby, George, *Sketches of Durham*, (1846)

Sharp, Sir Cuthbert, *The History of Hartlepool*, (1816)

Surtees, R., *The History and Antiquities of the County Palatine of Durham*, 4 vols, (1816–40)

Taylor, George, *A Memoir of Robert Surtees*, ed. J. Raine, (Surtees Soc. 24, 1852)

Thompson, A. Hamilton, *The Surtees Society, 1834–1934*, (Surtees Soc. 150, 1939)

Venn, J. and A., *Alumni Cantabrigienses*, 6 vols, (1922–1954)

Young, Arthur, *Six Months Tour through the North of England*, ii (1771)

Introduction

James Raine was born in 1791 at Ovington on Tees. His father, also James, was blacksmith there, as was his grandfather, "good auld Edmund Raine". Before her marriage, his mother Anne had been a visiting dressmaker. As a child she lived at Staindrop where she was educated in basic subjects including music by a Mr Facer who also taught at Raby Castle. Her father William Moore was an estate labourer, then a toll-gate-keeper and eventually a small farmer. He thought her much too good for the Ovington blacksmith.

Raine had aunts and uncles in the village; great aunts lived in their rooms at the Old Hall to which they had retired on becoming widows. His grandmother was living there when he was born. Some of his earliest memories are of her sitting at her spinning-wheel as she taught him her favourite hymns and told him stories of fairies, giants and local superstitions.

Ovington was a self-contained community. It boasted its own carpenter, butcher, tailor, stonemason and blacksmith. Local farmers rode to fairs and markets in Darlington and Richmond but mostly to Barnard Castle, where four fairs were held every year. Their wives carried butter, cheese and eggs to the weekly market. The men and women labouring in the fields were too far from the growing industrial towns of the West Riding to be aware of the higher wages tempting others from the land.

There was a dark side to life in the village. Poverty, sickness and, at times, near starvation threatened many of the inhabitants, but the local people looked after their own and the better-off farmers and the squire at Wycliffe were generous. On the other hand there was much rustic jollity. May Day and harvest were celebrated, often riotously; singing, card-playing and story-telling filled the long winter nights. Little had changed for centuries. Raine grew up in the midst of all this and knew nothing else until he was thirteen or fourteen. Fortunately, he was even then an eager listener and an acute observer.

After a succession of village schools he moved on to Kirby Hill free grammar school in 1804 as a weekly boarder. At this point his memoir ends. In 1809 he went to Richmond School. The Rev. James Tate was then Master, and he recognised in Raine a boy of similar background to himself. He set out to give him a grounding in the classics and "every attention". Raine found him "most learned, kind-hearted and amiable". While at Richmond other foundations were laid. He devoted his leisure to "the ardent pursuit of such information, architectural and historical, as might throw light on those relics of antiquity by which we were surrounded. We knew every church, every monumental inscription, every old coat of arms, within a ten mile circuit; and if our notions of architecture and its various features and periods were crude and fanciful, it was because there was at that day no correct guide in such matters for men or schoolboys." Raine stayed at Richmond School as an usher until Tate recommended him for the appointment as second master of Durham School which he took up in 1812 at the age of 21. He remained there until 1827. The Master, John Carr, was only five years his senior. A gentle academic, he was greatly loved by all who knew him and a good friend to Raine.

In that same year Raine met Robert Surtees of Mainsforth who had already heard of the young man's interests and enthusiasm. They immediately began exchanging information concerning their antiquarian research and an invitation to Mainsforth for Christmas sealed the friendship. Raine became a frequent visitor and often accompanied Surtees on his expeditions in search of material for his *History and Antiquities of the County Palatine of Durham*, the first volume of which was published in 1816.

In the following years Raine was to spend many weekends and part of his school holidays at Mainsforth, meeting other antiquaries and building on his already extensive knowledge. It was there he met Edward Blore in 1813. A young architect and illustrator living in London, Blore often stayed at Mainsforth while working on illustrations for Surtees' *History*. Within a year of their meeting, a correspondence had begun from which some of Raine's letters survive. These form the second part of this volume, 34 letters spanning the period from 1814-1824. They provide an account of Raine's increasingly crowded life, of local affairs and cathedral gossip. They also show in style and content the way in which he himself was developing and maturing. During that time he was ordained deacon in 1814 and priest in 1818, having become librarian to the Dean and Chapter of Durham in 1816. In 1822 he became rector of Meldon. He still accompanied Surtees on his expeditions including one to Scotland in 1819 when he met Walter Scott at Abbotsford. But, whenever he could, he returned home to Ovington.

Following his appointment as librarian he undertook too much work for others and greatly overtaxed his strength. This resulted in Whitaker complaining to Tate of Raine not answering letters concerning the final stages of his *History of Richmondshire*, while pressure of work forced him to abandon his offer to John Hodgson to help gather material for his *History of Northumberland*. He was mortified about this, "an offer which certainly could not have been made to the extent in which it had been understood. At that period, and for many years afterwards, the only portion of my time at my disposal for private purposes amounted to little more than twelve hours per week exclusive of Sunday."

In 1825 Raine was appointed Principal Surrogate in the Consistory Court and Diocese of Durham and in November of the same year a degree of M.A. was conferred on him by the Archbishop of Canterbury at the request of Bishop Barrington. He was now immersed in his own work, a massive piece of research into the life of St Cuthbert based on MSS and printed books at Ripon and York and culminating with his eyewitness account of the opening of St Cuthbert's tomb in Durham cathedral in 1827. Inevitably he came across a mass of "highly poetical fiction", much of which he recorded in lengthy and often entertaining footnotes. He gave his sources in detail and did his best to disentangle fact from folklore but some controversy arose when *St Cuthbert* was published in 1828. It was, however, hailed as a major work of scholarship and established his reputation as historian and antiquary.

1828 was a memorable year for Raine. He married Margaret Peacock, became the father of a daughter, Anne, and was installed as rector of the little church of St Mary in the South Bailey in Durham. In 1830 his only surviving son, James, was born and the first volume of his *History of North Durham* was published. Raine had been working on this for many years. Surtees had suggested it to supplement his own *History* and to cover various outlying districts such as Holy Island and Norhamshire which then formed part of the county of Durham.

In 1831, Margaret Raine was born and in 1834, Jane. It is from Margaret (later Hunt) that we have some idea of life in the Raine family between 1831 and 1840. Her memoir, like that of her father, was written in old age when she was living as a widow with her daughter, Violet, in London. This memoir forms the third part of this volume. Many months of her childhood were spent with her Peacock grandparents at Denton, old Thomas Peacock being a fearsome figure to a young child, and indeed to all his household. A rather different picture of him in the first years of his curacy at Denton forms the fourth part of this volume.

While in Durham the Raine children were largely confined to the nursery or garden in the charge of nursemaids and governesses. Their mother was often ill, their father always busy. He himself was very ill in 1832 when typhus fever raged through Durham. His old friend John Hodgson, then with the living of Hartburn near Meldon, wondered what on earth had become of him; visits between Durham and Mainsforth became less frequent. Surtees was depressed by bad weather, low rents and money matters generally. But he and Raine took an active interest in plans for the foundation of the new university at Durham, the Bill for which was given the royal assent in July 1832. They were involved in discussions concerning appointments but even these were attended by gloom and misfortune. They were deeply shocked by the death of John Carr who was appointed to the chair of mathematics in June 1833 only to die in the following October.

By the end of 1833 Surtees was far from well. It was said that one of his last pleasures was reading Raine's *Brief Account of Durham Cathedral* which had just been published: "a jewel of the first water" he wrote. The following January, a journey from Durham to Ferryhill on the outside of the coach in bitter weather was too much for him. He caught a bad cold, his condition deteriorated and he died on 11 February 1834. His sorrowing friend James Raine almost immediately set about the task of forming the Surtees Society. He was its first secretary and his work for it was to become the main preoccupation of his remaining years. He also agreed to finish the last volume of Surtees' *History* at the request of Mrs Surtees.

A detailed account of the founding of the Society is to be found in volume 150 together with a list of 152 volumes published up to 1938, each entry giving details of editor and content. Between 1835 and his death in 1858 Raine edited seventeen of the volumes published. In addition he shouldered most of the administrative duties involved in founding and running the Society. Small wonder that the Raine children saw little of their father.

In 1834 the Raines moved from the South Bailey to Crook Hall, their new home being described in some detail by Margaret Hunt in her memoir. The first letters and circulars sent out to prospective members of the Surtees Society were issued from Crook Hall. Raine was quite certain in his own mind what the objects of the Society should be and what Surtees would have wished. As his friend and admirer for over twenty years he felt greatly indebted to him for his help and encouragement generally and especially when he was first finding his feet in Durham. Nobody questioned the need for a suitable memorial, but the form which it should take was controversial. Some replied to the first circular saying that perhaps something in brass or marble with suitable inscription or a scholarship at Oxford founded in his name might be more acceptable. But, "the publication of inedited manuscripts, illustrative of the intellectual, the moral, the religious, and the social conditions" of northern England won the day. A satisfactory number of subscriptions was received and by the first annual meeting in 1835, the Society was in a self-congratulatory mood. Dr Fenwick proposed that "the thanks of the meeting be given to the Reverend James Raine for his services, the meeting being sensible that to his zeal, to his judgment and knowledge and to his extensive influence we are principally indebted for the highly prosperous situation in which the Society now stands."

As usual, Raine had taken on more than he could manage. In 1839, in addition to all his other commitments, he was struggling to keep up with his work for the Society. Subscriptions were falling into arrears and some of the volumes proposed for publication had been delayed. Not until 1842 were the affairs of the Society on a sufficiently even keel for him to be able to report "substantial progress". In fact, at the annual meeting, "in his estimate of the Society's achievements up to date, he waxed almost lyrical and ... not without some cause" wrote Hamilton Thompson in volume 150. Now that volume 200 has been reached, we can only speculate as to whether the Society would have existed at all had it not been for Raine's initial enthusiasm and continuing dedication. George Taylor, the biographer and friend of Surtees, certainly shared Raine's enthusiasm for the Society and helped him draft the original letters and circulars, but by then he was in his seventies, in poor health, and lacking experience as an antiquary or historian. Surtees had many other friends who admired his work but it is difficult to believe that any one of them possessed the qualities which Raine brought to the task. Without him, they would probably have settled for the scholarship or the memorial tablet.

Further volumes for the Surtees Society kept Raine busy while he continued to work on his own *History*. At last, in 1852, the *History of North Durham* was published, the culmination of many years of research which completed the volume first published in 1830. The Surtees Society volume for 1852 gave Raine particular pleasure. This was a new edition of the *Memoir of Robert Surtees* which had been written by George Taylor and dated 1839. In it Raine included many letters and poems by Surtees not previously published, as well as personal anecdotes of his own. But, pleasures of a different nature were now apparent. Raine's son, another James, was rapidly becoming a respected scholar and antiquary. He graduated from Durham University in 1851 and by 1855 had taken over the secretaryship of the Surtees Society; he had already edited Volume 26, wills from the archdeaconry of Richmond. Raine senior must have been highly gratified. His son's homespun classical education at Crook Hall had been followed by excellence at Durham School and a brilliant period at the university.

During his last ten years Raine undertook a number of lectures for other societies including the Yorkshire Archaeological Society and the Society of Antiquaries at Newcastle. He edited Volume 31, *The Obituary Roll of William Ebchester and John Burnby, Priors of Durham*, for the Society, his final undertaking for them, the preface being dated Crook Hall, 1856. He continued to attend their meetings until a few weeks before his death and found the company there to be most agreeable. But he gradually withdrew from society, reserving his energies for writing and the pleasures of bee-keeping.

In 1857 Raine was awarded the degree of D.C.L., a recognition of his long service in the ecclesiastical court and in honour of his literary and historical achievements. Also in 1857 he published the first volume of his *Memoir of the Rev. J. Hodgson*, the second volume being completed only just before his death. Raine and Hodgson had shared many anxieties over the years, including financial difficulties and struggles over tithes. When it came to publishing the results of their labours such men had to rely on subscriptions and when these fell short they had to abandon the proposed publication or dig into their own pockets. This was not always a viable alternative. In his introduction to *The History of Auckland Castle* (1852) Raine wrote with feeling that the rest of the history of the Palatinate could only be written "when there is enough zeal in the County to protect any future author, who may be inclined to finish the work, from that certain loss, which in modern years at least, has become too closely and seriously connected with topographical publications, and afford him reasonable compensation for his labour. The Author has had some painful experience upon this subject."

The heart trouble from which Raine had been suffering became more disabling. His doctor recommended a complete rest away from Durham so that there would be no temptation to undertake tasks which, however congenial, would try his strength. In April 1858 he was taken to Middleton One Row where he stayed for two or three months. On April 28th he began writing his memoir. He had only reached the end of his schooldays at Ovington when he had to lay aside his pen. On his return to Crook Hall his condition worsened and he died on December 6th after a brief illness.

We are told that the entire city of Durham went into mourning. On the day of the funeral all shops closed and an immense procession of mourners headed by the police and the mayor and corporation in their robes of office crowded up the hill to the cathedral where they were joined by members of the university and the cathedral clergy. Richard Hodgson, son of his old friend the historian of Northumberland, was one of the pall-bearers who carried Raine's coffin through the crowded nave to place it in the choir.

Raine had been a familiar, friendly figure in the streets of Durham and was known as something of a character. Those who knew him through their work had found him helpful and encouraging, though it was said that he could be quite sharp with anybody he thought might be wasting his time. All agreed that he was an incredibly hard worker. At various times his fellow historians, Surtees, Hodgson, Sharp and others, acknowledged their debt to the industry of "the indefatigable Raine". His sole motivation was his devotion to his work, backed by insatiable curiosity and a fervent wish to discover and preserve the past for future generations. Occasionally he was accused of carelessness, and in more recent times Sir Edmund Craster, when he was Bodley's librarian, complained that he did not always give authority for his assertions. In his defence we may mention the enormous amount of work which he undertook, sometimes leading to hasty or inadequate conclusions, and also the fact that he had received no university training. A lecture given by Professor Whiting in 1931 on *The Historians of Durham* provides further support: "The charge of inaccuracy is sometimes levelled against Raine, as against Surtees; but let us not forget that these men were pioneers, that when, for instance, they took up a mediaeval manuscript, they had none of the helps available for the modern student. Remembering this, our admiration for them tends to increase rather than diminish."

But Raine was not only a hard worker. He had a great love of simple pleasures and practical jokes, which he shared with Surtees. Their journeys were full of comic incidents, many described by Raine in his footnotes to Taylor's *Memoir*. He had the uncomplicated humour of a plain man. Like Surtees he detested hot drawing-rooms, nothing was more agreeable than an evening with a few friends of similar interests over a good joint of Willy Reed's roast beef. Throughout his life he remained a countryman at heart. His achievements were, therefore, all the more remarkable.

Description

Raine's memoir, firmly written and generally easy to read, occupies 189 pages of a memorandum book in hard covers, bound with marbled paper. Similar books are to be found among the Raine manuscripts in Durham Cathedral Library. Twelve pages at the end of the book contain headings intended to form part of the index. At page 60 a loose sheet of blue writing paper contains additional material; two pages are numbered 89, two more, 90.

Part 1.

Memoir of his Childhood
by James Raine

[*p. 1*]

Vita mea. Incipit Feliciter. Middleton One Row 28 Ap.1858

Ovington is a township in the chapelry of Forcett, a daughter of the great Saxon parish of Gilling near Richmond. The village stands high on the southern bank of the Tees, which rolls along far beneath in all its glory. Nothing in the whole of its course can be compared with its beauty at Ovington, from Wycliffe downwards to Winston Bridge. Banks high, rocky, here and there precipitous; well wooded, trees left to themselves to grow and fall and decay. Holly and ivy in abundance. Yew here and there only. Owls, gledes,[1] hawks, jackdays, jays, woodpeckers. Immediately behind the village the Tees flows imperceptibly in a deep dark bed in many places of great depth, called the Dubbock, dammed back by a stratum of mountain limestone. At the foot of this remarkable pool the water having regained its liberty expands its arms in a channel of great breadth with three islands of considerable size, one of them well wooded in its bosom [*cf. Addita 1*]. At the distance of half a mile the channel of the river again becomes contracted [*p. 3*] by impending banks and rocks equally well wooded and beautiful and through such scenery it struggles onwards for another mile to Winston Bridge and falls away into a softer country less characterized by such prominent beauties, but still of a very captivating character [*cf. Addita 2*]. The particular spot in the village of Ovington from which all these glories are best seen was once the property of the writer. From his very boyhood he had the judgment and taste to admire them, and it was his habit to wander alone for hours, almost daily, when not at school, by the rocks and in the woods which even at that early time of his life presented to him so many charms. It was not however until after a year's residence in Durham that he appeared to himself to appreciate fully their beauties. During that year it was his fortune to see and hear much of scenes and places which were believed to be unrivalled. He thought of home and its glories and the Tees instantly took its superior rank and character in his estimation.

---

1   The common kite, *Milvus ictinus*, or, occasionally, some other hawk or falcon.

The population of Ovington was then about two hundred. Three or four families were Roman Catholics and attended the chapel [*p. 5*] at Wycliffe. [...] The rest of the villagers, with the exception of two or three families of which ours was one, were heathens. We were four miles from our parish church, and therefore Wycliffe was the place which we attended. Thither, from my earliest recollection, my father walked at the head of his children, joined in the psalmody in which he was somewhat expert, walked home with Tom Jackson the parish clerk and left [*p. 7*] us to ourselves to seek birds' nests or amuse ourselves in any other way during the afternoon. [*p. 13*] And now for a few words about my "forebears".

[1. ANCESTORS]

[The Raines of Teesdale]

James my father was the son of Edmund, who was the son of Edward beyond whom I attempt not here to go. I remember in the house [*p. 15*] a rapier with a handle or hilt lapped with thread of silver which had belonged to an ancestor of my name, and certain tales of his having been a soldier in Ireland, and about a property I think called Naby somewhere on the west side of Stainmoor which had also belonged to him. I also have in my possession sundry small pieces of silver coinage of the time of Elizabeth and the Commonwealth [*cf. Addita 3*], which my grandmother Raine kept in a broken wine glass in her corner cupboard and which had come down from her husband's ancestors. But I was then careless about my fore-elders and the stories which she could have told me respecting them died along with her.

Edmund, my grandfather, died before my time but I have heard of him that he was a hard-working man at my father's trade, tall, thin, thoughtful, highly esteemed by his neighbours whom he would get round him in the evenings and read to them such books as he owned for their amusement or edification. In the summer evenings this was done in the open air, and Josephus's Wars of the Jews[2] was the book which of all others was most welcomed by the villagers and most captivated their attention. [*p. 14*] He had been well taught in

---

2   Most probably in the translation by W. Whiston, published in 1737, frequently reprinted and revised.

the ordinary rules of arithmetic. His school book embracing that subject was long tossing about in my father's house. I thought I had brought it away to Durham, but I cannot find it and fear it has been lost. The initial letters of the various rules and subjects were, after the fashion of old illuminated manuscripts, sometimes attempts at the heads of birds or beasts dying away into flourishes of the pen, and sometimes the mere bare letter itself but not inelegantly designed. A little colour was here and there thrown in and altogether it is a matter of considerable regret to me that this book has not been preserved [cf. Addita 4].

[p. 17] Edmund Raine was born at [blank] and baptized at [blank] [and] served his time, (ut dicitur) at [blank] and after having worked at his trade at various places such as [blank] was married at Gainford on the [22nd May 1756] to Margaret, daughter of James Williamson of Summerhouse "the bonniest lass in all Gainford parish, and everyone looked at her as she stood up to sing in the church." The new married couple lived for a while in Gainford in an old thatched house near the church which belonged to my grandmother's father and there her husband carried on his occupation until after a few years and a few children had been born they removed to Ovington. [p. 15] I have very frequently heard him spoken of by the old farmers and villagers with the most [p. 17] profound respect. Even after I settled in Durham in 1812 a labourer in Willy Reed's small farm called Michael Sewell who had sprung from Bowes and had lived as a farm servant with old Charlie Hanby at Little Hutton once asked me if I was not the grandson of "good auld Edmund Raine".

[p. 19] My grandfather upon his death in 17[84] left behind him my grandmother and four children (two or three had died of a fever): my father, a brother William who soon afterwards died of consumption at about 18 in 17[88], and my aunts Mary and Margaret. My father for a while carried on his trade for the benefit of his mother and sisters, but he soon took it into his head to marry and had a wife and children of his own to provide for. My aunt Margaret, the younger of the sisters went to live as a farm servant at Girlington with my mother's aunt Thompson [p. 31]. Aunt Margaret had been very handsome in her youth and she too like her mother was skilled in psalm singing. For many a long year it was her weekly duty to attend Barnard Castle market on the Wednesday to sell her mistress's butter and eggs etc. and she was known by the name of Girlington

Peggy. [*p. 28*] In 1806 [she became] the wife of Thomas Sayer of Stainton near Barnard Castle, a man who after various changes of place and occupation at last died in Durham in the house of Mr Scales of Crossgate who had married his sister and who after having lived with Dr Bowlby the Proctor as butler had become a hop merchant and was well-to-do in the world. After the deaths of Mr and Mrs Scales who were kind hearted, excellent people, aunt Margaret became the recipient of a small weekly allowance from a charitable fund at my disposal until she received an appointment as one of the widows benefitted by the will [*p. 31*] of George Ashton, a singing man in the cathedral whom I well remember [*cf. Addita 5*].

[*p. 30*] Ashton's father was a barber on Framwellgate Bridge and in a long string of rigmarole rhymes descriptive of Durham men and their trades was designated as "George Ashens Shaves all nations". Ashens was then the name of Ashton *in ore vulgo*. Ashton himself was a stately dignified person, and lived to extreme old age, having been during the whole of his life connected with the cathedral, first as a boy then as a man. He had a fine base voice and was highly respected. He remembered Mr Randall and was an intimate friend of Cade.[3] The portrait of the latter in my possession was purchased by me at his sale. The provisions which he made in his will for a few poor old widows will hand down his name as that of a kindhearted charitable man. Mons. Bouet became the purchaser of his house.[4] It was near the head of Old Elvet [*cf. Addita 6*].

[*p. 31*] Then she [Aunt Margaret] removed to Shincliffe to live with her daughter Ruth Brown the wife of [*blank*] Brown, the daughter of Thomas Sayer by a former wife. She did not however remain long at Shincliffe but returned to Durham and dying in Church Street she was buried at St Margarets in 185[2] by the side of her husband and sister [Mary].

[*p. 30*] Ruth lived for a long time in the house no. 2 in my parish in the South Bailey as cook to the Revd T. R. Shipperdson. She had money, and as the phrase is with persons of her rank she wished to change her condition, but she despaired of getting a husband in

---

3   John Cade (1734-1806) was an enthusiastic antiquary and collector; although not a member of the Society of Antiquaries he contributed several papers to *Archaeologia*.

4   Bouet occasionally helped Raine with illustrations; for his engraving of the Banner of St Cuthbert, see J. Raine, *St Cuthbert*, (1828), p. 108 pl. iii,2

Durham and gave up her place to try another locality. "Its all in vain" said she to her mistress "to try any longer. The quality's no better off than such as me. The Miss Burrells and the Miss Griffits is all getting mouldy like ony of us." She altered her mind however and got a respectable husband in the end.

[*p. 19*] [Aunt] Mary retired with her mother into a room in the Old Hall in the village. There they contrived to maintain themselves in a humble but contented way by spinning in the winter and my aunt Mary working in the fields in the summer months. At that period it was the custom for the farmers in the neighbourhood when they killed their pigs in the winter to distribute chines, spare-ribs etc. among their poorer friends and numerous were the presents of this nature which my grandmother and her daughter received from Girlington, Little Hutton etc. Few people were more [*p. 21*] respected in the village or neighbourhood.

[*p. 29*] After my grandmother's death in 1811, (she was buried at Forcett on the 8 Jan. not far from 80 years of age) my aunt Mary continued to live in the same house, doing the best she could for herself, and kindly assisted in various ways by my great aunt Thompson who had come to live as a widow in the house built by my grandfather Moore until she lost her benefactress in 1820. Upon going from Durham on the day after that event had taken place, I found the poor old woman curdled up by the kitchen fire in the bitterness of grief and despair. I cheered her up, however, by the promise of a small weekly pension, and upon my becoming the owner and occupant of the house in which my [Great] Aunt Thompson had died, she became my housekeeper during those portions of the year in which my duties kept me at Durham. She afterwards removed to Durham and there she died in 18[34] [*p. 28*] under the care of her sister, the aunt Margaret above spoken of.

[*p. 21*] My grandmother was handsome even in her old age, quiet, orderly and contented, regularly going through the morning and afternoon Sunday services of the church and seriously regular in her morning and evening prayers. Her favourite book for this purpose (she had many) was the Countess of Morton's *Devotions*.[5] I

---

5   The 14th edition of the *Devotions* of Ann, countess of Morton, was published in London in 1689; from it Horace Walpole quoted the remarkable expression "Lord wilt thou hunt after a flea", see W. T. Lowndes, *Bibliographers Manual of English Literature*, vi (London, 1860).

have her well-thumbed copy of this book, and from it I well remember her taking great pains to teach me the hymnal prayer to the Holy Ghost "Come Holy Ghost our souls inspire" as it is used in the ordination service [cf. Addita 7]. On Sunday afternoons Hannah Simpson, one of her neighbours frequently joined her and they spent a considerable time together in reading the New Testament. An ointment which she made from snow and hog's lard was in high request in the village and neighbourhood for scalds and burns and she knew much of the virtues of medicinal herbs for other complaints to which the villagers were liable. Of her stock of pewter dishes and plates she was very proud. They had been in use in her family in better times and she kept them duly arranged on their rack and as bright as silver. She was with difficulty persuaded to lend them [p. 23] to Mr Morrit of Rokeby when in 1804 or thereabouts he was giving a great dinner to the Teesdale Volunteer Infantry under his command of which my father was one [cf. Addita 8]. But I satisfied her scruples by so deeply marking upon them her initials with the point of my penknife that they could not possibly be mistaken for the property of another person. My grandfather Moore's stock of pewter which was still larger and equally burnished and prized was lent under the same precaution. The carter who brought back both the collections said that whilst in the case of the other collections there had been much confusion with respect to their owners, those of my two grandmothers had been so satisfactorily marked that in their case there had been no difficulty. [p. 24] My grandmother also had, for a person of her rank in life, a more than usual stock of fine linen sheets, pillowcases etc. in all probability of her own spinning in her younger days. Of these she would frequently lend a sufficiency towards the laying out of any poor person in the village.

[p. 25] During the period of which I am writing I was a sickly boy, fond of quiet, fond of reading such boys' books as fell my way, and most of my time was spent in my grandmother Raine's house so employed, or in making daubs of plants and flowers with a few colours which were given to me by someone whose name I now forget. The blue I used was nothing more than a cake of the blue used by washerwomen [p. 23] Her few books [were] chiefly of a devotional kind in which she spent much time. She also had two books in which I took great interest, the one a life of Christ ornamented at the head of each chapter with a rude woodcut of a very characteristic nature. That of the crucifixion was intended [p. 25] to represent not only the

event but also the darkness which overspread the land during our
Lord's agony and I shall never forget the effect which this strangely
depicted scene had upon my mind. I remember it as well as if I had
seen it yesterday. Another copy of this book has never since fallen in
my way. It belonged to the earlier part of the seventeenth century.
She also had a copy of Aesop's Fables, tattered and torn and
imperfect, equally ornamented with woodcuts, over which I used to
pore with infinite delight. This book which was of an earlier date has
never since come into my hands. [*p. 143*] I had during that period
spent every hour I could call my own by the wheel of my
grandmother Raine and, revelling in the glories of an immense
bundle of penny histories and ballads⁶ made myself intimately
[*p. 145*] acquainted with giants, witches, fairies and their doings, and
had the Seven Champions of Christendom and the ballads of Robin
Hood at my fingers' ends. In truth, I verily believe that of this latter
book in particular I could have repeated every word, such an
impression had it made upon my mind. But during all that time I
had enjoyed somewhat over and above the lore to be gained from
books.

My grandmother's stock of tales was very considerable, turning
chiefly on giants and ghosts with not a few touching tales of the dark
deeds of faeries and witches. From this stock she was at all times
ready to draw for my amusement. [*p. 144*] Many of my grandmother's tales had a religious object in view, the promotion of a due
observance of the sabbath day. One man continued to play cards
after the clock had struck twelve on a Saturday night. He was called
to the door and came not again, but his ashes were found upon the
dunghill the next morning. In another house the people were
continuing their game until a late hour. A stranger came in and was
prevailed upon to take a hand. A card fell to the floor. The master of
the house stooped to pick it up and saw a club foot beneath the table.
But giants and ghosts and faeries were the staple in which not only

---

6   Until about 1700, fairy-tales, mediaeval romances and popular ballads
    were published only for adults. This literature was condensed in a rough
    and ready fashion into the chapbooks published specifically for children
    and simple country folk. The stories which they told were part of an oral
    tradition and familiar to their readers. Chapbooks found in Ovington may
    have been printed in Newcastle by Thomas Angus whose printing firm
    founded in 1774 produced better quality books than other chapbook
    printers. Others were at work in Darlington and York.

she but every other house in the village delighted most to deal, and from this general prevalence of the mode of killing time only sixty years ago it is extremely easy to account for the way in which our ancestors spent their evenings even centuries ago before the invention of printing.

[Margaret Raine died in 1811 and was buried at Forcett on the 8th of January. She was then nearly eighty. The last of her family, John Williamson, died at Summerhouse soon after 1828 and was said to have left behind him a considerable property.]

[The Moores from Hartlepool]

[*p. 33*] My lineage on the side of my mother is not devoid of character or history. My grandfather William Moore was the son of Richard Moore and Miriam Allison and she was a member of an opulent family of merchants in Hartlepool some of whom were mayors of the town in their turns and men of substance and respectability. Sharp's *Hartlepool* contains many of their names.[7] Of Richard I have heard but little and that little is not to his credit. What he was, where he came from or what became of him in the end I know not. I have only heard the names of two children, William and Mary, but there were I believe more when her husband ran away and left her. I think she was then living in Stockton. Poverty and misery soon overcame her but she did the best she could to struggle against them. Once when she had no bread for her children she fell upon her knees to pray for help, and very soon afterwards a kind neighbour sent her a loaf. She always considered this as a special act of providence in her favour. She was a truly religious woman and she was justified in coming to this conclusion. [*p. 35*] Her husband however did not content himself with leaving her. He annoyed her by every means in his power. Upon one occasion of this nature she sent to him a copy of the 52nd psalm. At one time she had a lodger whom she called the peacemaker. When her children were misbehaving themselves this person would step in and support her

---

7   C. Sharp, *History of Hartlepool* (Durham, 1816), pp. 94-6, 201. Robert Allison was mayor of Hartlepool in 1760, William in 1765, Robert in 1768, 1773 and 1780. In addition, in 1755 Robert Allison was appointed one of the first trustees of the free school there. According to Sir Cuthbert Sharp other Allisons held positions of trust in the city until the mid nineteenth century.

authority. "For an ounce of pleasure take a pound of pain" was one of the sayings of her peacemaking lodger. Willy my grandfather was a wayward boy. When she had placed before him his bread and milk for his breakfast and he happened to be in a sulky fit he would refuse to take it, and gradually push the tin which contained the milk to the edge of the table till in the end it fell and the milk was spilled, he all the time growling and grumbling and saying "ye maybe think I's i't pet".

I must pass over many years in the history of this good woman of which I have nothing to record. When I knew her she was old and blind, living in Ovington with her daughter Mary who was also then a widow. She had been previously an inmate of Smith's Hospital at Easby[8] near Richmond, probably through the influence of Dr Zouch, [p. 37] rector of Wycliffe, with Mr Temple, master of Richmond School and vicar of Easby with whom the appointment rested, but upon becoming blind she retired from the hospital to reside with her daughter [cf. Addita 9]. [p. 39] Nothing could exceed her pleasure when she heard my voice in the cottage in which she lived. Her memory was good, and many a tale would she tell me with a moral at its end. She took a particular pleasure in teaching me Watts's Hymns[9] which I was not slow in committing to memory. Book we had none to refer to. Near her cottage was an open well into which my eldest brother once fell when he was five or six years of age, and her son instantly went with a spade in his hand and filled it up, to the great inconvenience of the neighbours. But he was a resolute man, and I am perhaps the only person now living who could point out its precise situation. [p. 38] There was also a gander in the village which in the gosling season made cruel and even bloody attacks upon the poor children of whose playground it had made itself lord and master. This he also destroyed. [p. 39] I well remember my great grandmother Miriam Moore being in my eighth year when she died. She was buried at Wycliffe on 30th March 1798, and I have a perfect recollection of the strongly built, manly figure of my grandfather walking after her coffin as it was carried on towels by the hand from

8   The almshouse known as Easby hospital maintained four old people who would otherwise have had to be lodged in a poorhouse, see R. P. Hastings, *Essays in North Riding History*, (Northallerton, 1981), p. 126.
9   The principal collections by Isaac Watts (1674-1748), the non-conformist hymn-writer, were *Hymns and Spiritual Songs*, (London, 1707), and *The Psalms of David*, (London, 1719).

Ovington to Wycliffe. [*p. 38*] She is properly called Miriam in the register. Her granddaughter the wife of James Allison and her great granddaughter, a daughter of this latter pair, are called Mille in the same record. The former, the daughter of John and Mary Harwood died in 1814 aged 59, and the latter in 1818 aged 20. In common parlance the name of my ancestress herself was always Milly.

[*p. 39*] This brings me to my grandfather. I have already told an early tale of his waywardness, and there were about him through life peculiarities not altogether inconsistent with this beginning. [*p. 43*] His education had been very limited but he was fond of reading, especially history. With his early life ... I am not much acquainted. He had been a sailor, whether in a merchant man or a man of war I know not. I do know however that he ran away from sea and was living as a farm servant in the [*p. 45*] parish of Wycliffe at a place now I believe called Thorp Grange when the Press Gang from Stockton having heard of his whereabouts attempted to recover him. When they knocked at the door and enquired if such a person was in the house he was the man to open it and answer in the affirmative without any surprise or hesitation. He happened at the moment to be without his shoes it being bedtime and he on his way upstairs. "I will send him to you in a moment" said he, and out he ran at the back door having snatched up his shoes, and was no more seen by the gang who returned without their man. The banks and rocks of the Tees would afford him secure shelter for that night, and he was too well acquainted with the country to be in danger next day. But upon consideration it is probable that he would before morning be many miles from the place. [*p. 44*] In after years, in my time, when a beggar professing to have been a sailor stumbled upon my grandfather in his rounds he would always give him money if he could box the compass. [About that time he was paying his addresses to Anne Dixon. His future sister-in-law and her fiancé considered the match unsuitable so told the Press Gang where William Moore was to be found.]

[*p. 45*] I know not where he and my grandmother were married but it was probably somewhere below Darlington, as my mother, their first child, was born in the chapelry of Sadberg and was there baptized in 17[64]. My grandmother had lived as a servant in this part [*p. 47*] of the county of Durham with a family of the name of Wetherell, and he and she would often talk of it as a district with which they were well acquainted. My hearsay information takes them next to Staindrop where one or more boys were born and died. I have a sort of notion that here my grandfather was employed by the Raby family in their parks or farms. He afterwards became a keeper of Turnpike Gates[10] at Winston and then at Greta Bridge. [*p. 46*] Once they lived for a short time, probably when under no turnpike engagement, at a small romantic cottage on the very brink of the Tees where its banks are very picturesque and beautiful, on the left hand of the lane on the road from Ovington to Winston. This charming little spot is called Fuster Gill. It was once monastic property, I think belonging to St Mary's at York, but at all events as its name is upon record in the Monasticon its owner may be easily traced.[11] It is not easy to conceive a more solitary or beautiful place than Fuster Gill. They were at Winston Gate when the comet of 17.. made its appearance and I have often heard my grandmother describe its appearance and the light it shed upon the house in which they lived.[12]

At both places [Winston and Greta Bridge] my grandfather saw ghosts in which he was a believer. At Piper-well-syke, a lonely place on the road from Winston Bridge to Caldwell, about a mile from the toll bar at the former place, a poor old woman had been murdered and could not rest, but manifested herself to passers-by in various shapes and characters, to my grandfather among the rest who, in his account of the matter, seemed to take her appearance to him as a matter of course coming as she did not with any wish to terrify him but in a friendly way. There is in general some foundation for tales of

10 When Arthur Young was in Teesdale he noted that "the tolls of the turnpikes for several paved roads do not rise higher than 3d per horse, for which sum they pave wide enough for one carriage. If this was quadrupled, they might certainly do it well enough for three, and then it would escape being cut up... Until better management is produced I would advise all travellers to consider this country as sea, and as soon think of driving into the ocean as venturing into such detestable roads."

11 Dugdale, *Monasticon* does not apparently record this property by name under St Mary's Abbey York, but does refer, pp. 548-9 and 567, to lands and property held by the abbey in the chapelry of Forcett, which included Ovington and Fuster Gill, while reference is also made, p. 603, to land in Ovington ("Ulwyngton super Teise") held by St Mary's cell of St Martins in Richmond.

12 The only comet of an appropriate date mentioned in B. Vincent, *Haydn's Dictionary of Dates ...*, is in 1769, "a most brilliant comet, first seen by Messier, 8th August".

this kind. In the present case I remember to have read somewhere of a real murder committed at this place. There stood by the roadside [*p. 49*] a solitary cottage in which dwelt a poor solitary woman who one night, more perhaps from fear than good will gave a night's lodging to two strangers who had demanded rather than requested admission to her house. During the night she heard them talking and other sounds meeting her ears which led her to conclude that they had not retired to rest in her spare room she determined to see what they were about. Peeping through the finger hole of the catch she saw them engaged in coining. She had hardly made this discovery before her inquisitiveness became known to them, and upon the principle that dead men tell no tales, they murdered her. I know the place where the cottage stood. Its foundations are easily traced but they are overgrown with grass and weeds.

He had another tale about what he once saw at Greta Bridge of a more fearful kind. Near the turnpike gate of which he was then the keeper stand a few small houses. In one of these lived two poor aged females of the name of Rokeby and of the lineage of that ancient house then nearly forgotten. These poor women had seen better days and they could doubtless have told many a tale of Rokeby and Mortham Tower[13] in bygone [*p. 51*] times. They lived much apart from their neighbours, by whom as a consequence of their age and exclusiveness they were held to be uncanny as the Scotch would term it. One night when it was known that one of these poor women was in the agonies of death, my grandfather was called out of his bed to open his gate, and upon looking along the road in the direction of the cottages what should he see in the very middle of it, opposite to the house of the Rokebys, but a huge fire around which some mysterious personages were moving whilst in the midst of it there appeared a human figure in the agonies of death. This was his tale,

---

13 Rokebys had lived in Mortham Tower since the fourteenth century. Early in the seventeenth century they sold some of their land to the Robinson family on which Sir Thomas Robinson built Rokeby a century later. He sold the property to the Morritt family in 1769. A headstone in Marske churchyard mentions Jane Rokeby, possibly one of these two poor women. She had two sons, William and Joseph, who were both killed in tragic circumstances in November 1771, "descendants of the gentle family of Rokeby". See H. Speight, *Romantic Richmondshire*, (London, 1897), p. 194; also G. Taylor, *A Memoir of Robert Surtees*, ed. J. Raine (Surtees Soc. xxiv, 1852), p. 362 n.

but the poor man had probably been that day at Barnard Castle market. At all events one of the poor sisters had died in the course of the night.

At the time of my birth my grandfather [Moore] was the occupant of a small farm in Ovington of perhaps 60–80 acres[14] and his residence was in a somewhat stately house at the extreme west end of the village on the north side with a deep and picturesque wood between it and the Tees. [*p. 39*] He was of the middle size, thickset and of a great [*p. 41*] bodily strength, ready to throw off his coat at a moment's notice and take vengeance of anyone who opposed him or gave him offence, real or imaginary. His strength and pugnacious tendencies were well known and few ventured to stand in his way. He frequently in his younger days came home from market with bruises but always victorious, and even to his last on such occasions he seldom returned in a state of perfect sobriety. [*p. 51*] His family consisted of himself and my grandmother and a man and maidservant. Two horses were sufficient to cultivate his farm; one of them was a brood mare and he frequently had a good horse to sell at Northallerton Fair of her produce. He also had two or three cows, a few sheep and the other live accompaniments of so small [*p. 53*] an establishment.

[*p. 57*] From the commencement of my recollection my grandfather was also the owner of two or three fields at the west end of Staindrop stretching from the Barnard Castle to the Langleydale road. These he kept in his own occupation. To the best of my recollection he had a lease of his Ovington farm which was to expire at Mayday, 1805.[15] In 1804 therefore, having no intention to seek for a renewal, he began to build for himself a small house upon a piece of ground lower down the village, sold to him [*p. 59*] for that express purpose by my Girlington uncle who had married my grandmother's

---

14 This was probably typical of the small farms around Ovington. When visiting the area in 1771 Arthur Young described a similar farm of 72 acres. Of these 30 were grass, 42 arable, and the rent was £30. There was one man and one maid; the stock consisted of 2 cows, 4 young cattle, 10 sheep, 3 horses and 2 oxen. He gave lists of labour costs, farm implements, provisions and labourers' expenses. He added that "poor rates are 8d in the pound, the employment of poor women and children is spinning a little flax and worsted; tea, to my great wonder, is but little drank here". See *Six Months Tour through the North of England*, ii,176-8.

15 Many small farms were let on an annual agreement. Where there were

sister. Between the two men there was as far as my memory goes at no time anything like hearty intercourse. He of Girlington was better off in the world, mixing much with breeders of shorthorns, and having annually at his house a great gathering of what was then called the gentlemen farmers of the district. My grandfather was stern and independent, caring nothing whatever for any man who gave himself airs (certainly some of my great uncle's associates were rather remarkable in this way) and I am not aware that he was ever invited to Girlington on these occasions.

[*p. 41*] In his ordinary demeanour he was a grave, serious-looking man of few words not mixing much with his neighbours, of great firmness of purpose and of considerable ingenuity in matters of a practical or mechanical nature. [*p. 53*] For a while after he took possession of his farm, his hedges were much broken for fewel especially in the fields near the village through which there happened to be a footpath. But he soon put a stop to such proceedings. He marked with his eye the stakes and rails which were likely to attract the attention of the thieves and with a large gimlet, made in them holes here and there which he filled with gunpowder, plugging up the opening with clay. Explosions were soon afterwards heard in the village to his great amusement. More serious tricks were apprehended from his ingenuity and his hedges were let alone.

[*p. 52*] To the villagers however my grandfather was always kindly inclined and ready to do them a good turn when it was in his power. I remember one in particular which reflects much credit on his memory. About the year 1800 corn was not only dear but bad and unsound into the bargain. The price was two guineas per boll and great distress prevailed among the poor people in the village as at this price it was utterly unattainable. There was to be had however in Newcastle, imported rye at a cheaper rate but how were the poor people of Ovington to be benefitted by this? My grandfather yoked his carts, went with them in person, filled them with this ship-rye as it was called, and sold it out at prime cost, freely giving the services of his man and horses and paying all the expenses of the expedition out of his own pocket. I have a distant recollection of this corn. It was

---

leases these were usually for 7, 14 or 21 years. The landlord provided the land, farmhouse and other farm buildings, and often paid for fences, upkeep of access roads and installations of a permanent nature. The tenant provided his own livestock, implements, waggons, manure and seed, and paid the wages of his servants and labourers.

small in grain, brackish in taste and not very palatable, but what could the poor people have done without it?

[*p. 92*] He himself had not had much education, he could however manage to keep his accounts in his own way. He was frequently in office in the township as overseer of the poor, churchwarden etc., and he was always in my time overseer of the highways for a considerable length of road under an act of parliament,[16] and when anything in particular had to be done in any of these departments I was his penman. He had a calculating head and my main business was to express in writing his ideas and his figures.

[*p. 41*] He would talk of bygone times in English history, of the foss or ditch which separated his farm from the rest of Wycliffe estate which he believed to be a trench dug out by men of war, not what it is in reality – a deeply dug boundary line. [*p. 43*] After Mr Headlam had begun to take notice of me in 1803 and had begun to lend me books, my grandfather read with the greatest avidity a history of Rome which this my first friend had kindly entrusted to my perusal. The character and exploits of Camillus captivated him beyond measure and he would talk of nothing else for weeks. [*p. 42*] A very favourite book with him was Ramsay's "Evergreen", a collection of early Scottish poems in two duodecimo volumes, a copy of which he had picked up at a sale at Staindrop.[17] There was in each volume a neat book plate with the name of Michael Watson who had been a draper or general shop-keeper. The "Advice Jock gied his Dan" a short

---

16 The annual vestry meeting of the parish rate payers at Easter elected the churchwardens. The surveyor of the highway and overseer of the poor were also chosen but the vestry meeting could only put their names forward to the justices of the peace who made these appointments. The surveyor had to rely on statute labour and the levy of a rate not exceeding 6d. in the pound for the provision of road materials. The overseer of the poor dealt with provision of weekly pensions, accommodation, clothing, fuel and medical attendance. Poor rates were levied weekly on the parish, the amount being fixed by the churchwardens and the overseer of the poor. They were often added to other small taxes for the repair of roads and maintenance of church buildings. This combined rate was borne by the farmers who were assessed according to the rents they paid, about 1s. 1d. in the pound in 1771 in the Rokeby area, see Arthur Young, *Political Arithmetic*, (London, 1774), p. 10.

17 Scottish songs and stories were very popular in the north of England, the broad dialect being well understood. Scottish drovers were still bringing

...

piece of epigrammatic wit in this book tickled his fancy exceedingly, and "The wife of Auchtermuchty" was clearly a favourite with him.[18] He could read most of the Scotch in these early poems with considerable ease. [*p. 43*] He seldom went to church, but he was a great reader of his bible on Sundays. I fear however that it was chiefly for the military history which it contains.

[*p. 55*] My grandfather Moore was an expert angler and I have spent many an evening with him by the side of the Tees. The Dubbock lay behind his house. He would take his stand at the head of this reservoir or long pool by the stream which ran into it, with the throstles and blackbirds singing high above his head and he would soon fill his basket. He made his own flies (a worm never came upon his hook) and these were his hail except when the may-fly was upon the water, and when that was the case there was an abundance of them under the thin stones by the side of the river. We boys all of us became fishers with such an excellent example before us but as to myself, I was [*p. 57*] never very successful. I remember a circumstance which once occurred to me in later years at my grandfather's favourite place at the head of the Dubbock. One evening my line became entangled in a branch of a super-impending tree, and all my efforts to set it at liberty were in vain. It was late in the evening. I therefore pulled and brake it leaving a yard or two of its end hanging down but far above out of my reach. Upon going to the place next morning, a bat was hanging at one of the flies and seeing that it was still alive I contrived by means of a long pole to pull down the branch and set it at liberty. It soon hid itself in a crevice of the rock above my head.

[*p. 53*] My grandfather was a keeper of bees, but knowing nothing of their natural history his success like that of many others was more the result of good luck and favourable seasons than of judicious management. [*p. 55*] I must not forget to mention that my grandmother's mead *vulgo* botchet was most excellent and she made

---

cattle to the markets and fairs of Durham and the North Riding of Yorkshire, and their songs had become part of the local tradition. Two volumes of songs by Allan Ramsay, *Evergreen*, in an edition published in Edinburgh in 1761, were among the books in Raine's library sold in 1859 after his death, according to the catalogue (in the editor's possession) of the sale by Mr George Hardcastle at Crook Hall, 28 Feb. – 3 Mar. 1859.

18 *Allan Ramsay: Works*, ed. B. Martin and J. W. Oliver, (Edinburgh, 1951); see also for example *Oxford Book of English Verse*, no. 448.

many a shilling from her beeswax. [*p. 53*] It was no doubt that from him my own turn for bee-keeping was derived as I never failed to be his attendant in his various operations in connection with his apiary [*cf. Addita 10*]. [*p. 41*] Without knowing anything of the principles of geology he had a geological eye and could [*p. 43*] tell in a moment where a spring of water was likely to be found, or where to look beneath the surface of the earth for mountain limestone or free stone. This latter knowledge was of considerable use to him in his capacity of surveyor of the highways in the neighbourhood.

[*p. 59*] I have no recollection of ever seeing my grandfather at Girlington except one Sunday afternoon when the bargain for the site of his new house had been completed and I was called upon, being then about twelve years of age, to read aloud to the two the deed of conveyance. Upon the ground so conveyed stood a primitive cottage covered with thatch with sides resting in the ground. [*p. 61*] [For the people living there] another house was found in the village and my grandfather began to build so early in the year 1804 if not in 1803, that the house was almost finished in the autumn of the former year when, in November, I think upon a Fair Day, he rode to Darlington to buy a few locks, window screws etc. which were wanting to complete his undertaking. Ovington on that morning saw him for the last time.

A few days before he had lost a favourite [*p. 63*] horse, a noble animal of great good nature and bodily strength which, having strayed from its pasture, had fallen down a steep place in Wycliffe wood, head foremost into a bog and had perished. "Accidents" said my grandfather "never come alone. Worse may follow." At Darlington he met with Kit Heslop, a man of great steadiness of character and respectability who had for many years been his servant but was at that time a sort of farm bailiff at Rokeby Grange. The two had a glass together, and perhaps more, but I never understood that when they left Darlington to ride home together my grandfather was what might be called tipsy. His pride was in a spirited horse. He rode one upon that occasion, and when the two were approaching Winston on the level road near Primrose Hill, "Now Kit" said he "for a gallop." Kit also was well mounted and away they went. At the east end of Winston there are two sharp bends in the road. The first they passed with ease but at the second, close by the gate leading up to the farm house occupied by Tommy Deighton, my grandfather lost his balance and fell to the ground his head coming into immediate contact with a heap of sharp stones of mountain limestone newly broken to mend the road. Upon lifting him from the ground all power of speech was gone and his body gave indications of great pain. [*p. 65*] He was instantly removed into the farm house where every kind attention was paid him, and the surgeon who had always attended his and our family, Joshua Watson a Quaker, was sent for from Staindrop.

The village of Ovington was on poor Kit's road home to Rokeby and he called at my grandfather's house with the sad news of the accident. My grandmother had often had alarms of this nature, but there was something about Heslop's manner of telling his tale which led her to suspect that this was no ordinary accident. She went therefore without delay to Winston and my father followed her. My mother had a few days before given birth to my brother John, and when my father returned home the next morning shaking his head and looking grave she too was inclined to think that he was making more of the accident than it deserved, remembering the numerous escapes which her father had had on former occasions. In her situation he did not like to tell her the truth for fear of the consequences, but the truth was soon afterwards obliged to be told. My grandfather died in the course of the day having never recovered his power of mind or speech, and a verdict of accidental death was returned by the jury with G. Ornsby's father who then resided at Darlington for the coroner. He was buried at Forcett on the 25th November 1804. I know not at present his exact age but he was far above seventy.

[*p. 75*] I now return to Anne Moore my grandmother on my mother's side. She and my great aunt Thompson were the daughters of Anthony Dixon and Martha Thompson. He was, according to the best of my recollection, something in the nature of a huntsman to the Milbankes of Halnaby, and she was the daughter of [*blank*] Thompson of Ovington, the farmer of considerable acres of land which in times of old had belonged to the Scropes of Bolton, and had descended through one of the natural daughters of the Earl of Sunderland to the Egertons afterwards Dukes of Bridgewater.[19] Martha Dixon died at an early age leaving behind her several children. Anthony married again at Richmond and his wife turned

---

19 The first earl of Sunderland and eleventh Lord Bolton, Emanuel Scrope, died 1630.

out to be a stepmother in the worst sense of the word. I knew three of the unhappy offspring of the first wife, my grandmother, my [great] aunt Thompson [*p. 77*] and Henry Dixon who lived to be an old man with some little substance and who died at Middleton Tyas in 18.. at an advanced age. Another, Anthony, was a soldier and died as I have heard at Westchester, a young man on his way to Ireland. I have heard that the second wife treated these children in a hard way and at last fairly turned them out of her house, but I know nothing or next to nothing of their sufferings. Jane the eldest was for a while housekeeper to her uncle Thompson at Ovington.

[*p. 79*] My grandmother was the pattern and perfection of a farmer's wife, always neat and clean in her person, cautious, prudent, economical, staying at home, never gadding about from house to house (I never saw her in any other house in the village than my mother's), no gossip, no encourager of people who run about with village news and lies. She could read and write, but nothing more, and yet her mode of expressing herself was singularly correct and thoughtful. Her temper was mild and conciliating and this happy disposition was frequently of great use to her in the wayward fits of my grandfather. [*p. 69*] When my grandfather died my grandmother came to live with us in a spare room in the house which my father had built in the preceding year and here she remained for a while until her own newly built house was dry enough to receive her. This was in the spring of 1805.

In the meantime as my grandfather died without making a will she took administration to his effects in the court at Richmond, made an immediate sale of his farming stock, and was permitted by her two daughters to take full possession of everything which had belonged to him, letting the fields at Staindrop under the advice of Thomas Harrison (her son-in-law) for the best rent which could be obtained. In 1807 she was joined in her house by her sister, who became a widow in the beginning of the year, and dying on Palm Sunday 1809 was buried at Forcett by the side of her husband on 29th March. [*p. 79*] She had been ill for nearly a fortnight. On Saturday, the day before her departure, I had come home from Kirby Hill School as usual with my empty basket upon my arm, and as I at that time when at home always lived with her and my great aunt Thompson, I was in the house when her gentle spirit took its departure to another world. I can never forget the earnestness of her prayers often uttered during her last agonies that she might die unto

the Lord. It has so happened [*p. 81*] that she has been the only one of
my relations up to the present time whom I have seen labouring
under the heavy hand of death, and I pray that we may all of us be so
prepared as this good woman to meet God in our turns.

I think I have said as much as is necessary on the subject of my
lineage down to my father and mother. I have had no boasts to make
nor anything of the tomfoolery of high blood to wade through or
deal with and yet I have mentioned names of men and women in my
pages to whom I look back with profound respect as those of sound
sense and integrity of which any pedigree might be proud.

[My Parents]

[When Edmund Raine died in 1784 his son James was 24. He carried
on his father's trade until in 1788 he married Anne Moore who was
then living with her parents in their cottage at Fuster Gill.]

[*p. 90*] After the departure of my grandfather and his family
from Staindrop my mother appears to have returned thither to learn
the craft of mantua making[20] in which she so far excelled as to gain a
great name for her skill in the whole neighbourhood. I have heard
her say that when they lived at Fuster Gill and she had to go to
Osmondcroft on the opposite side of the river to exercise her
vocation, my grandfather would go down with her to the Tees side
and carry her across it on his back, meeting her again in the evening
to bring her back in the same way.

At that time my father and she were within a mile of each
other, he a hard-working, sensible, good-looking fellow and she
handsome and singularly clever and captivating. The two appear to
have taken a strong liking for each other but my grandfather did
everything in his power to keep them apart. They were not however
to be disappointed in their mutual wish to be married in an
honourable way. Thomas Hanley of Little Hutton went with my
father to Richmond as his bondsman. A licence was procured. My
mother stole away to Forcett and they were married. My grandfather
had however in the meantime found out what was going on and
hurried to the church to prevent the union but he was too late in his
arrival. The poor young woman went with her husband to his own

---

20 A mantua maker was a dressmaker, mantua being a corruption of the
French "manteau" meaning mantle or loose dress.

family, to his mother and sister Mary and brother William, her own father refusing and her mother not daring to own her for many a long month. There she was living in a state of great unhappiness and in the want of many [*p. 92*] comforts to which she had been accustomed at home until one day, seeing her father in the village for the first time after her marriage, a miscarriage was the consequence and her life became in danger. All this I have heard from others. A reconciliation appears to have been brought about after this unhappy event, but certainly in my own observation, my grandfather Moore always looked upon my father with an eye which led me to believe that all had not been right between them. Things however gradually got right.

[*p. 81*] [My father] was a hard working, good natured, obliging man, prudent and proverbially honest in all his ways and fond of his children for whom he worked, I might almost say night and day, to bring them up in a respectable manner. He was of the middle size, full of quips [*p. 83*] and jokes which were always so good natured as to make him extremely popular in the village. When he laid aside his apron to walk in his fields, even the very children in the town (as it was called) would run after him in crowds and pull at his coat and feel glad of his notice. On the road he would sing them a song or find them a nest or do anything for their amusement. When he was inclined to go down the lane he had only to stand upon the hill in front of his house and give a loud whistle and the bairns would flock around him like bees. His education had been of a humble kind. He could manage however to keep his accounts daily upon a slate with great accuracy and transfer them to a book when the slate was full, but he seldom made out a bill at the end of the half-year. This was always the work of my mother who wrote a remarkably neat hand and in casting up accounts was always as quick as lightening.

My father was extremely remarkable for his queer old-fashioned sayings and phrases and proverbs which, as he brought them forward, were never dragged by force but always pat to the occasion, and his stock of good old Saxon and English words was very considerable. The Saxon prefix ge- was daily in his mouth. "I'll away gewrite" for instance I have heard from him a thousand times. When in a merry mood his face was a perfect comedy. His insight [*p. 85*] into character was keen and quick and he was seldom wrong.

His power of thought and memory were also of a high order and he was reputed to be one of the best players of whist (or whisk as it was invariably called) in the neighbourhood. Trumping was "shinning", a revoke was "shinning foul" and diamonds were "picks". Many of the "coat cards" had facetious names, and that of the ace of spades was not over decent. During the game he was always in the best humour, and when others were growling and grumbling at their bad luck he would often make use of a phrase which is very expressive and which I have seen used in the same sense in Peacham's Complete Gentleman.[21] "Cherish your cards", don't get vexed at them, make the most of them whatever they may turn up to be. (Peacham gives the same piece of advice with respect to the treatment of a refractory horse: cherish him, pat him on the neck, get the better of him by kindness.) My father's fondness for a harmless game of whist (they always played for love and not money) and his skill in the game made him a welcome guest in the evening at Girlington and other places after he had done his day's work. One night at a late hour as he was returning from a game at Wycliffe, he came upon what he believed to be a detachment of Sir William Brown's gang as they were sitting by the side of the footpath waiting perhaps for midnight. He was running quickly at the time and the men kept their seats. I have heard him say that Wycliffe church was that night attempted [p. 87] to be broken into, doubtless for its communion plate.

My father had a good tenor voice and would sing a good song as well as anybody. He took great pleasure in making himself useful in this way at Wycliffe church, and when in 1803 an attempt was made to revive the psalmody in that church which was rapidly falling into decay he took us boys along with him to the weekly practice, but nothing could be made of me.

[p. 90] The conversation in the church porch before the commencement of divine service was very characteristic of the men who assembled in it. They were chiefly the farmers or great men of the parish and their subject was generally the weather and the operations going on at that time in their fields. Bishoprig (the county of Durham into which a stone might have been thrown from the churchyard) was often mentioned, and to the best of my recollection there was always an impression that it was more highly favoured in point of rain and seasonable weather than the parish of Wycliffe. The proceedings of Adam Dale the farmer of Wycliffe Grange farm, a

---

21 H. Peacham, *Compleat Gentleman*, (London, 1622).

Roman Catholic and therefore not a goer to church, were always discussed as he had [*p. 91*] plans peculiar to himself which few in the parish were inclined to follow. It was a common saying with him that he would "make the seasons keep their time" and therefore he would begin to mow on a certain day and on a certain day he would put the sickle into his corn etc. His successes or failures in so doing were a common topic of conversation.

Now and then, as the parish was sitting in the porch, my father among them letting no opportunity for a little mirth be neglected, there would emerge from the wood into the churchyard a man who was seldom seen on such occasions, and he would say "Here comes Harry Hutchinson. I'll be bound to say he wants to borrow something of somebody." And so it generally happened. He wanted to borrow a horse or cart or something else on some day in the ensuing week, and he knew where he would be most likely to find the man he hoped would oblige him.

[When Tom Jackson's wife Betty died,] [*p. 9*] Tommy made a sale of his goods and the most extraordinary things were brought to light, things in short which might well have constituted [*p. 11*] the stock of a well-to-do merchant in the time of Queen Elizabeth such as is described in more than one instance in the Inventories published by the Surtees Society in its second volume. My father bought a church in wood with a steeple a foot and a half high, coloured externally after the fashion of brick, with windows too and a ring of small bells. This was a mousetrap, and when the mouse was caught the bells rang by some internal machinery which we children very soon pulled in pieces. My father also bought a mass of the Newcastle Courant for about the years 1740–60 with the quaint lesson-teaching woodcut of the devil sitting behind the horse and teacher. In an old coffee roaster of spacious size here obtained we long kept the meat, young birds etc. for our owls and hawks.

[Apart from recording that his father gave him a good whipping on one occasion when he had lied to his school mistress, Raine tells us little more about him. He never says directly that he was a blacksmith, only that once somebody came into their house while his horse was shod.]

[*p. 93*] My account of my mother Anne Moore must begin at Staindrop, where her father and mother for some time appear to have resided and where they lost one or two boys who died in their infancy. Here she went to school to a man of the name of Facer, a south country man I believe who had I think been brought into the north by the Raby family,[22] probably as a rudiment teacher in their family. He died in January 1826 at the age of 87, having for many years been schoolmaster at Staindrop, and one of his daughters was for many years the player upon the organ in the parish church. How long my mother continued at this person's school I know not, but she became under his care the writer of a very beautiful hand and an excellent arithmetician in somewhat more than the ordinary rules then taught to females. The most highly educated woman in the land could not have been more expert in spelling, and her reading aloud was worth hearing.

I know not whether it was at Staindrop but probably it was, and that too under Mr Facer's musical daughter, that she acquired the knowledge of playing upon the harp, more properly perhaps called a crowde [*cf. Addita 11*] strung not with tharm but with wire and played upon by a quill, the plectrum of old. Upon this instrument, when I was a little boy and her cares were few, she would often play on an evening and its peculiar sound still rings in my ears. She would also accompany the tune with her voice and Scotch [*p. 95*] songs were her favourites. My father had a musical voice and could sing divers good old Scotch songs as well as she could, but I do not remember that he ever joined her when she was musically inclined.

When I first knew her as my mother she was the great scholar in the village, writing letters for fathers and mothers to their absent children and their relations, and reading the answers which were received. This was an office which afterwards to a certain extent was exercised by me, my mother having her family affairs to attend to. I could tell many amusing tales of the correspondence which I occasionally conducted. [...]

During the autumn of the year my mother's powers were allowed on all sides to be unrivalled. At that time few farmers finished their harvest without a mell[23] supper, and dancing and "guising" were the glory of the evening. On these occasions [*p. 97*] the young men and maidens of the village would all of them bring the habitiments which they could muster to my mother. These she would throw into a common heap and clothe each of them in their turns in the most fantastic way so as to render their being known

---

22 Presumably the Vanes of Raby Castle, earls of Darlington from 1754.
23 The last cut of corn in the harvest-field.

even to their friends a matter almost of impossibility. Scotchmen were her favourite characters – i.e. in them she most succeeded. I remember the cunning way in which one lad in particular scratched his hands under her direction to indicate the country he came from. As the children of such a woman, so well educated for her station and of such an active mind, we boys had many advantages. It was her pleasure to make our school tasks easy and agreeable, to cheer us on in doing our best for ourselves in our evening exercises, and in giving us a helping word in time of need.

[*p. 96*] My mother had not been a traveller. Her farthest journey from home was to York to visit a young woman with whom she had become acquainted at Staindrop. At York she was taken by her friend to the theatre. "The Gentle Shepherd"[24] was one of the subjects performed on the night of her visit. She bought the book and, when my recollection commences I believe she could have repeated the whole of it. Mary Dawson, my mother's friend, married in York, became a widow and afterwards became the wife of a man called Christopher, a butcher.

[Great Aunt Thompson i.e. Jane Dixon who married John Thompson of Girlington in 1771. Raine several times mentions her acts of kindness to the poorer members of the family and to the villagers. As a girl she had been turned out of her home by a cruel stepmother.]

[*p. 77*] My [great] aunt Thompson was, I have heard her say, housekeeper for a while to her Uncle Thompson of Ovington, and in that capacity she made his cheeses, seasoned the whey which runs from the curds with savoury herbs, and placed the mixture at the door for a pleasant beverage to passers through the village. According

---

24 This play by Allan Ramsay was performed by a Scottish company owned by a Mr Mills whose family were the main performers. In *The Life of Thomas Holcroft*, ed. E. Colby, 2 vols (New York, 1968), i,169 Holcroft states that he joined this company which toured the north of England. "Though the loves of Patie and Peggy were a never failing source of delight on the other side of the Tweed, their English auditors grew tired of this constant sameness. They therefore, after the performance of *The Gentle Shepherd*, which was still the business of the evening, introduced a farce occasionally, as a great treat to the audience ... and by degrees, Allan Ramsay, with his shepherds and shepherdesses, and flocks of bleating sheep, were entirely discarded." This would be the company which Mrs Raine saw in York in the late eighteenth century.

to her account this was a great treat to the coal carters during the cheese-making period of the year. But she did more than that. I have heard her tell with great pleasure that in 1745 when she must have been about 17 years of age, the Duke of Cumberland was resting with his army for a day or two on the flat ground on the Yorkshire side of the Tees at Piercebridge on his road into the north to quell the rebellion. She baked a considerable number of large loaves out of her uncle's stock of meal, and sent them down on the heads of the villagers to the [p. 79] hungry soldiers.

[Great Aunt Mary, daughter of Richard Moore and Miriam Allison.]

[p. 69] She eventually married a tailor, but where I know not, of the name of John Harwood (there is a great cian of this name about Barnard Castle) [p. 71] and had a large family of sons but only two daughters. One of the latter, Jane, died at Hull unmarried in 179. and the other Miriam married James Allison the illegitimate son of a Roman Catholic priest at Wycliffe and in his latter days a carrier between Barnard Castle and Newcastle, but living in Ovington. Harwood was a tall, thin man, for some years before his death blind, and much given to eating chalk for what he called the heartburn. One of his sons Richard became a farmer upon the Crowe estate at Kiplin, another (William I think) became a tailor who lived for a while in Grays Inn Lane in London where he married, afterwards at Newburn or thereabouts near Newcastle and subsequently at Whorlton on the Tees where he died leaving two sons and two daughters. Of the former there are descendants in the village. The other sons of the blind tailor were all soldiers and some of them deserters. To one of them, before my day, my mother and father gave a hiding place for several weeks and I have heard them describe in feeling terms the horror of the poor man when strangers were seen in the village. Cuddy Harwood, one of them, was in the Durham Militia and having got [p. 73] his discharge fairly, became a sergeant and very useful in the Teesdale Volunteer Force under Mr Morritt of Rokeby [cf. Addita 12].

[After her husband's death Great Aunt Mary used to visit her old mother near Richmond.]

[p. 68] Once when she had been upon a short visit to her mother who was then an inmate of Smith's Hospital at Easby before she became blind, and was returning to Ovington over Gatherly

Moor, she met a man of whom she had reason to be afraid. She leapt upon a bank by the roadside and cried out over the hedge to a man she pretended to be ploughing in the adjoining field, begging to know what o'clock it was. Her assailant (if such was his intention) walked on his way and a real man soon rode up who going the same road and, having heard her tale, took her under his protection.

[*p. 73*] Mary Harwood was long a widow and lived upon an annuity of ten pounds a year for which she had sunk the £100 which had been bequeathed to her by Robert Allison of Hartlepool, her mother Miriam's kind relation. Her husband was a Roman Catholic and she became one too. [*p. 75*] For a while after his death she resided at Staindrop, but on returning to Ovington she relapsed to the Romish church. She was buried at Wycliffe on 31st October 1810 in the 82nd year of her age.

[Margaret Dent, a distant cousin by marriage.]

[*p. 139*] Margaret Dent was the sister of Thomas Harrison of Ovington Edge, and the two were the issue of Joseph Harrison by his wife [*blank*] who was the sister of John Thompson who, in 1771, the year of the great flood, married Jane Dixon, my mother's aunt. There was therefore somewhat of a connection between us and the Dents. [*p. 136*] The Dents had made some money by the carriage of coals from the Bishoprick into Richmondshire on the back of Galloways.[25] The Hindes in the more southern vale of Ravenswath had long and still carry on the same trade on asses. Hence the saying,

> A Dent for a galloway,
> A Hinde for an ass.

[*p. 137*] Margaret Dent was buried at Stanwick on 10th November 1842 at the great age of 92. It is very remarkable that 92 should be the year which so many persons, especially females, should reach once they have outlived 85. She was also the mother of several daughters, some of whom are still living having brought Caldwell into great notoriety by their cheeses which rival those made at Cutherston "where they christen calves." [*p. 136*] This saying is extremely common in Teesdale but few people seem to know its origin. I have heard that it took its rise from a wicked attempt of a

---

25 A small saddle-horse or pony.

Quaker to christen a calf in that village in contempt of Baptism. [*p. 137*] Margaret Dent herself was the mother of Jacky Dent as he was called (buried at Stanwick 7 May 1842 aet. 68) the clerk and confidential servant of Jonathan Raine son of Matthew Raine of Hartforth and also a well known barrister on the northern circuit a prizeman at Cambridge in his day and brother of Dr Matthew Raine at the Charter House School.

[Henry Thompson "my relation" was perhaps the brother of John Thompson of Girlington who had married Jane Dixon (Great Aunt Thompson).]

[*p. 118*] I have a very perfect recollection of Harry Thompson. He was a tall, thin, red-haired man and had been blind for some years. He had two sons, George who was steady and managed the farm, Hutton who was a profligate in every sense of the word ruined his brother in the end after the father's death, and Jane who married Anthony Robinson of Hutton Fields – another profligate who used his wife very ill and dragged down himself and his family into poverty and ruin. To raise a shilling for the alehouse, Hutton Thompson would write a letter to his poor old blind father as from an absent friend, would induce an old woman in the village to leave it at the house as if from the post office at Greta Bridge with which Ovington had only an accidental intercourse, and the blind man would pay the money and get this selfsame vagabond son not only to read it to him but if need be to write a reply. For some time this wickedness was not found out by George the brother. In the days of his eyesight, the father Harry sunk a well behind his house and found abundance of water. When the work was finished, his servant asked him what he was to do with the metal as they called it, or earth, stones etc. which had been dug up during the operation. "Make another hole to put it in" was his reply.

[2. SCHOOLDAYS]

[The Village Dames]

[*p. 97*] I think I have now reached the period at which my own history ought to begin. I bear about me a mark, on the right side of my neck touching upon my collar bone, which my mother used to [*p. 99*] look at over and over again when I was young in a very feeling and piteous way, and tell me of the narrow escape my life had had when I was a very infant. A cinder flew from the fire into my cradle when her back was turned and when she again cast her eye upon me I was on fire. A jug of water settled the matter in a moment but the mark remains. This was the first of my providential escapes. I have had others in abundance when I was not in so fit a state to be called away as a little child.

I have often heard that in my infancy I was always crying and I have no doubt such was the case. I was extremely delicate in my constitution and until I was about ten or eleven years of age I was annually troubled with a violent eruption on the back part of my head which was only removed by a seton[26] in my right leg, a nuisance which continued in operation for two or three years until it had done its duty.

And now for my schooling. To the man who once boasted that he might be compared to a calf which had sucked two mothers, as he had been at both Oxford and Cambridge it was remarked "no wonder that you are the great calf you are". Of university education I have no boast to make but if the various schools which I have attended have an equally fattening tendency, what a calf must I be, as I can [*p. 101*] enumerate nearly a dozen *almae matres* by whose milk I have benefitted. [...] Well, Thomas Harrison, had a relation [*p. 103*] in the village, his aunt or his father's aunt (the Forcett registers will settle this point, but I imagine the former) Betty Harrison, a venerable old dame, the name by which she was generally called, and she was my first schoolmistress. Her house consisting of only one room with a shallow open well in the passage was near to my father's and it was particularly convenient for such a youngster as I must have been when placed under her care. I have no very distinct recollection of her proceedings as a schoolmistress but I remember her teaching me my letters upon the battledoor as it was called, a piece of folding pasteboard having imprinted upon it the capital and ordinary letters of the alphabet [*cf. Addita 13*]. The old horn book had just gone out of use in schools and that which we used was no doubt called the battledoor because the horn book which it had superseded so strictly

---

26 Threads or horse hairs were twisted and drawn through the skin to keep open a wound or infected tissue.

resembled that instrument.[27] The battledoor itself, an implement of the shape of a spade but of wood and of one piece, was then in use in the village for beating clothes during the process of washing. [*p. 105*] My progress with the battledoor was I suspect gratifying to my schoolmistress as I remember receiving more frequently than anyone else of her scholars the neat little piece of tharf cake[28] and butter with which we were occasionally rewarded. I use the word "tharf" for unleavened because I never heard in my native village any other word applied to bread in that condition and it is interesting to see that John Wycliffe who was born within a mile and half of the place of which I am writing has that very word in his translation of the New Testament.[29] Indeed I have often remarked that I would undertake to read that translation to the old people of Ovington when I was a boy, from beginning to end, and not fifty explanations of words which had become obsolete would have been required. My father would, I suspect, [*p. 107*] have understood them all.

I well remember the pointer which did duty for each child in its turn, the stalk of a feather denuded of all its filaments, or by whatever name they are called. And now conscience calls upon me to tell a sad tale against myself. Good Betty had no clock, and one of us was daily sent out as noon approached to find out the time of day. My turn came in its course and the result was fearfully disgraceful. I reported that twelve, the hour of dinner, had arrived when in truth it was only eleven, and this I did knowingly and intentionally. A good whipping from my father was what I received as the just punishment of my falsehood. With the dame I was long in disgrace but we became friends in the end and the piece of tharf cake fell to my lot in return for my good lessons as usual.

About poor old Betty Harrison there were many peculiarities, and one in particular of a singular nature. At no time would she keep in the house the elements of fire. Flint, steel, tinder, and matches

---

27 Horn books, first used in the fifteenth century, consisted of single sheets of paper on which were printed the alphabet, numerals and the Lord's prayer. A sheet was covered with transparent horn and set in a frame with a handle. It was superseded by the battledore as described here which was less expensive to produce but, being unprotected, often had to be replaced.

28 Unleavened cakes of flour or meal, mixed with milk or water, rolled out thin and baked, not unlike bannocks.

29 e.g. Mark 14:1.

dipped in brimstone were then alone in use but not one of the four could be found in her possession. After she had dressed herself in the morning she would take [*p. 109*] in her hand an old shoe she kept for the purpose in which she had placed a few pieces of dry wood or other easily lighted material, and with this she would proceed to a neighbour's house, set her materials on fire and light her own fire with them on her return. There was something in the dame's mode of dressing which spoke of better times. Her head attire was different from that of any other poor woman in the village and she kept herself very much to herself not mixing with her neighbours [*cf. Addita 14*].

[*p. 113*] I do not suppose that I was more than a year one of Betty Harrison's scholars. Whether before my time she had exercised the vocation of a schoolmistress I know not, but I suspect she did not follow it for more than a year. Jane Hutchinson was to the best of my memory my next preceptress, but I do not think I could have been more [*p. 115*] than a few weeks under her care. She was a sharp active little old woman (the wife of a day labourer) and in her younger days had been very captivating and handsome. For this she had suffered as before her marriage she had been compelled under sentence from the court at Richmond to do penance in Forcett church for having had an illegitimate child.[30] Of all the people in the village, Thomas Harrison had been the only one who had gone to church that day to witness her shame and it was long her daily wish that she might live to see him visited in some member of his family with a similar disgrace. Unfortunately for him she had her wish as far as the disgrace was concerned. The shame of public penance was spared him, that sleeping lion the law ecclesiastic not having been aroused to do his duty.

And next comes Dolly Nicholson, the aged wife of an aged husband who had become a day-labourer until he was disabled by years. Dolly had the misfortune to be lame and as she was too old to work in the fields she fell back upon her scholarship. The few shillings she could weekly make by means of it would no doubt be a comfortable addition to their parish allowance. Some of Dolly's pupils were more advanced in learning than myself. They were

---

30 In the first half of the eighteenth century it was not unusual to find a man or woman "doing penance" in a church porch, clad in a white sheet, barefooted and carrying a white rod.

reading the Bible, the usual school book [*p. 117*] after the *Reading Made Easy*, and I well remember her teaching them to call pharaoh "proach". So much for poor Dolly's learning. I was in my fifth year when I was sitting at her feet and sucking in knowledge. This I remember from a particular çircumstance for which the Forcett register supplies the date. On the 26th June 1795 there was buried at that place my relation Henry Thompson, a farmer who lived in the village of Ovington opposite to my father's house and shop. The day was one of great excitement and curiosity to us youngsters as there was not only a funeral but there was to come into town a hearse, a vehicle which I for one had never seen and of which I had no correct idea [*cf. Addita 15*]. Dolly had promised to release us from our studies an hour sooner than the usual time that we might see the sight, but the usual prayers were to be gone through before we could be dismissed. The Apostles Creed had to be said in its turn, and when we were making unseemly haste to get through this part of our duty Dolly cried aloud "Dinnot gabble through't i' sike a hurry. It's impossible for God to hear you if gan on at that rate" and we had by her order [*p. 119*] to "start afresh and tak mare time."

Dicky and Dolly kept a gander and a goose upon the village green but they were in general unprofitable. I have heard the poor old man thus rhyming to himself as he was bringing the unproductive pair into shelter in an evening

Lag hyam, lag hyam,
Other geese hes geslings, ours hes nane.

The word hyam must be pronounced as a monosyllable and the *a* like the a in jam. Dicky was found burnt to death by his own fireside in 1802 and Dolly was blamed by certain people in the village for having pushed him into the fire. Her account of the matter, and she was believed by reasonable people and by the jury who sat upon the case, was that she had left him sitting quietly by the fire to go for half an hour into the house of a neighbour and found him dead upon her return. He was buried at Wycliffe on the 22nd August 1802, and she at the same place on the 1st March 1819 in the 87th year of her age. She was a resolute, right-minded, good principled woman and in her younger days before her marriage had shot her man, at least this was the story in the village. [*p. 121*] I have understood that Ulnaby near Piercebridge where she was a maidservant was the place where she performed this feat. One night she was left alone in the house, with no other protection than bolts and locks and a loaded gun, the latter at her own request. In the dead of night she heard a noise, found a man making his way into the house through a pantry window who threatened what he would do to her and her master's property and so she shot him at once.

My aunt Thompson who lived near this good woman's cottage in the village was exceedingly kind to her for many a long year during her widowhood. [p. 120] I must not forget to mention that Dolly Nicholson could sing a good song even in her old age. It must have been about the year 1815 that she sang to me with considerable feeling the song of Little Musgrave as it stands in Percy's Reliques,[31] but with a few important new readings. A copy of her version of the ballad as I then took it down from her lips is somewhere among my papers.

[p. 121] Here ends the history of my education under females. And now for a walk of a mile and a half at each end of the day and a schoolmaster and birch rod into the bargain.

[Schoolmasters]

In those days a village schoolmaster was in general but a very sorry stick, some poor man encouraged by the parish to which he belonged to try his hand in this way when he was on the point of being "troublesome". This was the term applied to those unhappy persons who were obliged by their necessities to have recourse to the parish for aid. If a man under such circumstances [p. 123] had the slightest knowledge of reading, writing and accounts, this was the line which the parish recommended him to pursue; and if a poor lad had in early life broken a leg or arm and had any turn for a book, the parish in such circumstances would send him to school to qualify him to act as schoolmaster and thus it would become a saver in the end.

There was a poor man of this sort at Hutton, a village to the south of Ovington and at a distance of a mile and a half [cf. Addita 16]. Hutton is another chapelry in the great parish of Gilling, and as it has generally been held by the same person as Forcett and was so much nearer to them than the former place, it was generally used by the Ovington dames for their churchings. The Hutton schoolmaster's name was Powell but he was better known as Auld Pow. He was a thin, weedy-looking, poor clothed old man who appeared to have

---

31 T. Percy, *Reliques of Ancient English Poetry*, (Edinburgh, 1767), 3,xi.

seen much hard work in the way of manual labour in his younger days. As his dialect was that of upper Teesdale he had probably been a miner in the lead-groves of that district; but his residence was Barnard Castle from which place he came to Hutton on Monday mornings and returned on Saturdays, crossing the Tees at Wycliffe boathouse. In the winter when there was ice upon the river, [*p. 125*] however strong it might be, even if it had been able to bear a cart, it was his custom for safety to bestride a long pole to keep himself out of the Tees if the ice should break beneath his feet.

His schoolroom was a wretched place, a mere hovel, paved with cobbles, covered with thatch and open to the roof. I should say that few of his scholars exceeded ten or eleven years of age. There might be twenty or five and twenty such as these, boys and girls, and when any poor child was guilty of giving birth to a noise from which an unpleasant smell might arise, the good-natured old man would do his best to spare the culprit by crying out "smo foat" (small fault). These words were frequently uttered during the course of the day.

As a scholar I was still a reader, and I do not think I could have had more than a summer of this man's instructions. I must then have been about five years of age. Markham's spelling book was then in high fashion, and I fancy it was my manual.[32] The going to Hutton school first made me acquainted with the wallet. My elder brother and I carried our dinner along with us every morning. At one end of the wallet was the solid part of our food, and in the other a tin bottle containing new milk from our own cow, perfect in its purity. We cared more for gooseberry or apple pies when they could be had [*p. 127*] than beef or mutton. When we were driven to the latter it was generally in a cold state, and the good woman [Mary Green the wife of Willy Green, a mason] at whose house we left our provender would boil for us a few potatoes for which a corner had been found in our satchel. In this convenience there was a bag at each end. It was slung over the right shoulder of him by whom it was carried, and it was tied by strings beneath the left arm. [...] He and his wife were excellent, kind-hearted people, great favourites at Girlington and

---

32 A wide selection of grammars and spelling books was available, see V. E. Neuburg, *Popular Education in Eighteenth Century England*, (London, 1971), ch. 3. As early as 1701 an anonymous text-book entitled *The Schoolmaster* described new methods of teaching three-year-old children. A revised edition of William Markham's *Introduction to Spelling and Reading English* was published by Peat & Son of Thirsk in 1856.

hence their becoming troubled with us youngsters. [...]

The next school which I attended was in my native village. There had settled in it, or rather had opened a school in it, a man of the name of Forster, who had the misfortune [*p. 129*] to have a wooden leg, the result of an accident, which probably first put it into his head to become a schoolmaster. Of poor "*wood-leg*", for this is the name by which he was generally known, I do not remember many particulars. I think he came from Darlington and I further fancy that he went home once a week like him of Hutton to Barnard Castle, but I recollect perfectly that under him I began to write. I can still see the penknife which he would place under my hand, edge upwards, that I might be compelled to hold my pen in a becoming way.

The making of a pen for each scholar was a solemn proceeding for this man. His first step was in each case to sharpen his knife upon his shoe. He then cut off the feathery part of the quill to a proper length, denuding one of its sides in a similar way. In the next place, with that part of the edge of his knife which is nearest to the haft he carefully scraped the bole of the quill itself which, having inserted into his mouth, he afterwards rolled in the scrapings upon his table obtained as above mentioned. A good rubbing of the quill so covered, by means of the breast of his coat, completed this part of the business. The cutting of the pen followed after the boy had been duly interrogated as to the kind of pen he liked in the way of splet [*p. 131*] or spawd etc. and then the lad was set to work to do his best, the master holding himself ready to wield his knife and amend the tool if it sprented or misbehaved itself in any other way. I do not remember the circumstances which took this master away or the time of his leaving us, but, from the dates and recollections of events, I had in May 1797 become the scholar, still a daily one, of a superior master and at a greater distance from home.

At the distance of about three and a half miles from Ovington, (a long way for a boy of not much more than six years of age to walk twice a day) on the way to Forcett but in the parish of Stanwick stands the village of Caldwell, a place of considerable antiquity and a member of the Fee of Scrope above alluded to. The place takes its name from a copious spring of cold and pure water which bursts out from the mountain limestone rock at the foot of the village, and the village itself is extensive and straggling with a large green and many gardens thickly set with plumb trees. [*p. 130*] The form of the village is as near as may be circular and in the shape of a bowl, the houses on two thirds of its circumference standing upon the edge of the summit and creeping down into the hollow with their gardens and plumb trees in great irregularity. It is nearly flat on the east. [*p. 131*] Two or three houses had pointed windows, and there was an old dovecot of the circular shape and massive walls peculiar to old manor houses. The village stands on the high road from the Bishoprick coal pits to Richmond by the Gatherly Moor and Gilling way, and there runs at its foot the famous trout stream which flows into the Tees [*p. 133*] at Croft, and which strange to say has no general name of its own but is called Hutton Beck, Caldwell Beck, Clow Beck etc. as it flows by the respective places which it visits. This stream takes its rise in the west, not far from Greta Bridge, and the trout in it however small are of the colour of salmon. My first acquaintance with it was at Hutton as we crossed it twice daily on our road to and from school at that place, and I have since caught many a good trout in its waters.

[*p. 135*] The school at Caldwell to which it was determined that I and my elder brother should go was in high repute. Its master was John Goldsbrough, better known by the name Jack Gaudy. He was a Barton man of the village of that name a few miles to the south east of Caldwell on the road to Darlington. Thither he went every Saturday afternoon to his wife and family, returning to his scholars every Monday morning. During the week he tabled with the farmers in their turn, such of them as had children at his school, but whether it was free of expense after the Westmorland fashion I do not know. [*p. 134*] Upon consideration I have no doubt the man lived free of expense or why his hebdomadal movements from house to house? (In Westmorland this privelege is called whittlegate).[33] [*p. 135*] He was a strong, hale, resolute man and about thirty-five or forty years of age, perhaps not so old, as boys invariably consider a man of forty an old man. He did not I believe remain long at Caldwell after we had left. Many years afterwards I heard of him at Hurworth where I think he died leaving a family behind him. There are still people of his name at that place, perhaps his descendants.

[*p. 137*] The point being settled that my brother and I should go to Caldwell school my mother took us there one afternoon in the

---

33 A country curate or schoolmaster could often exist on a miserable salary by means of whittlegate, entitling him to use his whittle or knife at the tables of his parishioners or the parents of his pupils for a certain number of days in each year.

spring of 1797 upon a voyage of discovery to learn terms and conditions and requirements. We were accompanied thither by my first preceptress, dame Betty Harrison who had a relation in Caldwell, the wife of a farmer of the name of Dent and a sister of Thomas Harrison of The Edge. [...] To a certain extent at the Ovington end of the road there is a footpath across the fields towards Caldwell in addition to that for carts and horses, and dame Betty and my mother took care to make us acquainted with both, the progress thither being made by the former and the return by the latter. The latter, among other purposes, served as the ancient corpse road to Forcett (I have seen many funerals go by that way) but on account of the bad state in which it was generally kept, [*p. 139*] it has I believe been disused for that purpose, the living finding it easier to carry their dead by the roundabout way of Old Bartle. [*p. 135*] Of Caldwell and its neighbourhood I have little more to say, save that with the exception of the usual men of handicrafts, its inhabitants were chiefly in the agricultural line, farmers or their labourers.

[*p. 139*] When it was settled that we were to trudge to Caldwell it was also thought best that we should not trouble the Dents with the deposit of our wallets but leave them at the house of an old Staindrop friend of my mother, Jenny Turton the wife of Nichol Turton, who always treated us with great kindness and was ready to cook for us or undergo any trouble for our sakes. [*p. 143*] We found the master in his school with a considerable number of scholars about him, boys and girls, some of them fourteen or fifteen years of age, and all of them intently anxious to have a look at us. There were perhaps few in the school younger than I was. Terms were asked, conditions stated, and before we came away the master presented my brother and myself each of us with a little book of the cost of a penny or two pence, glittering in the golden paper then in use for such juvenile treasures. My brother's gift contained a few figures of animals with a stanza beneath each. One only I remember.

> An elephant has bones of brass
> A castle on his back can bear,
> Just like an ox he eateth grass
> And drinketh up the river clear.

My present, the truth must be told, was *The Life and Death of Cock Robin* with cuts in wood of the wretched character of that period. Why, bless the good man, for two or three preceding years I had been able to read almost anything that fell my way. [*p. 145*] "Cock Robin" was something of a useless book, but it was kindly intended and it put me at once in love with my master.

The schoolroom, the seat of Jacky's domain, was if possible worse than that at Hutton above described. It was in every sense an uncomfortable place in itself, and more than this it was in danger of falling from old age. In this state of things, not long after I had become acquainted with it to record its demerits in after days, there came into this miserable place a gentleman, booted and spurred, attended by one or two farmers of the village, in all probability [*p. 147*] merely to pay an act of passing kindness to the master. But this was an opportunity not to be neglected. The visitor was the steward of the estate. The master feelingly pointed out to him the state of his school and the danger incurred daily by him and his scholars in assembling within its walls. Having finished his address to which the gentleman had apparently lent a careful ear, he begged his scholars, male and female, to stand up and join him in a respectful request for a place in which we could meet in safety. This was instantly done, we young and old repeating the words which fell from the lips of our master, and a promise was made which was afterwards fulfilled [*cf. Addita 17*].

[*p. 149*] The new schoolroom to which, through the kindness of Mr Clarke we were soon translated, was large and spacious. It had previously been a granary, and being above ground it was approached by a flight of stone steps on the outside. The wooden floor was a great comfort to us boys who had to walk a certain distance in all kinds of weather and often had to go into it in damp shoes. Before we quitted the former hovel however we had the scene of barring out[34] previous to the Whitsuntide holidays, a custom common to most schools at that time but now I believe obsolete. The event took place immediately before the commencement of the afternoon duties, after the hour of dinner. When the master returned [*p. 151*] at one-o-clock the door was fastened against him, we being all assembled in school. The scene was a new one to me and I remember being much afraid of the consequences. The parley soon began, angrily on the part of the master but firmly and respectfully on the part of the senior boys. The latter demanded the usual

---

34 This was more usually a Shrovetide custom. When the children had locked and barred the school against their teacher, master and children were free to join in traditional sports and games.

holidays with a day or two into the bargain. For a while he refused (why, I know not for I happen to know from experience that schoolmasters are as fond of their holidays as their boys) but at last consented in a dignified way; the door was unbarred and we handled our pens and slate pencils as usual.

As a schoolmaster Jacky Gaudy was considerably in advance of his period. His system of teaching was a good one and all his movements appeared to be the result of thoughtful consideration. With each class of scholars according to the progress they had made, every part of the day had its peculiar duties and after we had removed into the new school and had gained more room he had increased means and opportunities for the further development of his plans which were not neglected. By means of monitors selected weekly from the senior boys and by his own firmness the discipline of the school was kept up in an excellent way, and when correction [p. 153] was necessary a few slaps upon the open hand from a ferula, a piece of thin wood with a handle or shank of the same material, were found to be of great avail. After all, the punishment or rather the pain was slight under this instrument, but the children always roared out with all their might. The master did not discourage this noise as it was sure to tell upon the fears of those who had not undergone the punishment, and thus the firler as it was universally called even by the master became an object of terror to those who had never experienced its full effects, and kept them in order.

Here at Caldwell the usual *Reading Made Easy* was the preliminary book for beginners, but for those who were advanced in the art the Bible was very properly laid aside and there was put into their hands a collection of pieces in prose and verse from the writings of some of our best authors. From the copy I now possess of this book it appears to have been published at Darlington by subscription under the title of *Modern Beauties* in a duodecimo size.[35] To me it had many charms and even to this day I could repeat much of it both in prose and verse. I had not been long at Caldwell school before Walkinghame's Arithmetic[36] was put into my hands as it was thought I had acquired a sufficient skill in the mystery of reading and writing. Arithmetic was to me a new field and I set [p. 155] to work in earnest

---

35 Published by Heaviside of Darlington in 1793, see copy at Darlington Branch Library (Local History Collection).
36 F. Walkinghame, *The Tutor's Assistant, a School Arithmetic*, (London, 1751).

to master its first four rules, a victory which I soon achieved.

With the older boys in the school I was a great favourite, and first one of them then another would offer his services in making the initial flourishes in my account book in which were duly recorded the day to day results of my slate and pencil. I possessed this book until not long ago but I fear it is now lost. One of the lads who favoured me in this way with the embellishments of his pen was Tom Whytell who I think came from Eppleby. Upwards of twenty years later I stumbled upon this man as a head waiter in the Queen's Head at Morpeth. Poor fellow he died very soon afterwards a martyr to brandy, leaving behind him a widow and family in great distress. Another was a lad of the name of Shaw who came from Forcett, grew up to man's estate and then hanged himself in a state of lunacy. There was also in the school another James Raine, six or seven years older than myself, the son of James Raine of Forcett who having been a gentleman's servant or butler somewhere had opened a shop at that place, and the brother of William Raine whom I found in 1804 at Kirby Hill, of whom I shall have more to say hereafter.

Many of the articles which were used in the school were supplied to us by the master and upon them he would doubtless have a small profit. But his charges were not unreasonable and no-one complained.

[*p. 157*] Our doings as schoolboys were of the usual kind. Once however it was proposed by one of the seniors that we should raise the devil by a plan of which he had heard as being extremely successful for the purpose. During the dinner hour a circle was drawn with chalk upon the school floor within the limits of which such as desired to see the manifestation were bidden to take their stand. The rest were desired to leave the room. I was one [*p. 159*] who remained. Our leader then began to read the Lord's Prayer backwards, having informed us that at the last word the object of our curiosity would appear but without power to hurt us who were within the circle. The last word was said but the only appearance was that of the master who smelt no smell of brimstone, nor did he find out the wicked folly in which we had been engaged. Of our exploits on our road to and from school I have more to say and of a more creditable kind.

[*p. 161*] My brother and I were not the only two boys who went to Caldwell school from our village. No sooner had it been settled that we should become the pupils of Jack Gaudy than others determined to follow our example, some of them lads older than ourselves and we were happy in their company and protection. One of them [*p. 163*] Cuddy Harwood jun. was the grandson of my grandmother Moore's sister Mary Harwood and therefore our relation. The school fees for many of these poor lads were paid by charitable people who could hardly have made a better use of the money they had to spare. An aged housekeeper at Wycliffe Hall paid for such as were Roman Catholics, my great aunt at Girlington was charitably minded in the same way, and there were others who imitated her example.

Cuddy appeared one day at school in a pair of new shoes and in the course of the morning he frequently disappeared beneath the table. Seeing this movement repeated half-hourly, the master sent for the lad up to his desk and begged to know the meaning of his proceedings. "I've gotten a new pair of shun" said the boy, "and my mother telt me to change them as oft as I could and I was deing as she bad me." The shoes were not made for each foot as at the present time, but from the same last, and the mother's advice was good. But a daily compliance with it would have been sufficient. Poor Cuddy became a soldier like most of his uncles and died before he was twenty years of age far from home but where I know not.

[*p. 164*] Once during my connection with Caldwell school the alehouse keepers and a few of the young farmers got up two or three horse races for saddles, bridles etc. The sport lasted for one day and with the master's permission and under his directions we schoolboys wrote the hand bills or notices of the event which were circulated in the neighbouring villages. We were all of us permitted to attend and my father came down to take care of my brother and myself upon the ground. I have a very distinct recollection of the gingerbread watches covered with leaf gold with which we were tempted.

[*p. 165*] We had not been many weeks at Caldwell school when one evening as we were returning homewards we met a man running to that village to carry the sad news of the death of their son to a father and mother. Kit Fenwick an apprentice to Harry Hutchinson our village carpenter and a native of Caldwell had been drowned that afternoon in crossing the Tees a little below Wycliffe at the foot of Howberry, a remarkable rock with a rapid stream and a deep pool below it. Kit was a lad universally beloved and at the time of his death was probably about 18 or 20 years of age. After his body was found it was taken home to his poor father and mother and was buried at Stanwick St John's on 27th May 1797.

[*p. 179*] I have gone through Caldwell scores of times since my connection with it as a schoolboy ceased and I have always looked upon the place with an affectionate and grateful eye. Soon after that event [*p. 181*] a new school was built in the middle of the village and since that time the convenience of the people has been further consulted by a new chapel on account of the distance of the village from Stanwick St John's, the parish church.

[*p. 185*] I do not remember the precise circumstances which led to our removal from Caldwell school but I believe it was owing to the situation in which Thomas Harrison the farmer at The Edge at this period found himself placed. He had a large family of boys and girls, chiefly of the latter, and to a person of his slender income education at a distance might have been inconvenient if not out of the question. Neither do I recollect through whose recommendation a man of the name of John Bonner came to teach school in my native village but I am inclined to connect his advent with Thomas Harrison as our school belonged to the latter and was of precisely the same character as that at Hutton and our first at Caldwell. It was a small room, open to the roof, covered with thatch and paved with round stones gathered from the Tees. It had originally been a stable and for a while before it became a seat of learning had been occupied by John Burrell. It was the most northern house in the last row of the village, and behind it on the old Tunstall estate and on the brow of the ravine separating the village from The Edge was a clump of fine old Scotch firs of such an age as to have become stately [*p. 187*] in size and graceful in form.

To the best of my recollection Bonner was a man of perhaps fifty years of age and one who had evidently seen not a few ups and downs in life. I believe he was born somewhere in the Scorton country and had been educated at Barton under a man of the name of Stelling, a master of great fame about 1750 and afterwards who walked about in a scarlet gown and made many scholars. Bonner had afterwards gone to America but in what capacity I know not. After returning home he had been in the service (perhaps as a steward) of a family of the name of Michell, the patrons of the living at Haslingfield in the county of Cambridge one of whom purchased the estate at Forcett about the year 1783. Bonner was in the service of Mr Michell that year as he was one of those who took part in removing to Forcett the body of the purchaser's father from Haslingfield where it had previously been interred to Forcett. Of his history after that until his settlement at Ovington as schoolmaster I know nothing save that he had formed an improper connection with a loose woman at Manfield by whom he had a large family of illegitimate children. To this place he went away every Saturday and returned on Monday morning. This man was by no means the person for a mixed school of both sexes [*p. 189*] and all ages. He was a sound mathematician, a neat penman, and much above the ABC department of his vocation.

[How long Raine stayed under Mr Bonner is not recorded but we know that by 1804 he was at Kirby Hill School and later attended the well known grammar school at Richmond.]

[Country Pleasures]

[Raine refers above to his habit of wandering alone for hours when not at school, often in the woods by the river. Sometimes he watched the fishermen, occasionally there was a different form of entertainment.]

[*p. 103*] The women of the village would carry their dirty linen and pans down through the woods to the Tees side, would kindle a fire with the wreck of floods or the fallen branches of trees of which there was always abundance, would boil their water, make the ravine [*p. 105*] ring with the battledoor and return home in the evening with their habitiments not only washed but dried into the bargain. If the process was prolonged till the shades of evening were creeping into the ravine and all work in the fields was over, they were generally joined by the young men and lads of the village and the echoes of mirth among the rocks and the combination of sounds was extremely striking.

[*p. 159*] On the whole way from Ovington to Caldwell there was only one solitary house and in consequence during the breeding time of the year the road was rich in birds' nests. We failed not to take every advantage of our opportunities in this way but I have no recollection that we were so cruel in this amusement as boys are in general. We refrained from robbing the nests of redbreasts from the belief that if we did so our cows would give blood instead of milk.[37] I

---

37 It was considered very unlucky to kill or maim a robin or to take eggs from the nest. Country people said that if you killed a robin you would break a limb before the day was over.

myself was always averse to robbing and, young though I was in comparison with the others, I had considerable influence with my comrades. I remember that on one occasion when we had found a blackbird's nest, I administered a solemn oath to each of them upon the catechism (the only *good* book we had about us) that he would neither rob the nest himself nor tell of it to others. To add to the solemnity I made each boy in his turn take his stand upon a large boulder stone of granite lying in the ditch and repeat the words of the oath after my dictation. [*p. 158*] The monitors were of the party. Precious fellows, no doubt, to keep us out of the way of harm! [*p. 56*] During my first few years at Durham it was now and then the sport of school boys to go down to the Prebend's bridge and angle for swallows with rods and artificial flies over the battlements. In general they were very successful but after some difficulty I put a stop to their cruel amusement.

[*p. 159*] We were not without our superstitious [*p. 161*] observances. We would not eat a bramble berry or bumblekite after Holy Rood day because we had heard and believed it was a custom with the devil to go from hedge to hedge putting his foot upon the fruit.[38] We also took pleasure in now and then laying two straws cross-wise upon the footpath to bother and mortify the witches.[39]

We had another amusement on the road of a different kind. There had been (and perhaps there was even then) a clergyman at Forcett of the name of Johnson. This man was a great smoker and was generally occupied in this way on his road from village to village in his walks round his parish. He would light a pipe in one village and proceed with it in his mouth to another. When, however, the pipe was exhausted, he did not throw it away neither did he carry it home in his pocket. He hid it in a holly bush or some place of apparent security, and the searching for Parson Johnson's pipes in the hedges was a constant object with us on our road.

---

38 As well as Holy Rood Day, 14th September, northern folklore also associated the devil's pollution of blackberries with 29th September, Michaelmas day, see J. Wright, *The English Dialect Dictionary*, (1898-1905), i: A C, p. 441 *sub* bumble-klte. On 11th October the devil was supposed to have fallen into a blackberry bush and to have cursed it for scratching him; it was therefore unlucky to eat blackberries after that date, see I. Opie and M. Tatem, *Dictionary of Superstitions*, (Oxford, 1989), p. 29.

39 Stems of bracken are probably meant here. These were often used as a charm against witches.

[The solitary farmhouse which the boys passed on their way home was occupied by a man called George Wheatley.]

[*p. 179*] [He] was a sad thorn in our sides. In the field in which his house stood grew the best rushes on the road, and when on our return home in the evening we were inclined to make a cap or a whip he would sally out upon us with a gun and put us to our heels.

[*p. 25*] My books were got as I could. A few were gifts [*p. 27*] by my mother after she had been at Barnard Castle or Staindrop, sixpenny books in gilt backs such as Jack the Giant Killer, Tom Hickathrift[40] etc., but another source was occasionally open to me in which happily I could choose for myself. Once in about two months there came into the village from Barningham I believe, a man called Tom Barnes who had been a soldier in his youth and wore a red coat. His trade was rag gathering, buying hare skins, selling pins, needles, tapes etc., but he always had in his basket a few penny books such as were then popular, tales of giants and fairies, ballads etc. It was his custom to announce his arrival by the blast of a tin horn at the head of the village, and this blast had a magical effect upon me the moment I heard it. With the penny in my hand which my mother never failed to give me to get rid of my importunity, Tom's basket was ransacked and a new book was the prize. [*p. 26*] Tom was in the habit of making a proclamation at the head of the village after blowing his horn "Gether out your rags ony a' ye 'at hes ony."

There was another itinerant bookseller with whom I sometimes dealt, a man who had been a pig-jobber and in consequence rejoiced in the name of Pig Tommy. His name was Oates and he lived at Winston. With Pig Malley, his wife, this man travelled from village to village in the neighbourhood selling a few articles of coarse earthenware made at Ramshaw near West Auckland, and now and then he had a few books in his basket. [*p. 27*] In the absence of novelties I could always fall back upon an old tattered, well thumbed copy of Robin Hood, the whole of which I could have repeated at one

---

40 Tom Hickathrift was said to have been a giant of enormous strength who defended the marshlands of Norfolk but also was kind to the poor and weak. There is a gravestone, eight feet long, said to be his in the churchyard of Tilney All Saints in Norfolk. He is supposed to have stood on a river bank three miles from Tilney and hurled his huge gravestone, saying that he wished to be buried where it fell. This, conveniently, was in the churchyard. See J. and C. Bord, *The Secret Country*, (London, 1976), p. 89.

time. All these studies (if they may be dignified by such a name) were carried on in the room of my grandmother Raine whilst she was at her wheel, every now and again telling me a tale or singing a song which had been current when she was young.

[*p. 16*] I remember that when we were children, I must I suppose have been eight or nine years of age when a large collection of toys was sent to us from York by a person of the name of Williamson a relation of my mother. There was a thrift box for each of us and there were also books of a religious character such as explanations of the catechism, tracts published by the Christian Knowledge Society etc.[41] The donor promised to come and examine us in the catechism and I for one was duly prepared but he never made his appearance.

[*p. 60*] There had been a maypole in the village from time immemorial. This was periodically taken down and re-erected amid rejoicing and jollification. Everyone subscribed to raise the fund for a tansy cake, an enormous plumb cake flavoured with tansy.[42] Even the passers through the town were laid under contribution. A chain was stretched across the road at its western end where the passage was a narrow one and no-one was allowed to go on his way without giving his mite to the maypole and the tansy cake. The day of rejoicing I think was Easter Tuesday. Crowds assembled from the neighbouring villages. There was ale drinking (spiritous liquors were not sold in the town) tansy cake eating and dancing upon the green. The maypole was re-erected and hung with garlands, and the fun terminated by choosing a mayor to remain in office until the next festival. Harry Page was always the man, and he always had a facetious speech for the occasion. He was duly chaired upon a handbarrow and, being always re-elected, he was as a matter of course called "My Lord" by

---

41 The S.P.C.K. was founded in 1699. A twelve volume collection of their tracts was published in 1800. These were generally very dull and stern in content and presentation.

42 Raine may be wrong in his dates here: the maypole was apparently put up for 1st May, whereas tansy cake was part of the Easter celebrations. It was made from tansy, a herb with yellow flowers and bitter green leaves, said to contain properties which encouraged miscarriages and, according to an early herbalist, "to purge away from the stomach and guts the phlegme engendered by eating of fish in the Lenten season", see W. Coles, *Adam in Eden*, (London, 1657), quoted in J. Brand, *Popular Antiquities*, i (London, 1841), p. 104. Not surprisingly tansy cakes were liberally coated with sugar.

man, woman and child till the day of his death.

[*p. 133*] A field or two to the west of Caldwell the limestone rock rises up to a considerable height and cropping out towards the south, in a thick wood of natural elder, thorns, whin, etc., divides its strata into several yawning fissures which afford excellent shelter for foxes. This place is called by the ancient and appropriate name of Foxberry and has long been a favourite cover of the Raby hounds. The view from this elevation is extensive and the scene on a hunting day is very striking, especially after the fox has broken cover and is making his way over the low country at the feet of the spectator. I have frequently witnessed this scene, and well should I like to see it once more. But this may not be. I could once run after the Raby fox hounds with the swiftest of the swift, but I am now nearly sixty eight years of age and am detained at Middleton One Row by a pair [*p. 135*] of swelled legs, the result of a disordered action in my heart.

[3. OVINGTON FOLK]

[When James Raine was born in 1791 there were about 200 people living in Ovington. Many had lived through the greater part of the century.]

[*p. 169*] Harry [Hutchinson the village carpenter] once had as apprentice, a lad whom the pen of a ready writer has rendered immortal. Mr Squeers, in reality George Clarkson, served his time to Harry Hutchinson at Ovington as a carpenter.[43] [Harry was] [*p. 165*] a man advanced in years and a great character in his way. He was a man utterly without education but with no small share of worldly wisdom, knowing well his own interest and not very scrupulous in pushing that knowledge beyond proper bounds. He was the coffin maker for the village and its neighbourhood, and on the day [*p. 167*] of the funeral when the company was assembled he invariably had the same routine of grave sentiments suited to the occasion. "All man's mortar" was one of them and he would occasionally add the remainder of the truism but also in his own peculiar phraseology.

---

43 Clarkson had a school at Bowes Hall, a farm at the east end of the village of Bowes. The character of Wackford Squeers in Charles Dickens, *Nicholas Nickleby*, is generally thought to have been based upon William Shaw, headmaster of Bowes Academy, but it is possible that it was a composite picture of several masters in the area, perhaps including Clarkson.

"All man's mortar, here today and here aghyan tomorrow." Here was a strange perversion of the Christian adage "All man's mortal, here today and gone tomorrow." This is somewhat like a gravestone at Rock or Remington in Northumberland upon which the words *memento mori* are written "me men tomorrow".

Harry had a large family of grown-up children, he had also apprentices but neither he nor they ever went near a place of worship, save and excepted as above. My uncle Thompson for whom he worked when his services were required once remonstrated with him on the example which he set to those around and instanced the poor lad Kit above mentioned saying at the same "Kit, I'll give thee a shilling if thou can say the Lord's prayer." Kit blushed and hesitated, well aware that the shilling could be no shilling [*p. 169*] to him, but his master encouraged him with all his might and tried to set him going. "Come Kit man begin and addle thy shillin, our father, our chart i' heeven." [...]

Betty, Harry's wife was also a singular person, full of much mischief and cunning and taking pleasure in setting her neighbours by the ears together. Her usual caution after having put some base tale into circulation was "mind and dinnot give up your author, if ye de I'll clap my foot on't." Willy their youngest son was a mild good-natured lad who came by his death in a melancholy way. The wife of John his elder brother died of a virulent fever. The relations of the poor woman did not arrive in time to see the face of their relative before the coffin was closed, but they came before the procession had left the village and made it their earnest request to see the face of their relative for the last time. Every objection was properly raised to such a proceeding but Willy, sympathising with their desire, [*p. 171*] consented to do his part in satisfying their wishes. The coffin was set down upon the village green, he as the carpenter who had made it unscrewed the lid and exhibited the face of the poor woman to view but he was struck upon the spot with death. He caught the fever and was himself buried at Forcett within five weeks. These things happened in August and September 1825, Willy being then in the 35th year of his age, a man who would have been a scholar if he had had the opportunity. A gentleman he already was in his heart.

[*p. 61*] Hannah [Page] was a distiller of herbs such as balm and mint. She was the widow of one of the men to whom my grandfather Edmund Raine read aloud in the evenings from Josephus etc. Dying

in the year 1819 at the great age of 101 she was the first person over
whom I read the funeral service happening to have walked down
from Ovington to Forcett on that day (the 7th July) to pay an
afternoon's visit to Mr Heslop. [*p. 60*] Hannah had been born and
brought up in a district in which *q* was pronounced *wh*. She would
talk of a whart of milk, and the good times in which the spoon would
stand erect in a whart of pease podish (porridge). No complaint was
ever mentioned incident to the human frame under which she
herself had not laboured. When in the work field the conversation
between the men and women haymaking or reaping took a turn this
way, her account of her sufferings under her various maladies was
marvellous. The small pox was once in the village and Hannah was as
usual full of detail as to what she had undergone from this
complaint. My uncle Thompson in whose field she happened to be
working said to her in his quiet way "Had you ever the fiend pox
Hannah?" Her answer was instantly "Oh honey twenty times" to the
infinite amusement of the knowing ones. Hannah was also a doctress
in her way.

[Hannah Page had two children, Harry and Martha. She lived with
Martha and her bastard son in a primitive cottage on land bought by
William Moore in 1804. The old cottage was pulled down and its
occupants were rehoused in the village.]

[*p. 61*] Martha Page was a great thief, stealing anything she
could lay her hands upon in a quiet way. Jacky her bastard son was
a poor, half-witted, decrepit cursing and swearing creature whose
father had been Ninian Gascoigne of Middleton One Row. Martha
died in 1825 at the age of 71, and Jacky her crooked son, who could
never walk but pulled himself round on a stool, in 1814 aged 41.

[*p. 60*] Harry [Page] who lived in the village [was] a married
man with a family and quite a character in his way. He worked at the
highways for his livelihood, shaved the men on Sunday mornings
and knew everything that could be known about the remarkable
racehorses of the day. [*p. 62*] The house in which he lived was a
parcel of the glebe land of the vicarage of Gilling. He had a standard
jargonell pear tree in his garden (the only tree of that kind in the
village) and he made a good deal of money from its fruit in
favourable years. He knew precisely the time to gather them. He then
wrapped them up in blankets, and when they were ready sold them
for a penny a piece. Harry's was the only house in which I ever saw

the primitive oven [*p. 64*] in use among our cottage forefathers.[44] It was made of cast iron, circular in shape like a pan, with a strong lid of the same material, and of the depth of an ordinary pie. After the article to be baked had been placed in it, it was suspended over the fire by the randle balk and reckon crook. The next step was to kindle a good substantial fire of wood and coals upon the lid, and in due course out came the pie or loaf of bread or whatever it might be, properly soaked and browned, as in these days it would have been in an oven.

[Harry Page attended the church at Wycliffe and was one of the men who assembled in the porch for a gossip before the service.]

[*p. 87*] [He joined] in the attempt to revive the psalmody in that church which was rapidly falling into decay. [...] His mode of writing music was somewhat peculiar. He ruled the lines for his bars at a distance of not much less than half an inch from each other. He then poured his ink into a teacup, and scorning the use of a pen would dip the point of his forefinger into it and make a dab upon his lines where each note in its turn should stand. In the case of open notes he had some contrivance which I forget. Then he would put in tails and ligatures and his work was done.

[*p. 62*] On a Sunday morning about the year 1820 as I was on my road to officiate at Hutton church, I found him in a situation of which he appeared to be heartily ashamed. He had given up shaving on Sundays for a better, I mean more lucrative occupation, that of carrying out joints of beef for the Ovington butcher. On the day in question, Harry's horse had stumbled in a very nasty dirty part of the road between Hutton and Girlington, his basket had fallen to the ground and its contents were covered with mire. There he was with his jack-a-legs scraping the mud from his shoulders of mutton and fillets of veal with all his might and main and trying to make them decent before presenting them at the house for which they were intended. "A bad job my Lord. So much for sabbath breaking" said I as I passed by. He blushed and shook his head, but made no remark in reply. This was the last time I saw poor Harry Page, Lord Mayor of

---

44 A kail pot was used for boiling vegetables for broth and also as an oven for baking bread, pies and cakes. The randle balk, or reckon bauk, was a bar in the chimney from which an iron chain was suspended. From this hung a reckon crook on which to hang pans and kettles.

Ovington, a good-natured, kind-hearted man in his way. He was buried at Forcett on the 14th of November 1821 in the 53rd year of his age.

[Tom Jackson, shoemaker and parish clerk and his wife Betty.]

[*p. 7*] He was a tall thin man of grave aspect and of few words. He was I suspect not obliged to work for his bread. The house he lived in was his own and it was the impression in the village that he had money. I can never forget his wife, Bet Jackson. I see her distinctly, a short, quick-eyed, shrewd woman enveloped in mystery. It was the common belief that she had been a member of a notorious band of robbers who had, under the heading of Sir William Brown, as he was called, kept the county of Durham in particular in a state of perpetual alarm. I think mention is made of him in Sykes *Local Records*,[45] and the stories about him in the neighbourhood of Auckland and Witton-le-Wear are still numerous. One of Brown's favourite exploits was to break into parish churches and to steal the communion plate which up to his time was generally kept in a box in the vestry. In many cases he was but too successful.

But whatever [*p. 9*] Bet Jackson's early history might have been, there was something about her indicating that she had come down when she became the wife of a cobbler. The room in which she and her husband mainly lived made a very strong impression upon my mind. It was of large size, and its walls were literally overspread with utensils of copper such as dish covers, jelly shapes and everything conceivable in the way of necessaries in that metal accommodated to or necessary to the kitchen of a man of rank and fortune. Here and there also upon the walls were suspended many articles in the same material of a purely ornamental character. I remember in particular a figure of what the old woman called King William on horseback, about five or six inches in height, and I have a recollection of various other ornaments of the same character.

[*p. 11*] Betty was famous for her punctual attendance at the funerals of her neighbours, and still more famous for the quantity of funeral cake which she would eat on these occasions. There was a story that upon her deathbed she gave orders for two holes to be made in her coffin, one at each end, [*p. 13*] so that when the devil came in

45 John Sykes, *Local Records; or, Historical Register of Remarkable Events*, (Newcastle, 1824), does not have an entry for William Brown in its index.

at one end to claim her as his own she might escape by the other. She was buried at Wycliffe on the 29th January 1802 when I had just entered upon my eleventh year. Her husband left Ovington, married again, died at Lane End near Hutton and was buried at Wycliffe on the 6th of February 1807 aged 80. The two occasionally visited Mr and Mrs Wilkinson at Thorp Hall in the parish of Wycliffe, and upon their departure Mrs Wilkinson who was [blank] would say "Good night Bet. Good night Tom. Good night Bet and Tom." The house in which Jackson lived at Ovington was previously occupied by a man called Adam Lodge. He had his coffin made for several years before his death and used it as a cupboard for his bread, cheese etc.

[Betty Harrison, venerable old dame and schoolmistress.]

[p. 109] I remember her talking frequently of a brother she called Uvvy who had died at York at an early age. I have since read an inscription in memory of Ovington Harrison in the account of the epitaphs once to be found in the churchyard of St Olaves in that city.[46] This is doubtless the youth whom the poor woman lamented, and perhaps for a good reason as in him she had probably lost not only a brother but a friend.

How she lived, whether in the end she had to receive help from the parish or whether the family at The Edge assisted her I cannot tell, but to the best of my recollection her relations never went near her and so she struggled [p. 111] on in her small room until 1806 when she was buried at Forcett among her ancestors. She had been unwell for some time before she died. Happening to be home from school and hearing that the poor woman would probably not live until my return at the end of another week, I ventured to go into her cottage to sympathise with her in her sufferings and in truth, to bid her farewell. To my surprise I found her room full of people, young and old (none of her relations were among them) who had been brought together by idle curiosity to see the poor woman take her departure out of the world. She was in bed taking no notice of those around her, but breathing heavily with what is called the death rattle in her throat, a noise caused I believe by the collected mucus from which the sufferer has not strength to free himself. The people talked with each other in whispers. One woman got a prayerbook and read

---

46 Untraced.

it in silence and all waited in fear to hear the last sound from the poor sufferer's throat and see the last beating of her ailing heart. At last Cuddy Harwood my relation said in a somewhat louder tone than that of a whisper "There's pigeon feathers [*p. 113*] in her bed, she cannot die."[47] In a moment, as if by instinct without further deliberation, he and two or three of the women wrapped the poor dying woman in her bedclothes and placed her in her old armchair before the fire so that the spell being broken she might die in peace. But still she could not die. There was the same deadly sound and the same glazed eye and I could bear it no longer. A while afterwards the wife of Thomas Harrison of The Edge came in, thanked the people for their kindness, and clearing the room replaced the sufferer in her bed where she lingered for a day or two longer and died in peace. Only once in the interim had she strength to speak and her words were these: "This old heart of mine takes a great deal of pulling down." She was however incessantly occupied in mental prayer.

[Thomas Harrison one of the Ovington farmers was Betty's nephew. His farm, Ovington Edge,] [*p. 101*] is an ancient freehold of perhaps 80 or 100 acres belonging for centuries to a family which had born the name of Ovington itself, the Ovingtons of Ovington, and of which the heiress had, soon perhaps after 1700, given with her hand to a man of the name of Harrison. It stands upon the roadside at the east end of the village but separated from it by a deep and at that time well wooded ravine, its situation being partly upon the edge of the ravine here spoken of which runs into the Tees at right angles and partly upon the high bank of the Tees itself. The owner of this property in my early days was a Thomas Harrison a man of remarkable acuteness of mind, wonderfully resembling in face the portraits of Bishop Horsley,[48] and in point of intellect by far the first man in the village. Dr Zouch had noticed him much when

---

47 This old superstition also applied to game-bird or dove feathers. If these were found to be in the mattress or pillow of a dying person, either they or the invalid would be removed. If, however, it was hoped to prolong life just a little longer, feathers would be placed in the bed. This was often done in the hope that relatives coming from a distance would arrive in time to say their farewells. See I. Opie and M. Tatem, *Dictionary of Superstitions*, (Oxford, 1989), p. 309.

48 Raine presumably refers to engravings in the many publications of Samuel Horsley, successively bishop of St Davids, Rochester and St Asaph, died 1806.

rector of Wycliffe and had made use of him in his botanical researches in the neighbourhood.[49] Having a family of children into the teens he was eventually obliged to sell his small estate to the family at Wycliffe and become a tenant upon their estate of a farm of no great extent at Hutton. [*p. 184*] One son, Thompson Harrison, a youth of perhaps seventeen, had been for some time attending the free school of Kirby Hill with which I myself afterwards became so well acquainted. This young man afterwards went out to Cacos one of the Bahama islands as a sort of clerk and eventually removed to St Vincent where he died, having only once paid a visit to England after his mother and father had removed to Hutton. Thomas Harrison [*p. 101*] died at Hutton, and was buried at Forcett on the 28th Jan 1826 in the 79th year of his age.

[Mary Bilton, widow of William Bilton, tailor.]

[*p. 60*] The old woman in the village who was most consulted [as a doctress] was Mary Bilton who was an old querulous widow living upstairs in the ancient house of the Tunstalls[50] called the Old Hall in what must have been the best room which commanded a full view of the Tees and of its splendid scenery from Ovington down to Winston Bridge. [*p. 18*] It was an edifice of spacious size of the Charles the second period but with no architectural characteristics, had always been covered with thatch and had been inhabited (perhaps built) by a junior branch of the Tunstalls of Wycliffe, of rank enough however to intermarry with the Radclyffes of Dilston

---

49 Thomas Zouch (1737-1815) was rector of Wycliffe 1770-95. F. Wrangham, *The Works of Thomas Zouch. With a memoir of his life,* (York, 1820), records that "he divided his hours between the duties of his profession, the care of his pupils, and his pursuits in natural history. His botanical excursions more particularly, among the romantic scenes of his new neighbourhood, contributed at once to enrich his collection and to strengthen his health." During that time he was working on his *Life of Isaak Walton,* (1796). See *Gentleman's Magazine,* Jan. 1816, for other publications.

50 The Tunstalls once owned the Wycliffe estate. The last member of the family, Sir Marmaduke Tunstall, a well known ornithologist, died in 1790. Although they were Roman Catholics, they held the gift of the living. Sir Marmaduke was a close friend of the rector Dr Thomas Zouch, a Cambridge naturalist with whom he had much in common, see above, and he left behind him an extensive ornithological museum which Bewick visited several times in search of reference material for his birds, see M. Weekley (ed.), *A Memoir of Thomas Bewick,* (London, 1961), p. 116.

[*cf. Addita 18*]. [*p. 60*] When this ancient woman made her appearance in the open air, which was seldom, she had so many wrappers about her head that it looked more like a haycock in point of size than part of a human body. In her latter days she was a Roman Catholic (one perhaps of the porridge pot[51] converts) but she had been baptized at Wycliffe church in 1731 and was married there in 1753 to William Bilton a tailor of Ovington. Mary Bilton died in 1812 and was buried at Wycliffe on the 11th of March.

[Bartholomew Elwin was her father. He] was a labourer upon the farm at Wycliffe occupied by the Tunstalls themselves, the owners of the estate. He terminated his existence by his own hand with a razor in the barn in which he was threshing because the allowance of ale to which he thought he was entitled was curtailed. I know not the year when this was done but it was probably about 1750 or 1760. After an inquest had been held and a verdict of *felo de se* had been returned by the jury, the body of this unhappy man was buried upon the Girlington farm at a lonely place where a lane branches off to Caldwell from the road from Ovington to Hutton. Here the last Mr Tunstall who died in 1791 or 1792, who was a great planter of ornamental plumps (this is a more correct word than clumps), planted three patches of trees and in digging the ditch of that in the field nearest to Girlington, the men came across the coffin of the suicide. The place where the lanes meet is known as Old Bartle. In my younger days few people of a timid character liked to pass Old Bartle, but I never heard of a ghost. In 1802 or 3 I shall have to write of another three lanes and three lords' lands near Ovington in connection with what had in all probability been child murder an event which made a very great noise in that quiet country and in which I myself then a boy of 11 or 12 had some little to do.

[John Burrell, day labourer, and his wife Nancy.]

[*p. 171*] In May 1798 in our second year at Caldwell school, as we were idling and birdsnesting on our way home in the evening an empty cart overtook us on which had been that afternoon carried to

---

51 There are several references to the temptations of the porridge pot. This was symbolic of the inducements offered to possible converts to catholicism such as sheeps' heads and blankets which were apparently offered by the owners of the Wycliffe estate. Gifts of money or jobs on the estate were also offered, such bribes meeting with considerable success according to surveys carried out in 1781 and 1820.

their resting place in Forcett church yard the remains of John Burrell
an aged man who had died in the village. John had been for years
racked with the rheumatism, a disease which almost invariably
attacks in their old age men who in their early years have set bad
weather at defiance and have thought little of standing up to their
knees in water for hours in ditching operations. This was invariably
called rheumatis. Catechism was pronounced in the same way by all
my schoolmistresses. John had a [*p. 173*] wife Nancy Burrell, and the
two had many years before my time migrated southwards from
Lanchester in the county of Durham where there is still a family of
that surname. In his pains John would cry out "scrat me, Nanny,
scrat me" and Nancy would too frequently exclaim, weary no doubt
of the operation, "the deevil scrat ye John, ye're nivver dune."

After my settlement at Durham, a place with which she had
been well acquainted, Nancy was always rejoiced when I returned to
spend my holidays in my native village and when about 1814 or 15 I
told her that since I had last seen her I had paid a visit to the Roman
camp at Lanchester, in which she had doubtless played as a child, her
joy was prodigious. Who has not experienced feelings of this kind?
Who that is wearing out his years far from home has not his own
Abana and Pharpar [*2 Kings 5:12*] which he may never see again and
upon which he ponders with a painful pleasure. Nancy was buried at
Forcett on the 31st Oct 1824 wanting only three of an hundred years
of age, having maintained herself for many years after her husband's
death by weeding in the gardens at Wycliffe Hall. My aunt as long as
she lived was very kind to her and Nancy was one of the infirm
people who met in her house on the Tuesday after Christmas day,
Easter Sunday and Whitsunday to receive the Holy Communion
from the curate of Forcett.

[*p. 95*] Willy Gibbon a young lad in the village had a love affair
at Chester-le-Street. My brother Anthony who was born in 1795 and
was therefore four years younger than myself was in his day the love
letter writer for all the young men in the countryside. Anty duly
managed Gibbon's part of the correspondence and brought the
business to a happy conclusion. The marriage took place, and for all I
know to the contrary Willy's grandchildren, nay, perhaps he himself,
may still be flourishing in that place. [*p. 94*] Willy's father had been
the gardener at Wycliffe and dying young was buried at Hutton on
11th February 1799. I was at Girlington on that day and I remember
going to the bank top to see the funeral pass by.

Nancy his widow struggled hard with poverty and a few young children until in the process of time, one of the latter having become a servant in the nunnery without Micklegate Bar and the remainder having "gone to place", she removed her mother to York where she died in 1832 at the age of 76 and her body was brought to Hutton to be buried. The York daughter had when a girl a protuberance upon her upper lip which grew larger as she grew in years. I saw her in York in 1857 coming out of the Roman Catholic Chapel in Blake Street with a lip of an enormous size of a dark bloody colour and very painful to look upon. Before their removal to Ovington, Willy and his wife had lived as servants with the well known Toby Heyrick of Gainford who, as the wife once told me, was fearfully afraid of ghosts.[52] When he came to be gardener at Wycliffe he was probably, like his successor, brought under the influence of the porridge pot.

[Cuthbert Watson, the successor in question, was] [p. 87] a most regular attendant to practise on weekdays and sing on Sundays [at Wycliffe church. He was] a Staindrop [p. 89] man, nearly related to Mrs Cundill the wife of the vicar of Stockton and afterwards of Coniscliffe. Watson had learned his art in the gardens at Raby and when he came to church he was constantly attended by a huge black and white water dog or mastiff which lay in the porch till the practising or morning service was over. All on a sudden however the dog began to come alone, and at last it came out that Cuddy had bartered his Protestant religion for the bailiffwick of the Wycliffe estate (this was the porridge pot by which he had been tempted). Eventually upon the death of Mr Constable, there was left to him for life the farm in Ovington upon which my grandfather had lived and which, having been a late acquisition to the estate, was not included in the general entail by which it is now held by Sir Clifford Constable. The poor dog long continued to come to church, I believe during the remainder of his life, and every Sunday morning in the church porch before service was the cause of remarks upon the absence of his former companion.

[p. 90] Soon after the death of Mr Constable (once Sheldon) his templar, Watson presumed to think himself a fit person to dine with his widow Mrs Constable; but upon presenting himself one day at her table along with her dinner she spiritedly told him that his proper place was in the servants' hall. This I had from Miss Sanderson

---

52 Heyrick was well known as "a jolly parson who loved his God and loved his dinner", see T. C. Eden, *Durham*, (London, 1952), ii, 292.

of Durham who was staying in the house at the time [*cf. Addita 19*]. Poor Mrs Constable, she was I believe one of the Fermors of Tusmore, [*cf. Addita 20*] lost her life through the mistake of inwardly taking what was intended as an external application. [*p. 89*] Watson is still alive, [*cf. Addita 21*] has had his portrait painted and engraved, has received other testimonials from a "grateful tenantry" and has long been known for his bigotry and intolerance by the name of the Pope of Ovington – a name originally given [*p. 90*] to him by Tom Harrison of Stubb House on the opposite side of the Tees of whom I could write anecdotes by the score.

[The Ovington Witch]

[*p. 64*] Tommy Deighton had an aged relation in the village who was a witch and played strange tricks with the carts and horses which were leading coals through the town from Bishoprig into the North Riding. The drivers of the carts however found out a charm which operated in their favour. A witch has no power over anything when a piece of mountain ash is present and they got them whip shanks of rowan tree (the vulgar name of this wood) and passed through the village without harm.[53] In her rage the old woman would sing in a whining tone

> Woe to the lad
> With the rowan tree gad

but her words were harmless.

[All that we know about Tommy Deighton is that he lived at the farm house at the east end of Winston to which grandfather Moore's body was taken after his fatal fall from his horse.]

[4. NEIGHBOURING VILLAGERS]

[The Turtons of Caldwell. Raine came to know several families in Caldwell while he was at school there. He and his brother left their wallets with Jenny and Nichol Turton.]

[*p. 139*] How long Nichol lived I know not but he once, about

---

53 The mountain ash or rowan tree was believed to have special properties and many country folk wore crosses made of rowan to protect them from evil and annoy the witches, see Brewer, *Dictionary of Phrase and Fable.*

1802 or 3 nearly lost his life in the second field from Ovington on the footpath road to Caldwell. It was midwinter and an extremely frosty night but there was no snow on the ground and no moon. He had left Ovington for Caldwell as the evening was coming on but he had not far to go before it became dark and he lost his way. Not arriving at the time at which he was expected, one or two persons were sent out to seek him and they reached Ovington without having met him [*p. 141*] on the road. An alarm was immediately raised and two parties started from the village, one by the field path, another by the cart way, in search of the poor man whom neither party expected to find alive as it was then late and the frost was intense. They on the footpath however, upon going into the second field heard a man's voice. "Jenny ye auld b... oppen t' door." Another half an hour would have silenced Nichol for ever.

Of Jenny I know no more after we left Caldwell school until the year 1830 when in the beginning of that year I had gone to Staindrop to see the body of my poor old friend Dr Sherwood of Snow Hall placed in its grave, and at his request to read the burial service over his grave. Jenny who had retired to Staindrop in her widowhood had heard that I should be present on that occasion and had tottered into the churchyard through the snow to give me her last look after an interval of upwards of thirty years. I was much grieved when I heard that she had been present and I had not known of it. She did not live long after that day, as she was buried at Stanwick near her husband on the 26th of August 1830 in the ninety fifth year of her age.

[The Wheatleys]

[*p. 173*] The village of Caldwell is remarkable for having sent out two youths [*p. 175*] to that place of enterprise and commerce Newcastle, who were singularly prosperous in their day. A few fields to the west of the place on the Ovington road stands the solitary farmhouse mentioned above where in my schoolboy days lived a man of the name of George Wheatley, the father of three sons and a daughter. One of these sons, I believe the second, Matthew, had constructed for himself a galvanic machine upon which he would operate for the benefit of those who had sprains or any other malady for which electricity was supposed to be the remedy. In other respects he was an ingenious, thoughtful lad, and there being some connection between his father and Newcastle (he was I believe a Freeman of that place) he had removed thither to engage in trade, and dying in [*blank*] left a considerable fortune behind him which is now in the hands of Matthew his son [*cf. Addita 22*] the philosopher.

When a little boy, Matthew was once lost, and his mother ran about the premises for a long time seeking him like a woman demented. "Matthew honey, where is thou, my honey Matthew, what has become of you?" The words "Mother I's i't duckhill (pronounced without the aspirate "h") eating sugar" relieved her fears. A similar loss ended in a different way. Once in a later year, in my hearing, a poor woman at Ravensworth had lost her child, and in hopelessness at ever seeing the boy alive again she was wringing her hands and running from place to place near the mill and crying [*p. 177*] "My honey bairn, I've offens used tha badly, but if I had tha aghyan I'd nivver lay hand o' tha mair." "Here he is" said a good woman who was aiding in the search, and the mother's cry was instantly changed. "Thou d...d deevil, I'll murther tha."

Tommy Wheatley, the eldest son of George was what the world would call rather soft. He would come into Ovington now and again with a horse to be shod, and coming into the house in drab with shining metal buttons would take his seat with no other greeting than "Here's a fine day." A clean pipe would then be given to him and he would sit and puff away in silence. Once in his hearing the conversation turned upon a neighbour who had won a large sum of money at a cock fight. To everyone's astonishment Tommy broke mouth and said in a drawling way "A wish a'd knawn he would win." "Why Tommy?" said my mother. "Because a'd hey axed him to let ma gan halves." And he relapsed into his usual silence.

[*p. 176*] Cock fighting was then in all its glory. When I was in the neighbourhood of Ulverston in 18.. I was told that a grave ecclesiastical question had once been settled by appeal to a cock battle. The chapelry of Pennington was vacant, but there was a dispute who should present a clerk to the vacant benefice – the vicar of Ulverston the mother church, the church wardens, the four-and-twenty, or the parishioners at large, and recourse was had to a Welch Main.[54]

---

54 J. Wright, *The English Dialect Dictionary*, (1898-1905), iv: M-Q, p. 13 records "main" as a northern term for a match in cock-fighting, but *Ibid.* vi:T-Z, p. 430 "welsh-main", only from Lancashire and Cheshire, as a term for a medley of "up-and-down" fighting, or for a method of voting until only two are left in.

[*p. 177*] To Nancy Wheatley the sister, I was once sent with a present of honey from my grandmother Moore, and right delicately did she receive it. She put a shilling in my hand and said, "Take this and put it in your pocket. School lads are always in want of pencils."

[Their father] [*p. 179*] was a man without much education, but then much was not required for a person in his way of life. When times were good Henry Eeles the butcher at Caldwell bought a pianoforte for his daughters. George Wheatley thought this a piece of great presumption, and this was his speech when he and the butcher had their first meeting after the purchase had been made. "Whya, Harry, how's this? Is't true – they say thou's bought thy dowters a hyana?"

[Fortunatus Lennis and James Gordon]

[*p. 178*] I must not omit to mention another Caldwell man with a singular name and with some peculiarities of character. Fortunatus Lennis was a small farmer and somewhat given to reading. His wife was Frances Gordon the daughter of the wine merchant at Gilling, and she was the aunt of James Gordon who died under her roof at Caldwell at an early age, having edited for the Surtees Society the Townley Mysteries [Volume 3, 1836]. Mr Gordon had been brought up as an attorney at Hull, had settled at Richmond and afterwards at Durham in that capacity. His removal to Durham took place in consequence of having been appointed under-secretary of the society above mentioned, and the first fruits of his labours was the book I have alluded to, an undertaking which gave him very great pain upon his death-bed. He was a highly religious man, and it grieved him to think that he had been instrumental in bringing to light such apparent profanity as the book contains. Mr Gordon was a good classical scholar and deeply read in northern grammar and literature in general [*cf. Addita 23*].

Lennis had a son whom he sent to Kirby Hill school (long after my time) but the poor youth died in 1829 at the age of twenty before he had an opportunity of converting his scholarship to any useful purpose. Fortune the father died in 1842 aged 85.

[Ralph Hardy, a poor old man of Caldwell]

[*p. 157*] With the people in the village we Ovington boys formed few acquaintances but there was one man in particular called

Ralph Hardy to whom we would often go during the dinner hour and listen to his horrifying tales. He had been in the American war, and had been taken by the natives, and had narrowly escaped being scalped. Every day this poor old man had something new to tell us of the scenes which he had witnessed, and many a night was I sleepless from his tales. He lived to the very advanced age of 102 years and was buried at Stanwick on the 31st March 1812.

[Vipond] the carpenter would sometimes prevail upon the master to give us a holiday. He was of the good old Cumberland line of Vipond,[55] but "Weepin" was his common name at Caldwell. His wife was Mary the daughter of William Wigham and Alice Thompson of Ovington, who were married at Wycliffe in 1735 and Alice Thompson must have been the aunt of my great aunt Thompson and my grandmother Moore.

[Kit Heslop, a man of great steadiness of character and respectability, for many years grandfather Moore's servant and later a sort of farm bailiff at Rokeby Grange.]

[p. 67] He must have been not far from 35 years of age, a steady, active man with his master's interests at heart and attached beyond measure to us boys with whom he would play as a child like ourselves. Many a ride he gave me upon his back. When I next saw him he was acting as a hostler to Mrs Sunderland who kept the King's Head,[56] the chief inn at Morpeth. His delight at seeing me in Morpeth was great and when a few years afterwards (in 1822) I became rector of Meldon we saw each other more frequently and had many a crack with each other about bygone times. The head waiter in the same inn Joe Whytell was another of my old acquaintances. Poor Kit died of brandy and water, unmarried, having been until he settled at Morpeth a man of great sobriety. His body was brought to Pittington to be buried by William Heslop his brother who had lived as a farm servant with the "real Mr Newby" of West Thorpe when Kit lived in

---

55 Raine printed two twelfth-century charters of William de Vieuxpont concerning property at Horndean in south-west Berwickshire, see *North Durham*, Appendix pp. 36-7. For the family's lordships, including Alston in Cumberland, see G. W. S. Barrow ed., *The Acts of William I King of Scots 1165-124*, (Edinburgh, 1971), pp. 181-2.

56 Previously referred to as the Queen's Head.

my grandfather's service. William had migrated into the county of Durham, had married well, and had become a man of landed property at Sherburn in the parish of Pittington.

[*p. 58*] [John Newby was] the farmer of West Thorpe under Mr Cradock of Hartford.[57] He was called "the real" from a circumstance which is enough of itself to indicate his character. Not far from Staindrop on the Winston road, on the west side of the lane is a farm house called G. B. House from having those initials in coloured tiles upon its roof, the initials of George Bowes of Streatlam its builder and owner. The tenant of this farm was a man of the name of Newby, and one day as our friend of West Thorpe was riding to Staindrop near this house he was met by a man who enquired if Mr Newby did not live somewhere thereabouts. "There may be such a man, but I am the Real Mr Newby" was the answer which he received. Newby pretended to write poetry, and once when Dr Sherwood and I had been driven into his house by a thunderstorm in 1816 or 17, he read to us one of his compositions at which we were highly amused. We were on a walking expedition from Ovington to Rokeby, for an account of which see my *Versus Barnabaei* & *Life of Surtees*. "Turrim Mortham Rokebeiam etc."[58]

[*p. 17*] Old Charley Hanby, [farmer of Little Hutton] looked on Christmas Day as the day of the year to be devoted to holy gratitude, a day on which not one "hands turn" was to be done by his servants. His cattle were duly and plentifully fed the evening before, he headed his whole family to church and afterwards the day was spent in peace and thankfulness.

---

57 Sheldon Craddock is listed as owner of the "gentleman's seat" of Thorpe Hall in E. Baines, *History, Directory and Gazateer of the County of York*, (1823), ii,604.

58 Anon., *A Dysshe of Sottleties, ryght richelie seasonid; or, A Goodlie Garland of Duresme Evergreens, plaited by the Ingenious*, (Durham, 1818), unpaginated, contains "Iter Barnabaeum", addressed to Robert Surtees and dated Jul. 1815, beginning "Turrim Mortham Rokebeianam". For a brief account and example of the "Drunken Barnaby style"^, in which many letters between Raine and Surtees were written, see *A Memoir of Robert Surtees*, (Surtees Soc. xxiv, 1852), p. 127. Richard Brathwayte (1588 ? – 1673) wrote *Barnabee Itinerarium*, a popular record of English travel in doggerel verse, commonly called "Drunken Barnabee's Journal"; among several editions was one by Raine's friend D. Haslewood, librarian to the dean and chapter of Durham, printed in London by J. Harding in 1818

[The Greens of Hutton, where Raine and his brother went to school for a time.]

[*p. 127*] The good woman who kindly permitted us to eat our dinner in her house, and now and then did a little for us in the way of cooking was Mary Green, the wife of Willy Green a mason who had left his own country at Wolsingham [in Weardale] to take part in the building of Winston Bridge in 17.. and had after it was finished settled at Hutton and was much employed upon the Wycliffe estate [...] Hodgson Green their eldest son had for some time been paying his addresses to my mother's maidservant. They also had a son called Ralph, and I observe that a man, a mason called Ralph Green of Wolsingham was called before the High Commission Court at Durham in the time of Charles I, not for his good deeds.[59]

[5. THE NOTABLES]

[John Bacon Morritt of Rokeby Hall, a man of great influence in the area.[60] The Teesdale Volunteer Infantry was under his command. Sir Walter Scott used to stay with him at Rokeby when writing the poem of that name.]

[*p. 73*] Barnard Castle was long a favourite place from which the Durham Militia drew its recruits, and when they quitted the regiment from age or other causes they almost all of them became great fishers in the Greta and Tees. With respect to the Greta, and Mr Morritt and Sir Walter Scott, I told an amusing tale of the doings of these Barnard Castle anglers to Mr Howitt which may be found in his book of visits to remarkable places in the north of England, and it is worth referring to it.[61]

---

59 One Ralph Greene of Nether Bitchburn (near Wolsingham) was accused in 1628 of railing and brawling in the churchyard and also of calling Dorothy Hutton widow a "turne coat", see W. H. D. Longstaffe (ed.), *The Acts of the High Commission Court within the Diocese of Durham*, (Surtees Soc. xxxiv, 1858), pp. 15–16, but he is not there described as a mason, nor apparently in the original (Durham Cathedral MS Hunter 16 fols. 6v-36v).

60 See the introduction to *The Letters of John B. S. Morritt*, ed. G. E. Marindin, (London, 1914); also, for the free education that Morritt provided for the poor children of Rokeby, R. P. Hastings, *Essays in North Riding History*, (Northallerton, 1981), p. 185.

61 W. Howitt, *Visits to Remarkable Places*, (London, 1840), esp. i,109.

[For another story concerning Morritt and Scott see *Addita 12*.]

[Mr Michell of Forcett Park bought Forcett Park in 1783 and brought his father's body with him from Haslingfield where it had previously been buried.]

[*p. 158*] In 180. Lord Darlington's hounds were hunting in the neighbourhood of Forcett. The fox made his way into Mr Michell's park, the dogs followed, and Mr Jadis was the only horseman who followed the dogs. Mr Michell was a man of many peculiarities and the rest of the hunters thought it best to keep out of his way. The fox made his way to the principal gate of the park which leads to the mansion house from the village. The dogs and Mr Jadis were at his heels but the gate was locked, no-one ever visiting the owner of the mansion, and how to keep up the pursuit Mr Jadis was at a loss to know. At length there appeared Mr Michell clothed like one of the labourers upon his estate, and no sooner had he come into sight than he was ordered in somewhat uncourteous terms to open the gate. He stumped and strunted,[62] told his name and turned his back, leaving Jadis to ride back and make his exit by the way he came. The next morning there was a challenge at Raby, but with Michell there was considerable [*p. 160*] difficulty as he was not acquainted with one single gentleman in the countryside whom he could ask to be his second. He therefore sent for a sturdy farmer of the name of George Hodgson, one of his own tenants a man who knew just as much about the laws of duelling as he did about the laws of the [*blank*] Tables, and what is more, the very man who ought to have inhibited his landlord in his bloody designs for he was the constable of the township. George however felt himself bound to comply, in fact his very farm depended upon it.

Never perhaps since the days of Don Quixote had such a pair issued forth with their deadly weapons to do a deed of chivalry. But before he sallied forth to quell impertinence, Mr Michell bethought him that he probably might not return, and thinking it fit and proper to be prepared for death, he sent for my old friend Mr Heslop whom for some time he had only seen once a week, and telling him what he was about begged him to do his best in preparing him for another world. Heslop, shocked beyond measure at what he had

---

62 Raged and insulted.

heard, ventured to remonstrate, first against the duel itself, and then against the wickedness of the proceeding for which his presence had been requested. Mr Michell became impatient, but making no [*p. 162*] reply, pointed to the pistols upon the table. At this Heslop, knowing his man and reasonably considering his own life in danger read a prayer or two, more applicable to the poor madman's state of mind than to the bodily danger to which he was about to expose himself, and was suffered to depart in peace. Michell was in such a state of excitement that he probably paid no attention to what was said. Prayers were prayers, and he was satisfied. But had the curate refused to open his lips it is probable that he would have been shot on the spot. The duel took place in a field near Barford on the Yorkshire side of the Tees. Michell winged his man, an apology was made, and the constable of Forcett brought off his landlord victorious.

[*p. 158*] About the year 183[2] there was a duel between Sir Hedworth Williamson and Mr Braddyll on the Sedgefield road during an election for the northern division of Durham. Sir Hedworth's second was Mr John Fawcett, a magistrate for the county. Mr Fawcett was not removed from the roll. [*p. 162*] A Durham justice of the peace, and a Forcett constable connived at a proceeding which might have ended in murder.[63]

[*p. 13*] [Dr Zouch was] rector of Wycliffe in my earliest childhood. [*p. 12*] He had become rector there under peculiar circumstances. The advowson belongs to the family at the Hall – then Marmaduke Tunstall Esq the eminent ornithologist and antiquary, now Sir Clifford Constable, and having in 17.. become vacant by the death of [*blank*] the next turn not having sold fell by law to the university of Cambridge.[64] Dr Zouch was then a fellow of Trinity College and a well-known naturalist. He became a candidate for the

---

63 On September 27 1832 Mr Edward Richard Gale Braddyll, the candidate for election in Durham County north division fought two duels. The first was at 7 a.m. with Mr Bowlby, candidate for South Shields, the second at noon with Sir Hedworth Williamson a Durham city candidate. Each duel was the result of objections to speeches made. Nobody was injured. See W. W. Bean, *The Parliamentary Representation of the Six Northern Counties*, (Hull, 1980), p. 102.

64 On the Tunstall family of Wycliffe and repeated changes of name to Constable, see *Victoria County History: Yorkshire North Riding*, i (1914), p. 139; as Roman Catholics they were debarred from making presentations

...

presentation and he obtained his object.

One of my earliest recollections is this gentleman in the pulpit at Wycliffe in his great full-bottomed wig, in conformity with the clerical fashion of the time. He was for some years deputy commissary of the Archdeaconry of Richmond, and, presiding in the court there, visited and gave charges to the clergy *virtute officii*. He was also a magistrate for the North Riding, and as in the simplicity of his character he could not believe that anyone would tell a falsehood, when he had to adjudicate in this capacity in a quarrel which had taken place in the neighbourhood, he who could first tell his tale invariably gained the victory. There was therefore [*p. 14*] always a race between the real culprit and the aggrieved party. Mr Munday, rector of Winston a few miles down the river, acted upon a different plan in similar cases. He would show the plaintiff and the defendant into a room in which there were bread and cheese and ale in abundance upon the table. He would then say "I am going out for a quarter of an hour, but [you] had better take something to eat and drink and, if you can, make it up between yourselves before I return." The quarter of an hour he would then make an hour, and when he at last came back he saw smiling faces and was told they would give him no further trouble.

Dr Zouch was a tall athletic man of great strength. I have heard that in his younger days at Wycliffe he would walk through a thin hedge and stride over a stiff one, caring nothing for hedges and stiles. Once a set of Mountebanks made their appearance at the rectory and begged to exhibit on the lawn for the benefit of Mrs Zouch, himself and the servants (he had no children). Leave was given and when the doctor and his household were enjoying the fun, one of the itinerants stole away, entered the house by the back door and stole from the spit a piece of beef which was roasting for dinner. The man did not return but took to his heels with his prize. When the performance was over and the beef was missed, chase was given, and it and the thief were overtaken at Ravenswath.[65]

---

to benefices of which they owned the advowson. T. D. Whitaker, *An History of Richmondshire* i, (London, 1823), p. 200 states that Zouch was instituted in 1770, being preceded by Thomas Robinson and followed, in 1793, by John Headlam.

65 Presumably Ravensworth, 6 miles to the south-east.

Dr Zouch left an heirloom behind him at Wycliffe, a portrait by Sir Antonio More of Wycliffe the reformer, since engraved by Dr Vaughan in his memoir.[66] He was succeeded by Mr Headlam in 17...[67]

---

66 The Flemish painter Anthonis Mor was commonly known as Sir Anthony More in England, which he visited in 1553 or 1554, see *Oxford Dictionary of Art*, (Oxford, 1988), also R. Strong, *The English Icon: Elizabethan & Jacobean Portraiture*, (London, 1969), pp. 117-8. On his portrait of Wycliffe and its similarity to a woodcut used by Bale, see Whitaker, *Op. cit.*, p. 197; also R. Vaughan, *Life of Wycliffe*, 2 vols (London, 1825).

67 See note [64] above.

Addita

Addita in the handwriting of James Raine the younger are indicated by [J.R.:]

1. Upon the opposite bank of the Tees stands boldly, with an extensive view Osmondcroft with all its ancient history, from its name a Saxon settlement, a gift to the monks of Durham[1] by Robert Fitz Meldred Lord of Raby the descendant of Northumbrian kings, and the ancestor of the Nevilles.

2. I remember communicating to Mr Surtees for the 4th vol. of his History some peculiarities of the Tees in this part of its course which he briefly noticed in his pages, I think under Winston or Osmondcroft.[2] These are in my possession and it may be well to copy them here as in my opinion they are worthy of being preserved.

3. [J.R.:] and also a locket in shape of a heart with the head of Chas I on it – now mine.

4. The same custom of writing the initial letter of a new subject was prevalent in my time, as my own books (such as are *to the fore*) will shew, and no doubt it had descended from the manuscript period of our history, before I mean, the invention of printing. It is still in force in the initial letters of title deeds, the *interlacing* of which has come down to us uninterruptedly from the Saxon times. My grandfather's book was in 4to. the sheets having been added from time [to time] within a loose back of paper.

5. [J.R.:] See Carleton's Durham Characters for an account of G.A.

6. [J.R.:] My mother lived for some years in a house some doors below it, next to the passage down to the Racecourse.

7. An inscription in it states that it was the property of ... who was my grandmother's father and lived at Whorlton.

8. The men wore upon a small brass plate connected with their trappings the letters T.V.I. Teesdale Volunteer Infantry and once

---

1 See *Durham Cathedral Priory Rentals I: Bursars Rentals*, ed. R. A. Lomas and A. J. Piper, (Surtees Soc. cxcviii, 1989), p. 212.
2 Apparently under Osmondcroft, see Surtees, *History of Durham*, iv,I,37.

upon Mortham Bridge in my hearing one soldier said to another, neither of them could read, thou cannot tell what them letters stand for. Nëa says them nowther can thou. Thou wrang there said the first speaker, they mean John etc.

9. In the meantime viz in 17.. the last of the Allisons of Hartlepool died leaving behind him ... [*J.R.jun. adds*:] I have the copy of the will and a pair of silver sugar tongs which belonged to him, marked with the initials of himself and his wife.

10. With me however it has been a matter of study and observation, and if the sum and substance of the experiments and observations which I have made on the subject for upwards of forty years should ever see the light in the shape of a sixpenny hand book for the special use of bee-keepers in the northern counties the peculiarities of the climate being among things of a local nature taken into consideration it might probably be useful to those who have neither time nor mind for anything above a mere brief guide on the subject. At all events such a little book is much needed in the north.

11. [J.R.:] ? a dulcimer.

12. Let me record here a saying of Scott to Morritt during one of the visits of the poet to Rokeby. The two had walked together from Barnard Castle to Rokeby one morning after breakfast and in passing through the church yard Morritt had directed Scott's attention to a public house sign exhibiting a picture of Burns the poet, which said he is believed to be an excellent likeness. "How long has it been there?" asked Scott. "Perhaps two or three years" was the answer. "Then" said Scott, "take my word for it is no like Burns. Rabbie Burns would not have stayed so long on the outside of a public."

13. Let me here narrate a tale which Mr Tate would often tell in a place of no less dignity and decorum than the school of Richmond when it was in all its glory.[3] The speakers are an A.B.C. dame at Richmond and "my son Tommy" as he called him, now vicar of

---

3   James Tate (1771-1843) became master of Richmond School in 1796; at Cambridge his pupils were so successful that they were known as "Tate's invincibles". In 1838 he became rector of Edmonton, a living in the gift of the Dean and Chapter of St Paul's. See L. P. Wenham, *Letters of James Tate*, (Yorkshire Archaeological Soc. 1966), and L. P. Wenham, *Biography of James Tate*, (County Record Office Northallerton, 1991).

Edmonton, and the accompaniments the *battledoor* and *pointer*, it being understood that Tommy had had one or two previous lessons which he had taken care to forget.

"Now Tommy, what's this letter?"

"I cannot tell mistress."

"Tommy thou soon forgets. But I'll tell thee t' first letter. It's A."

"Well, A then."

"Now Tommy what's this?"

"I cannot tell that ather, mistress."

"Why, what tengs thee Tommy?"

"Waps mistress."

"No no Tommy, bees."

"Why B then."

"Now Tommy what's next?"

"I've forgotten."

"Why what do I de with my eyes?"

"Squint, mistress."

"No no, thou monkey, see Tommy, see."

"Why C then."

"Now Tommy here's another : what's this?"

"I tell ye what, mistress, its nae use your plaguing me. When ye knaw far better yoursell, what d'ye aks me for?"

14. She had a few devotional books, and a few prints framed but not glazed – of two only I remember the subjects. The first was the view of Darlington church which was if I am not mistaken drawn and engraved by Bailey, and of which there is a reduced copy in Hutch[inson's] *Durh*[am][4] and the second a general view of the town by the same artist.

15. It is the custom for the parish clerk of Forcett to attend at the house from which the funeral proceeds, however distant it may be from the church and accompany it thither singing a psalm (in which he is duly accompanied by others) not only in the village itself but in those also (if any) through which the body passes. This is a very affecting ceremony. Frank Lawson was the clerk at Forcett when I was a child and he also as well as Harry Hutchinson would moralize

---

4   See the octavo edition of W. Hutchinson, *History and Antiquities of the County Palatine of Durham*, iii (1794), facing p. 185, or thereabouts. John Bailey (1750–1819), agriculturist and later engraver.

especially over the burial cake and the ale. In the case of an aged person he had a rhyme of his own making which he never failed to deliver with great effect.

When a man comes to three score and ten
It's time he came back to Forcett again.

A funeral on its road to the church was in my younger days treated with much reverence. Every male person who happened to meet it took off his hat and stood uncovered till the very last person in the procession had passed him, and from the sex of the first person who was so met the people foretold the sex of the person in the village who was next to die. If a male, a female, and vice versa.

16. Hutton Magna or Hutton Longvillers from a family of that name seated at Hornby Co. Lanc. to which it belonged till the reign of Edward I when it was carried by Margaret the heiress *ea asse* of John Longvillers to Galfrid second son of Galfrid de Neville Lord of Raby.[5]

17. Among the rest of the supplicants there stood up on that day a little pale-faced, sickly looking boy and said and did as he was bid like the rest of his schoolfellows. What strange things take place in the course of time. Between this boy, after he had grown up to a man's estate, and that gentleman in boots and spurs there sprang up an intimacy which terminated only with the death of the latter, and right glad was the former to be solicited by a large body of grateful gentlemen in a southern part of the kingdom to tell the truth respecting his friend in a Latin inscription to be engraved upon the most magnificent piece of testimonial plate which he has ever happened to see in the course of his life. [*J.R.jun. adds:*] I remember it well. Mr Clarke was the father of Wm. George Clarke, fellow of Trinity, who spent the latter portion of his life in the Station Hotel, York.

[*J.R. continues:*] Testimonials were not so common then as they are now. What the hand then gave it gave with a willing heart. Now they are becoming bywords and in most cases with justice. Nowadays in nine cases out of ten they either proceed from a suggestion by the would-be recipient himself, or from some unhappy flatterer who has his own private gain in view.

---

5   See *Victoria County History: Yorkshire North Riding*, i (1914, repr. 1968), p. 84.

18. See a paper on this latter family by J[ames] R[aine] junr. in the *Archaeologia Aeliana*.

19. [J.R.:] Mr T. A. Shipperdson saw in his room a row of books with white paper labels. On the first of these he wrote "Betty Sanderson's Sins?" I remember her.

20. [J.R.:] Some years ago an attempt was made, greatly encouraged by Leonard L. Hartley, to publish the pedigrees of the R.C. gentry. It came to nought. A pedigree of Fermor of Tusmore was printed and was sent down to me from the Herald's College to examine. Whilst it was lying upon my table the workmen employed by the Corporation, near the church of Bishophill Junior, in the roadway, which had been taken from the churchyard, broke into a brick vault in which there was an elaborate lead coffin-plate of a Mr Fermor who had been buried there. They brought it to me and as they were Irishmen, I told them that the gentleman was a R.C. like themselves and unless they replaced the plate he would haunt them. They almost ran out of my house with it.

21. [J.R.:] I saw Mr Watson in Ovington and he was told who I was and was civil. A rather tall man with a brown dress coat. He was very civil. It was he who destroyed the old deeds of the estate. He put them into a disused malt kiln and burned them.

22. [J.R.:] I remember Matthew W. of NC seeing him at the Soc[iety of] Ant[iquaries]. He came up to me and said he was a relation of mine.

23. [J.R.:] He left my father by will a number of books among which were two old York service books.

Part 2.

Letters from James Raine to Edward Blore, 1814–1824

Introduction

Edward Blore (1787–1879) had already illustrated his father's *History of Rutland* and other county histories when he first met Raine at Mainsforth in 1813 while working on illustrations for Surtees' *History*.[1] His detailed architectural illustrations were greatly admired, and his reputation reached Sir Walter Scott whom he met in 1816. Scott immediately engaged him to design the exterior of his house at Abbotsford in the Gothic style.

During the early years of this correspondence, Blore was working alongside Turner and other artists on Scott's *The Provincial Antiquities and Picturesque Scenery of Scotland* (1818), managing the production of the book and at the same time providing all the purely architectural illustrations. He was also working on his own book *The Monumental Remains of Noble and Eminent Persons*, which was published in 1824. By then his opinions were being widely sought by those who shared his enthusiasm for the Gothic style, including Thomas Rickman, an acknowledged authority on the subject.[2] In addition, he undertook to provide illustrations for Raine's projected *History of North Durham* which was eventually published in 1830. By 1824 Blore's architectural practice based in London was growing extensively, his later work including designs for buildings in capital cities throughout the world.

The temptation to edit the earlier letters has been resisted. The writer often rushes from one subject to the next and back again, but this reflects the immense excitement of young Raine, at 22 in his first job, making a wide variety of new friends in Durham and at Mainsforth, and in headlong pursuit of the history and antiquities of the northern counties which were to be the preoccupation of his life.

The letters are printed *in extenso*, except that after the first one, the opening and closing compliments are mostly omitted. Blore's address changes from time to time and this has been included at the

---

1   On Blore and his works see H. M. Colvin, *A Biographical Dictionary of British Architects 1660–1840*, (London, 1954).
2   *Ibid.*

head of some letters. The few blanks which occur in the text are the result of damage which probably occurred when letters were opened carelessly.

1

Edward Blore Esq., No. 10 Upper Tichfield Street, Fitzroy Square, London.

Ovington, not far from Romaldkirk, Yorkshire.
Jan[uary] 9 1814

My dear Blore,

I have long and anxiously expected to hear from you but in vain. If I recollect rightly, you certainly promised to write to me long before this. What can have become of you? Your friend Mrs Robinson is offended at your long silence too. This I had from Mr Surtees whom I left in good health three weeks ago. We have at present a most severe storm of frost and snow, so I am completely shut up, with no books except a few in which I am to be examined by the Bishop of Durham next September.[3] I don't know whether you have heard that the Dean and Chapter have determined to engrave their seals, and have requested me to make out an index.[4] I am afraid it will be a long time before I can put their request in execution, in consequence of my new engagement to superintend Mrs Wharton's boarding house as poor old Wharton died some time ago of a mortification in his foot.

We were obliged to leave Durham a few days before the commence[men]t of the holidays as the scarlet fever had been some time in Durham and had attacked two of our boys. By a letter which I had received a few days ago from Willy Reed I find that Mr

---

3   i.e. as an ordinand.
4   The muniments of the Dean & Chapter of Durham contain one of the best collections of medieval seals in Britain; they were the source of most, if not all, of the 198 engravings of seals issued on 12 plates with Surtees' *History*, see vol. iv,2 pp. [clxvii]–clxxvi.
    On 20 November 1813 Chapter ordered that records be delivered to Raine against a receipt and that he be thanked for his great trouble already taken and "for his future offer to make an index of the records", see Dean & Chapter Muniments, Act-Book 1800–18.

Barrington has taken the title of Lord Viscount Barrington in consequence of the death of his elder brother in France. Willy also informed me that he has got the premium at the Agricultural Meeting for another fat pig. Poor Clarke has been appointed organist at Worcester and has consequently left Durham. You I dare say will be sorry at this because if ever you condescend to visit Durham again you will be in want of a chess mate. Poor George has lost his wife too, a severe misfortune as she has left him two little children.[5] B[isho]p Nesfield asks what has become of you. I was invited to dine there a few days before I left Durham with Captain Allen, Wolfe the Gaoler etc. I need not inform you that I was engaged.

Since your departure I have become a member of the Book Room. I like it very much. The members of the Antequarian Soc[iety] at Newcastle[6] have held their first annual meeting a few days ago. There is a long puff in the Newcastle paper about it. I have seen a few sheets of Mr Surtees's book.[7] Pray how does it go on? What plates are in the hands of the engravers and what are you about? You will confer a very great favour upon me by answering me these questions as soon as possible, at least before I go to Durham which will be on the 24th; don't do as you did your friend Major Anderson.[8] Mrs Phillpotts[9] has had another son. Smith the verger is dead. Mr Barrington's butler succeeds him. We have had a contested election[10] concerning which I can tell you some good stories when I have the

---

5   Patrick George, curate of Bishop Middleham in 1810, later minor canon of Durham, keeper of Bishop Cosin's Library and first University Librarian, died 1834.

6   The Society of Antiquaries of Newcastle upon Tyne was established at a meeting on 6th February 1813. Raine became a member in 1815.

7   The first volume of *The History and Antiquities of the County Palatine of Durham* (1816).

8   Presumably Major George Anderson of Newcastle. A letter from Surtees to John Hodgson of 31st December 1821 stated "Now is there spirit enough in Northumberland to raise a fund for illustrating your pages ... I should really hope it only wants setting a-going, and that Major Anderson would not stand single in such a list", G. Taylor, *Memoir of Robert Surtees*, (Surtees Soc. xxiv), p. 402. Surtees and Anderson both subscribed to Hodgson's *History of Northumberland*.

9   Presumably wife of Canon Henry Phillpotts, see note 12 below.

10 The polling for this election took place between 1st and 10th December 1813. George Allan (Tory) gained 440 votes, George Baker (Whig) 360 votes.

supreme felicity of seeing you. Pray write to me very soon and tell me when you are likely to come to Durham.

> I am my dear Blore yours very sincerely
> J.Raine, Ovington, Greta Bridge.

2

Durham Feb. 5 1815

You will naturally imagine that I was somewhat surprised at being told that you were expected at Mainsforth – but I was still more astonished when informed that you had departed for London after the short visit of two days. We are all conjecture. One lady, a friend of yours, suggests that you have formed a resolution of marrying and that the object of your expedition to Mainsforth was to ask Mr Surtees' opinion on such a knotty point. Another says that you wished to pay a short visit to "somebody" who is the object of your affections. In short one entertains one opinion and another another. All I conjecture equally remote from the true one. Your next visit I trust will be of longer duration.

[*drawing of coat of arms*]

These are Mr Carr's arms which he will be much obliged to you to get cut in the same way as ours.[11] He wishes the seal to be as small as you conveniently can – for common use.

Frye who will bring this letter with him to town will return in the course of a month or five weeks. May I therefore beg of you to get the seals done so that he may bring them down with him. It will be the most convenient way. I am scribbling this after having ate a hearty dinner of Willy Reed's roast beef so that you must excuse the inelegancies and want of thought which everywhere betray themselves.

Mr Phillpotts[12] whom I saw accidentally yesterday tells me that he dined at Mainsforth a fortnight ago and that he had some

---

11 John Carr (1786–1833), headmaster of Durham School in 1811.
12 Canon Henry Phillpotts (1778–1869), canon of Durham 1809–20 and 1831–69, and bishop of Exeter 1831–69, see also note 44 below.

conversation with Mr Surtees concerning the index.[13] He begged me to show him the plan which I drew up and seems more anxious about the matter than before. However I have come to a determination to having nothing to do with the matter except they will allow me to have the charters ...

Durham is at present quite gay. I am engaged every evening this next week. Don't forget to send with the seals an acc[oun]t of what we are indebted to you. Let me conclude this rambling letter by earnestly requesting to hear from you very soon ...

3

Durham May 9th. 1815

The sole reason which prevented me from answering your last letter was the daily expectation of Frye with my seals, when I might be better able to tell you what I thought of them. However as Frye arrived yesterday without them I take the very first opportunity of informing you how much I am pleased with your impression taken technically too with vermillion as I perceive. May I beg of you that you will immediately upon the receipt of this pack them up with addition of paper so as to make a small parcel and send them to me by the mail not forgetting to send the invoice as Geo[rge] Andrews would say.[14] M[esse]rs George and Carr are upon the tiptoe of expectation for theirs also and if they are finished you will be kind enough to forward them with mine.

Smirke left us last Sunday after a fortnight's stay.[15] He met with only a cold reception, at least the Treasury locks did not open with such facility as heretofore. He only drew the royal seals as far down as John and that only in outline for wood engraving so we have I think nothing to fear from Master Lysons.[16] There is no perfect seal of the

---

13 Cf. The projected index of the Dean & Chapter's muniments mentioned in Letter 1 and Letter 3 at note 20.
14 George Andrews, publisher and bookseller of Saddler Street Durham.
15 Richard Smirke (1778–1815), antiquarian draughtsman, eldest brother to Sir Robert the architect, Sir Edward the lawyer and antiquary, and Sydney the architect.
16 On 15 October 1814 Chapter had given leave for Mr Richard Smirke "to take drawings of such seals of our early Kings as shall be wanted for the

...

Conq[uero]r but there are two different ones of Rufus on one of which he calls himself *Willm fil Willi Regis*.[17] I think you did not observe this. Smirke seems exceedingly anxious to find the seal of the Empress Maud. However I was inexorable. Mr Surtees wishes to have a facsimile engraving upon one of his plates of Bishop Ranulph's charter which I enclose for you with Mr S's request that you will superintend the matter.[18]

I have not had any conversation with Mr Phillpotts[19] lately on the subject of the index[20] yet I think they have still the disposition to do it and that when you come we can easily settle the preliminaries as I think I am inclined to concede the point which seems to be the only obstacle. You of course have heard of Miss Emma Robinson's dangerous illness.[21] Surtees on his road from Hendon[22] to Mainsforth yesterday told me that she was considerably better. You are also I suppose acquainted with Darnell's intended marriage with Miss Bow.[23] Must now conclude with requesting you to send off the seals immediately as I think they are sure to arrive safe ...

Woodifield[24] told me the other day that he had some money to pay you on the Dean and C[hapte]r acc[oun]t and at the same time told me he was ignorant where to find you. If I can be of service to you in this matter – command me.

---

embellishment of a work about to be published by Mr Lysons", see Chapter Act-Book. Samuel Lysons (d. 1819), Keeper of the Records in the Tower of London, co-author with his brother Daniel of *Magna Brittania; being a concise topographical account of the several counties of Great Britain*, 6 vols, (1806–22).

17 No such seal has been identified in the Chapter's muniments.
18 Bishop Ranulf Flambard's seal is engraved Surtees, *Durham*, i Plate I top centre.
19 Canon Henry Phillpotts, see notes 12 above and 44 below.
20 See Letter 2 at note 13.
21 She was sister to Surtees' wife.
22 Near Sunderland.
23 William Darnell, rector of St Mary le Bow Durham 1809–15, vicar of Stockton 1815–20, canon of Durham 1816–31, was a member of the committee set up by Surtees in 1812 to administer the subscriptions raised to finance the illustrations for his *History*.
24 Matthew Woodifield served the Chapter as travelling bailiff and bailiff of its property in Elvet, Crossgate, Merrington and Billingham.

4

Durham Aug[ust] 13 1815.

What in the name of wonder has become of you? A considerable time has elapsed since I last addressed you requesting you to forward our seals by any safe conveyance but no seals have made their appearance. If your only object in sending me such a beautiful impression was to tantalize me, your end has been gained. I have suffered enormously. Every time I open my desk my seal stares me in the face and reminds me to go to the Mail Coach Office to enquire for a parcel from London. Pray put me out of pain. Patrick George is a great deal worse than myself and Carr more impatient than either of us. Do let me hear from you in the course of a day or two.

Emma Robinson's death has been a dreadful blow to Mr and Mrs Surtees. They with Mr and Mrs Robinson are at present at Harrogate. However it is their intention to be at Mainsforth in a few days. It seems we are not to have the pleasure of seeing you down this summer. What can so materially have altered your plans? Poor Smirke's death was sudden and shocking. I hope this will be a warning to you not to brave danger as you did last winter in your peregrinations. Of course Lysons will not be much benefitted by his sketches as they were in many instances imperfect and to be completed from memory.

You have doubtless heard of Viner's death and of Gamlen's appointment to Heighington and Croxdale,[25] so that Tom Shipperdson has nothing to do at present. Report says that we are in a few weeks to lose Darnell as the Bishop has given him Stockton. I am as George Andrews says quite in the dark with regard to Surtees' history. Pray tell me how John Nichols[26] and the engravers go on and what you have been doing all this time and recollect that the correspondence which you solicited failed first on you side. This is Sunday evening, on Thursday or Friday I hope the clerk will answer

---

25 Revd Samuel Viner (1739–1815), principal surrogate in the Consistory Court of Durham. Revd Samuel Gamlen, one of the original vice-presidents of the Surtees Society.

26 John Nichols (d. 1826), publisher, known as "The Father of English Typography", was succeeded in the family firm by his son, John Bowyer Nichols (d. 1863); his son, John Gough Nichols, was first co-treasurer with Henry Allan of the Surtees Society.

in the affirmative to my enquiries after a small parcel. You see I am very impatient.

I have [at] last come in contact with Sir C Sharpe in consequence of being obliged to visit Hartlepool for the sake of my health. I have long epistles from him almost daily on the subject of his *History*.[27] The persons employed to recolour the cathed[ral] have taken great pains in freeing the altar screen and B[ishop] Hatfield's canopy from old plaster and I think with very great success.[28] The improvement in sharpness is obvious. I think I have told you all the news...

5

Durham October 7 1815

You will discover from the *"dorsum rotuli"* as Bowlby[29] would say that my seals have arrived safe. Before I proceed any further pray accept my sincere thanks for the great trouble you must have had and at the same time let me inform you that I am quite in raptures with them. George and Carr are becoming very impatient in consequence of having seen mine. If it is not too late Mr Carr begs me to inform you that he does not wish his to be so very large – at least not larger than my large one.

According to your request I send you herewith the £39 18s. due to you from the Chapter and, as you in one of your letters told me that the cost of my large seal was £6 14s., I have included that sum in the note together with £1 for the crest, making in all £47 12s the receipt of which pray acknowledge immediately as I shall be fidgetty. If the bill when you find it turns out to be more than £6 14s. I can easily make up the deficiency at any future period.

And now let me inform you of a circumstance which I think

---

27 Presumably a reference to Cuthbert Sharp (1781–1848), *History of Hartlepool*, (1816).

28 G. Ornsby, *Sketches of Durham*, (1846), p. 51 "The rich painting and gilding with which not only these shields but all the tomb, with its canopy and screenwork once glowed, has been partially brought to light by the careful abrasion of the many coats of whitewash under which they were hidden."

29 John Bowlby, Chapter Registrar.

will draw from you a letter of congratulation. Bow[30] vacated by Darnell's acceptance of Stockton has been given by Mr Bowyer the Patron in the most handsome manner to our worthy though eccentric friend Tom Shipperdson. I know you will rejoice at this. Surtees who has been staying nearly a week at Shipperdsons was overjoyed. Though he did not know Mr Bowyer yet he immediately called upon him to thank him for his kindness to Tom, who bye the bye was completely beside himself the whole day. The next piece of news is that Frye has resigned his minor canonry being just upon the point of marriage with a Miss Waring sister to Mrs Faber of Longnewton his nearest neighbour. She possesses two good qualifications – she is beautiful and has a fortune of £70,000. What do you think of all this?

I have since I had the pleasure of seeing you made some discoveries at which I flatter myself you will in no small degree rejoice. There is beneath the B[isho]p's Castle a beautiful Roman crypt consisting of enormously thick pillars with capitals richly ornamented with dragons etc and supporting rude circular arches.[31] Besides there is at Hart the most delightful font I ever saw. It is in excellent preservation and is in every respect worthy of the most conspicuous place in Mr Surtees' book.[32] There is in the ch[urch]yard a font still older which has been turned out to make room for the one abovementioned. I was quite delighted to hear from Henshaw[33] that it is your intention to visit us soon. Pray don't delay any long time ...

6

Durham November 22 1815

I lose no time in informing you that Mr Carr is very well satisfied with his seal and requests me to beg of you to forward it

---

30 i.e. the rectory of St Mary le Bow, Durham.
31 Raine refers to the late eleventh-century Romanesque "Norman Chapel" at Durham Castle, depicted in Surtees' *History* Plate 80 (vol. iv final plate).
32 Although Surtees decribes this font in his *History* vol. iii p. 96, and refers to a Plate, none was included, see the List of Plates, see *Ibid.* iv,2 pp. 171–3.
33 Presumably Dr Henshaw, organist and choir-master of Durham Cathedral.

along with Mr George's immediately. That is as soon as ever it is convenient to yourself. You will of course send the engravers' bill along with them. Your information concerning Dr Whitaker[34] gives me great pleasure and if the thing had not so much the appearance of a job nothing would be wanting to the satisfaction which I feel with regard to his intentions. Pray how is he doing Leeds I mean as to plates etc., on this head I am rather afraid also.

Mr and Mrs S[urtees] are both exceedingly well. This acc[oun]t I had from my neighbour the Rector who walked over the other day. George, Miller[35] and myself were yesterday at the sale [of] Jones the broken Sunderl[an]d banker. The font at Hart is exquisite. You must be muzzled or else you will devour it. Mr S[urtees] has come to a determination to print the Coldingham papers, seals etc. after Durham if the D[ean] and C[hapter] cannot be roused to the work themselves[36] ...

I will endeavour to give you a good impression *in dorso rotuli.*

7

Mainsforth Dec[ember] 21 1815

I trust that ere this the Pittington plate has arrived in safety.[37] I have now got out of the bustle of Durham and am no longer saluted with the rattling of trunks and the noise of boys gasping for holidays. Miller and Tom Shipperdson are amusing themselves, the

---

34 T. D. Whitaker (1759–1821), author of *History and Antiquities of the Deanery of Craven* (1805), and *History of Richmondshire* (1823), also published a second, enlarged edition of R. Thoresby's *Ducatus Leodiensis* ..., (Leeds and Wakefield, 1816), having married, in 1783, Lucy daughter of Thomas Thoresby of Leeds, "a kinsman of the celebrated antiquary".

35 James Miller, minor canon of Durham and vicar of Pittington; see also Letter 30 below.

36 In the event the major part, pp. 1–114, of the Appendix to Raine's own *North Durham* comprised texts of charters in the Chapter's muniments, but with far fewer plates than he had originally hoped, see *Ibid.* p. viii. Further Coldingham materials were published by Raine as Vol. 12 of the Society's publications (1841). Chapter granted Raine access to the original documents on 20 November 1816, see Acts.

37 Surtees' *History* includes no plate solely devoted to Pittington, but features of the church are found *inter alia* in Vol. I plates 19–20.

one with chess and the other with the *Christian Observer.* Mr Surtees is reading an account of the battle of Waterloo so that I am left unoccupied.

I naturally turn to the plates etc. for the *History of Durham* and proceed to point out a few inaccuracies in the view of the choir in the cathedral.[38] They are very trifling however if it can be done without much difficulty, they may as well be rectified. The figures at the Litany desk are quite out of plan. When the minor canons officiate upon it it is brought forward and stands opposite the approach to the minor canons' seats on the left hand of the plate. Besides no boys with surplices sit so near the pulpit. Their place is where you have introduced the ladies etc., in which place some are permitted to sit except the boys in question. These I allow are trifles but when the plate might be accurate without much trouble you will I think agree with me that these inaccuracies might as well be removed. The plate is beautiful and in every other respect as far as I am a judge perfectly correct.

I had no opportunity of answering your numerous queries in my last and must now therefore proceed to inform you that I have been unusually silent for the last half year, that the bees have made a considerable quantity of honey and that Willy Reed killed an enormous pig the morning before I left Durham. "These are important points" and have been answered with all due attention. Tom Shipperdson and Mr Yorke[39] had a serio-comic debate last night with regard to doctrine etc. However they have parted good friends today. The latter has gone home to eat a heron shot by Mr Robinson. Miller accompanies me to Darlington and probably to Dinsdale tomorrow. I have given the seal-engraver's bills to George and Carr though it is probable that you may hear no more on that subject till my return from the holidays ...

---

38 Surtees' *History* Plate 72 (given with vol. i) has, in its published state, none of the figures of minor canons at the Litany desk, surpliced boys or ladies etc. that Raine criticized. For further problems with this plate, see Letter 9 below.

39 Thomas Yorke, vicar of Bishop Middleham from 1813; Mainsforth lay in his parish.

8

Ovington 8 Jan[uary] 1816

Another discovery has been made at Staindrop. Stothard who was there some time ago found out that the female who wears a coronet rests upon lions which have hitherto been concealed in the ground.[40] Tis a strange story yet I should hardly suspect Mr Sherwood Sen[io]r my informer of having made a mistake.[41] Perhaps Mr Stothard,[42] if you are at all acquainted, will permit you to examine his drawings, which will give you some idea of the matter.

I have since I left Mainsforth confined myself pretty closely in copying the North riding of Yorkshire, to wit from Dugdale's Visitation in 1665.[43] I have however this day brought my labours to a close and it is my intention, a laudable one surely to devote the remaining fortnight of my holidays to idleness. In consequence of Dr Zouch's death there have been some few changes in the College at Durham. Mr Darnell is to be the new prebendary and Mr Phillpotts is the person promoted.[44] Mrs Ingram succeeds to the whole of the Doctor's cash and Mr I[ngram] to his estate in Teesdale.[45] At this I know you will rejoice. Since writing the above I have got a letter from Haslewood[46] in which he describes the joy at Durham in consequence of Darnell's return from Stockton ...

40 The effigy may be that described in Surtees' *History* iv,1 p. 129, and cf. Plate 59 in which one of the female effigies wears a coronet.
41 Thomas Sherwood, antiquary and friend of Surtees, lived at Snow Hall near Gainford; he also practised as a surgeon in Bishop Auckland.
42 Charles Alfred Stothard (1786–1821), antiquarian draughtsman, prepared ten parts of *Monumential Effigies of Great Britain*, (1811).
43 Raine's transcript of Dugdale's *Visitation of Yorkshire* (1665–1666) was used by Robert Davies of York for his edition, Surtees Soc. xxxvi (1859).
44 The second of the prebendal stalls fell vacant by Zouch's death on 17 December 1815 and Henry Phillpotts transferred to it from the poorer ninth stall, to which Darnell was instituted on 12 January 1816.
45 John Ingram, vicar of Hartlepool, was the nephew of Dr Zouch.
46 Dickens Haslewood, Chapter librarian.

9

Durham February 4 1816

I have this moment arrived at Durham from Mainsforth where previous to my departure your parcel had arrived. It has been a matter of real grief to me to hear the two plates of the Cathedral so violently abused by those who, had it not been that they had heard of some trifling deficiency, would never have made the discovery themselves with regard to the cloister door.[47] It was your wish that they should protest against it and therefore it was necessary that they should see it. At the same time I must confess Mr Darnell acted very injudiciously when he submitted to their inspection the inside view of the choir also.[48] Dr Gray and Mr Phillpotts are the only two prebendaries with whom I have had any conversation on the subject both of whom seem to have formed an opinion of it as a finished plate. I accordingly told them that that was by no means the case and that even a few alterations trifling in themselves would give it quite a different appearance. They both fully acquitted you in the most unequivocal terms and bore the amplest testimony to the correctness and beauty of the original drawings. I am afraid the only person to blame in this vexing matter is Mr Darnell who has erred without the slightest intention of so doing.

Having seen the impression which reached Mainsforth today I shall certainly call on one or two of the Preb[endaries] tomorrow and state the wonderful improvement which has been made not in consequence of any suggestion of theirs but in pursuance of the original plan in its engraving. Mr Surtees has acted in the most gentlemanly manner on this occasion and not one slightest particle of blame ought to be attached to him. You may expect a letter from him in the course of a day or two on the subject. Lambton is most beautiful – what will it be when finished.[49]

---

47 Surtees' *History* Plate 73 (given with vol. i).
48 *Ibid.* Plate 72 (given with vol. i). See Letter 7 above for Raine's criticisms of it. Canon William Darnell acted as Surtees' representative on the committee which had been set up to deal with the allocation of funds given by subscribers for illustrations to his *History*, see G. Taylor, *Memoir of Robert Surtees*, (Surtees Soc. xxiv), p. 150.
49 *Ibid.* Plate 35 (given with vol. i); in a letter to Raine of 7th Jan. 1821 Surtees says that he still reserves his "unqualified preference of Lambton to anything of Turner's", see Taylor, *Memoir* ..., p. 400.

Since I last wrote to you I have begun to etch under the inspection (for I don't say tuition) of Mr Busby[50] and I must beg you to forward to me as soon as possible in the ... of a letter an impression of the plate which contains the churches of Houghton and Easington.[51] It is a material point to have something handsome and correct to copy from and that plate certainly answers the description. You may, if you please also send the plate which contains Pittington monum. Horden etc.[52] Poor Mrs Robinson is far from well, the rest of the worthy family are all in good health ...

10

Durham March 4th 1816

Many thanks for the Easington plate which arrived at a very acceptable time. I so far please myself in etching that I am afraid it will take up too much of my leisure hours for the future. As you kindly promise to be of any possible use to me pray send me a set of points of diff[erent] sizes as those I am at present using are most villainous ones. If Mr Surtees has a parcel to leave London in the course of a day or two enclose them in it, but if not you will particularly oblige me by forwarding them per mail without delay.

I herewith send the amount of the seal engraver's bills and am requested by the Reverend Gents to convey to you their warmest thanks for the trouble which must unavoidably have fallen to your share in their concerns. Mr Surtees who has this moment left me is very anxious to know if you received a sum of money from Mr Taylor of Sunderland so pray satisfy him on this head as soon as may be. He has been dining with the Shipperdsons. The young unmarried gentlemen in Durham have all (if common report may be credited) taken leave of their hearts and some of them of their senses. Carr is to be married to Rose Hopper, George to Miss White and her £20,000, Penson the new minor canon to Miss Alderson and Miller to Miss Smales. With regard to the first and last fame I think may not be believed but I think that there can be little doubt respecting the other

50 T. L. Busby, artist and engraver; see Letter 12 below.
51 *Ibid.*, vol. i Plate 18.
52 *Ibid.*, vol. i Plate 19.

two. There is to be a ball on Wednesday which will (as Miss Shipperdson, your dear friend Miss Shipperdson says) put the matter to the test.

I wish you could continue to enclose a few pieces of copper in Mr Surtees' parcel of octavo or duodecimo size. I am most amazingly annoyed in procuring it here. I shall not fail to send you the first favourable proof though it will be totally eclipsed by the beauty and elegance of your own performances. You know I am not guilty of paying compliments. Therefore value the above. Pray remember me kindly to Frye and tell him the Durham news. So much have the good people of Durham to talk about now that he and his concerns are never mentioned. At this I dare say [he will] not be sorry. Let me conclude this rambling epistle ...

Pray remember the points and I sh[oul]d like to know if the contents have arrived safely.

11

Durham Ap[ril] 3 1816

In the first place accept my sincere thanks for your kindness in sending me a timely supply of copper. The only desideratum was the manufacturers demand against you with which I must soon be favoured.

Upon receipt of Dr Whitaker's prospectus[53] I lost no time in writing to him to inform him of the treasures at Durham relative to the district of Yorkshire. I mentioned particularly the archiepiscopal and other seals, accurate drawings of which I told him were in your possession and that it would be very difficult if not absolutely impossible for a stranger to gain admission to make fresh drawings. I told him of the mass of information in my possession relative to Richmondshire and gave him to understand in pretty plain terms that I would give the whole up to him provided you were engaged as his draftsman.

His very gentlemanly answer to my letter informs me that he had too lately become acquainted with your merits to engage you exclusively, but that very fortunately he was at liberty to solicit your

---

53 See note 34 above.

assistance in drawing seals etc.[54] This result of my correspondence gives both Mr Surtees and myself great satisfaction and I trust you will have no objection to accede to a plan which can be put in execution with so much ease to yourself and which will give such an additional interest to the work.

You have drawings of almost all the seals which are worth engraving so that the trouble to you will be but inconsiderable. I write to him again tomorrow to give him a list of charters etc., and I dare say you will ere long hear from him on the subject. I think I can refer you to many more seals in the public offices in London[55] so that I trust it will be an advantageous concern to all parties. Mr Surtees gave up the archiepiscopal and other seals willingly. As to the Dean and C[hapter], I don't believe they have any idea whatever of engraving their remaining seals so that I think you cannot do better than turn your drawings to advantage. Leave must be obtained not only for the seals but also for the charters. This I will undertake to procure as soon as I know your determination. I shall desire the Dr. to write to you immediately on the subject. He comes to call upon me at Durham in the course of a week or two when matters can be settled. Many more seals will doubtless make their appearances in … families in the District. At least the town chest of Richmond must be examined. Perhaps it is your intention to make your appearance among us when the first part of the magnum opus has fairly made its appearance. Pray consider these things and let me know the result speedily …

12

Durham May 26 1816

Dr Whitaker who is now at Richmond is very anxious to get my papers into his possession but as permission cannot be obtained before Saturday the next Chapter day and as from conversation

---

54 Whitaker's *Richmondshire* does not include engravings of seals, nor any engravings by Blore, its illustrations being mainly "after Turner", by a wide variety of engravers.

55 Until the Public Record Office was created under an Act of 1838 many buildings were used for the storage of central government and legal records.

which has taken place between Mr Surtees and Mr Darnell it appears that permission will scarcely be granted except upon condition that you furnish drawings of the seals, I must earnestly beg you that you will by return of post inform me whether you have had any communication with him on the subject. Dr W[hitaker] from all accounts seems to be anything else but a Surtees or a Clutterbuck[56] and from the brevity and style of his epistles and from many other latent symptoms of the great man I am not much inclined to disturb myself about him. If however matters can be so arranged that your seals and my transcripts can go together, let them go and much good may they do him. I shall defer answering his last cold letter till I hear from you which must be on Thursday or at farthest on Friday. Pray tell me what has become of the *History of Durham* and when may we expect to meet it at Farewell Hall as we do other worthies.[57] The *Hist[ory] of Hartlepool* [by Sir Cuthbert Sharp] is to be published in the course of a day or two. What a book! Pray get a sight of it as soon as possible, 't will do you good to read it.

Carr, Miller and myself yesterday visited the peninsula [i.e. Hartlepool] so blessed with an Historian. Ingram who is still there paid us every attention and devised various amusements for us. In particular we were regaled with a trip in the lifeboat and with the exhibition of Cap[tain] Manby's rope and mortar.[58] Ingram gave me also a very particular account of the discovery at Staindrop.[59] Stothard it appears suspecting something to be beneath the slab caused it to be raised when to his no small astonishment it was found to be supported by 4 lions in a couchant posture. From their disposition he conjectured that the number had originally been 8, and since that 2 if I am not mistaken have been discovered in houses

56 R. Clutterbuck (1772–1831), topographer and author of *The History and Antiquities of the County of Hertford*, (London, 1815–27).
57 Farewell Hall, 2 miles south of Durham, beside the turnpike road to Darlington, is said to have taken its name from the fact that it was the point at which the city authorities bade farewell to the assize judges, having previously greeted them at a corresponding point north of the city known as the Salutation; conversely notables arriving from the south were met at Farewell Hall, and in particular several bishops of Durham during the eighteenth century on their first visit to the city.
58 George William Manby (1765–1854) invented, among other life-saving equipment, the apparatus for firing a line from a mortar to a shipwreck, see C. Sharp, *History of Hartlepool*, (1816), p. 204.
59 See Letter 8 above.

in Staindrop and two more tossing about in the church.

If we are to have the pleasure of seeing you soon you will of course improve your drawing upon the spot. Haslewood who has this moment left me tells me that no fewer than 12 marriages are talked of in the Durham circles. Oh club of scandal, how long wilt thou imagine lies and mischief! Busby is now at Hartlepool engraving the views of Durham for Andrews. He seems to have an idea of publishing the Hartlepool costume which would certainly be interesting.[60] Pray write soon and tell me everything respecting the probable time when I may expect the *Hist[ory] of Durham* ...

13

Addressed to Edward Blore at Edinburgh
Durham Nov[ember] 23 1816

The question with regard to the records was gloriously settled last Wednesday the day on which the great annual chapter was held.[61] Mr Darnell was kind enough to manage the matter and at his request it was determined that every facility of access should be afforded me to the originals and that the manuscripts in Mr Surtees's possession might be given up to me. But this was not all, a plate of seals was promised, doubtless at Darnell's suggestion and therefore all is now over.

My next transmigration will be into a folio. Since I saw you I have transcribed almost every record from the boxes which contain North Durham and nothing now remains but a few pickings from the Coldingham papers. I have found many interesting armorial seals which you do not seem to have noticed and of course I have with my pencil attempted to preserve a recollection of them. Have you drawn the large armorial seal of Vescy which occurs connected with Farne?[62]

---

60 T. L. Busby, *The Fishing, Costume and Local Scenery of Hartlepool in the County of Durham*, (1819).
61 Chapter Acts 20 November 1816 accords with Raine's account here, but on 14 January 1817 Chapter rescinded that part of the order concerning a plate of seals, "no plate of seals having been ever proposed to be given to Mr Surtees".
62 Raine most probably meant the seal of William de Vescy, attached to *North Durham*, Appendix no. DCXCVIII, but that of Agnes de Vescy, *Ibid.*

...

Mr Surtees who has commenced his weekly attacks upon me promises me a *Inieta Clamacio* de Norham next Saturday. He wishes you would return by Coldingham and Halieland if you have time though you are not to visit the Farne islands so late in the season.

I am thinking of drawing up a prospectus next week which should I think be neatly printed in the way of a circular – and besides it should appear in the Edinburgh, Newcastle and Durham papers, and also in the *Gent[leman's] Magazine*.

Do you wish your name to appear in it in any other way than as connected with the decorations? Pray let me know upon this point as soon as possible. Perhaps you would like to see it before it be made public.

Darnell was ordered to draw up the resolution and from the brief sketch he gave me of it it was done *amplissimis verbis*. Bowlby no longer jealous of a young antiquary told me today unasked that the resolution was on its road to the Dean for his approbation. This is merely pro forma. He promised me a copy in the most good natured manner ...

14

Addressed to Edward Blore at Edinburgh
Cover: December 12 1816
Durham Tuesday Evening

I am at last enabled to send you a copy of the prospectus which is I think very neatly printed. You will observe a few alterations which render the plan more intelligi[ble in so] far they are improvements. Will you be kind enough to see it printed in that Edinburgh newspaper which has the most extensive circulation and send me an impression. I like the seal very much only there is a trifling blunder which will easily [be altered.] The arm instead of being na[ked should] be covered with little pellets. As soon as this is put right pray forward it to [the] coach as speedily as may be for Bryan will take his departure on the 22nd and I should wish him to

---

no. DCC, is a possibility, see W. Greenwell & C. H. Hunter Blair, *Catalogue of the Seals in the Treasury of the Dean & Chapter of Durham*, (1911–21, as *Archaeologia Aeliana* 3rd series vii–xvii), nos 2540 and 2537, and plate 29.

take it home with him. Trusting to hear from you soon ...

Thank Mr Thomson kindly for his intended present.[63] Perhaps he would be so obliging as to take the trouble of circulating a few impressions of the prospectus if forwarded to him. Mr Surtees has desired me to inform you that if you can conveniently introduce Ralph Sherwood now a med[ical] student at Edinburgh to Walter Scott he will be greatly obliged to you.

[A proof of the prospectus for *The History and Antiquities of North Durham* accompanied this letter.]

15

Addressed to Edward Blore at Edinburgh
Cover: Durham March 22 1817

This comes greeting with £24 10s in its belly. £20 from Mr Surtees and £4 10s the amount of your demands against me for the two seals. It grieves me to inform you that the Coldingham charters cannot be sent to Mr Thomson during your abode in Edinburgh for when last in the treasury for the express purpose of taking out the boxes which contain the early Scottish records I was totally unable to lay my hands upon them.[64] Where you have put them I know not and I am therefore compelled to wait till your arrival at Durham before I make another attack. Think not that I was easily driven from the place of seals. I heard many a complaint of the damp above and below before I sallied forth with half my errand. I have however transcribed one of Mr Thomson's charters from the cartularies which shall be sent to him immediately if he cannot wait for a transcript of the original.

Pray give my best comp[liment]ts to R. Sherwood. To him I am a grievous debtor and I know not when I shall have the opportunity of fulfilling my epistolary promises. The fact is, I devote the whole of my leisure to Bowlby's storehouse most liberally thrown open to me upon all occasions. Time was when I was looked upon by that arch

---

63 Thomas Thomson, Deputy Keeper of the Records preserved in the General Registry in Scotland.
64 On 8 February 1817 Chapter had "agreed that Mr Raine be allowed to take out of the Treasury boxes labelled *Comitum de Dunbar & Instrumenta publica de Coldingham*", see Acts.

labeller as a dangerous intruder but now I have every facility afforded me in the most goodnatured manner. This is the age of reform.

When in the name of wonder are we likely to see you at Durham. I am half inclined to think that we shall meet upon the Border in June next. I think I told you that Mr Burrell[65] has been kind enough to hire a house at Bambro' within a stone's throw of my kingdom where we are to spend the Midsummer Holidays. This is but one link in a long chain of kindnesses. I was at Newcastle the other day examining nearly 1000 coins found in Bamboroughshire. They consist entirely of pennies of Henry II and Stephen some of which have been struck in Berwick.

Pray let me hear immediately of the safe arrival of this epistle and its contents and perhaps you will tell me when it is probable we may see you here ...

Bye the bye, your old friend Sanderson alas is dead and buried.

16

Addressed to Edward Blore at Edinburgh
Durham May 31 1817.

As our midsummer holidays are fast approaching I am very anxious to hear of your intended motions before I come to any final determination with regard to my own.

I have already, I think, told you that Mr Burrell has taken a house at Bambro' for a few weeks purposely on my account, and as his lease will commence on the first of July, I must as in duty bound present myself before him at that time. I am requested to convey to you his warmest wishes that you will be one of the party and you will not I trust disappoint us. Our vacation will commence on the 24th of June and though I have received a most pressing invitation to spend the few intermediate days at Broomepark yet George has partly persuaded me to accompany him to Edinburgh for a few days. Tell me therefore, suppose I should muster courage to cross the Tweed could you so manage matters as to be able to return with me to Bambro' and stay there a few weeks? On this condition and this only will I come to Edinburgh and therefore I am exceedingly anxious to

---

65 Presumably William Burrell, F.S.A., 1773–1847, whose seat at Broome-Park, 5 miles south-west of Alnwick, is mentioned in subsequent letters.

hear from you on the subject. If you knew a seventieth part of the immense interest taken by Mr Burrell in our pursuits you would I am sure almost fall down and worship him. Besides it will be of the greatest importance to me to have you at my elbow on the Border. Your long delay in Edinburgh induces me to hope that you have been waiting for this very purpose and therefore my only request is that you will lose no time in enabling me to answer the Lord of Broomepark's kind invitation to us both.

Since I last heard from you I have been most diligently employed in our never to be exhausted mines here and I am now busily engaged in smoothing and arranging matters for the approaching visitation. Perhaps you would prefer meeting me at Broomepark at the beginning of the holidays when we may spend the intervening week before we take up our abode at Bamborough. The plan shall [be] entirely of your arranging and therefore pray let me have timely notice. Ralph Sherwood will never forgive [me] for my apparent neglect of him and his amusing epistles. Pray make all the apologies in your power for me for I can assure you that had I time for the least epistolary correspondence I should be by no means disposed to forget him.

We are just as dull as ever at Durham and such is the state of our society that I really consider myself very fortunate in having a pursuit which occupies the whole of my leisure ...

17

Addressed to Edward Blore at Edinburgh
Cover: June 29 1817
Broomepark Saturday morning.

According to an arrangement of Mr Burrell's which will detain us a day on the road, he and I will not reach Bamborough till Wednesday next the 2nd of July and therefore I give you notice accordingly. You may either defer your visit till that day, or if you cannot conveniently alter your plans Mrs Burrell who will be at Bambro' on the 1st will I am sure take care of you till our arrival. Hoping very soon to have the pleasure of seeing you ...

18

Durham Dec[ember] 7 1817

I send you herewith £24 8s. which I have at Mr Surtees's request got from Andrews for you. Let me hear of the arrival *quam primum.*

I have also in the mean time had some communication with Mr Burrell on the subject of the castles and as he cannot make up his mind on the matter till benefitted by my advice, I am to request that you will stop your proceedings till the holidays when we shall have an opportunity of talking the matter over together. He himself would wish to have them framed, but Mrs Burrell and Miss Forster prefer the portfolio. Bamborough, Dunstanborough, Alnwick and Warkworth are to be the subjects and you shall hear more on the matter in the course of a few weeks.

Accept my best thanks for your prompt attention to my seal. As we take our departure on Tuesday the 16th I hope to receive Broomepark and Bolton as soon as may be after this reaches you.[66] The seal may be sent at the same time as from your account it must be already finished.

The vicarage of Brantingham near Beverley which is now vacant has been offered to Carr by the Dean and Chapter and if he should decline it which is somewhat probable, your friend the antiquary is to be the rector. At least so says one well skilled in the mysteries of the chapter house, but this is of course *inter nos.* Tell me therefore what you know of it as you have perambulated Howdenshire.[67] A history of that district must of course follow North Durham if I am transplanted.

You will observe no small disparity between the date of Mr Surtees' epistle and that of this scrawl. The delay has been occasioned by George Andrews who wished for more than a bare day's notice.

When at Mainsforth last week I found Surtees considerably indisposed in consequence of a fall from his horse a few days before. He was however on the high road to recovery and I have since heard

---

66 Raine appears to be referring to work being carried out by Blore for William Burrell of Broome-Park and his wife Eleanor, daughter of Matthew Forster of Bolton.
67 Howden, some 17 miles south-east of York, was the centre of a long-established ecclesiastical jurisdictional peculiar belonging to the Chapter of Durham. It included the church of Brantingham.

good accounts of him.

Turner has I dare say ere now reached town with his drawings of Raby, Gibside, Hilton and Streatlam. Lambton[68] has done all this. Would that some heavy pressed wight would show his face in North Durham ...

19

Durham Dec[ember] 16 1817. Tuesday evening.

I have just time to state that I set out tomorrow morning for Teesdale instead of Tweed dale. This alteration of my plans has been brought about by Mr Burrell who will be absent from Broomepark till the day after Xmas day. On that day however (the 26th inst.) I shall return through Durham on my road to Broomepark. The drawings will have arrived by that time and may I hope to find my seal also? I cannot be sufficiently thankful for the trouble you have had with it. When I am vicar of Brantingham I will repay you in full. On this subject I have nothing further to communicate. The matter is still undecided and Carr has set out to see the place this day before he can make up his mind on the subject.

Andrews tells me that you are not likely to have any difficulty with regard to his note. He sends up £150 to his agent in London in the course of a day or two to cover that and similar demands.

I think that I can partly explain the mystery of the Edinburgh portraits. Ralph Sherwood on his road home some three months ago left with me whether I would or not 3 proof impressions of Walter Scott for you. Two of them are still in my custody and the third Mr Surtees carried to Mainsforth some time ago intending to satisfy every demand which you might make upon his purse for it. So stands the matter. The two in my possession shall be forwarded to you if you require it.

---

68 Plates of Gibside and Hylton Castle were issued with Surtees' *History* vol. ii, as Plates 36 and 28, and of Streatlam Castle with vol. iv, as Plate 57. John G. Lambton, later Lord Durham, subscribed £52 10s. to the fund raised for illustrations for Surtees' *History*, see Taylor, *Memoir* ..., p. 150.

I shall have great pleasure in recommending Mr Cooke's *Bot[anical] Mag[azine]*[69] to Mr Burrell who will I dare say purchase it immediately. Mrs Surtees seems to regret the want of English names to the plants and the descriptive part is certainly meagre. The plates however are a sufficient recommendation ...

20

Durham 14 Jan[uary] 1818

It gives me great pleasure to hear of your intention to visit us at Bambro'. We shall muster about the 2nd or 3rd of July and as our stay will only be a fortnight pray arrange matters in Edinbro' so as to be with us as soon as may be. Mr and Mrs Surtees are at present at Broomepark on their return from the north without any intention of joining us at Bamborough. Our holidays commence next Saturday, but I shall in all probability remain here till the end of the month. We must contrive to visit Coldingham and Bedlington, and drawings of the Farne Islands etc. remain to be made so that I shall have work enough for you ...

21

Cover: Durham January 26 1818

Your expostulatory epistle reached me the other day at Berwick after a somewhat roundabout journey and in reply to it I must begin with begging your forgiveness for not informing you of the safe arrival of the two drawings etc.

Mr Burrell has requested me to convey to you his most sincere thanks for the great favour you have conferred upon him and also to inform you that he has made up his mind with regard to the four drawings which he expects from you – Bamborough, Dunstanborough, Alnwick and Warkworth are to be the subjects and the size is left for your own choice. Mr Forster of Lucker is

---

69 There appears to be a confusion here between *The Botanical Cabinet*, (1817–33), illustrated by G. Cooke, and *The Botanical Magazine*, vols 1–14 by William Curtis, 15–53 by J. Sims, and 54–70 (new series 1–17) by Samuel Curtis; both are referred to in Letter 21.

somewhat impatient for his two views of Bamborough. I have however told him not to expect them till midsummer as you are over head and ears in business. Mr Burrell rode to Dunstanbro' to seek your Indian rubber but without success. A large reward has been offered to the finder and therefore you may hope to meet again.

You gave me such a miserable impression of my seal that I can form no idea of its execution. Now that I have returned to Durham will you be kind enough to send it to me as soon as possible. You know how impatient I am and when I tell you that I shall expect it on Wednesday or Thursday next you will not I am sure let me break my heart with disappointment.

I have had a rich harvest in my kingdom of North Durham. Independently of having examined the title deeds of many of my loyal subjects I have made most copious extracts from the parish registers of the whole of Islandshire in Alnwick, Bambro' and Lesbury into the bargain so that my labours in collecting materials are drawing rapidly to a close. Nothing can exceed the flattering attention with which I have been received and as I have made considerable additions to my list of worthies which I intend to print as soon as possible will you take the trouble of procuring a copy of the list of names handed to John Nichols, and send it me with the seal, or at least as soon as may be afterwards.

As I confined myself to Berwick and Islandshire I had no opportunity of visiting the vicar of Norham, who I understand arrived in Durham a few days ago to spend two or three months with us. Nothing can exceed the beauty of the seal at present used by the Corporation of Berwick. It seems to be about the time of Henry VI and the architecture with which it is graved is inimitable. I shall procure an impression next midsummer which must be graven. The corporation records are exceedingly curious but I have made no extracts from them as it is my intention to spend a week or a fortnight there at Midsummer.

Mr Burrell happens to possess a copy of Curtis and therefore conceives it unnecessary to become a purchaser of Mr Cooke.[70] He is however trying to procure a subscriber for the copy which you sent him and I have no doubt of his succeeding. He either has or will speedily write to you on the subject as he is much obliged to you for

---

70 See Letter 19 note 69.

telling him of the book in question and it would have given him the greatest pleasure to have become a purchaser of it had he not possessed Curtis which is perhaps better accommodated to him. He wishes to give you an unlimited commission with regard to any splendid book you may think worthy of his shelves and in particular he requests you to put his name down for a copy of Mr Baker's *Northamptonshire*.[71] I the other day received a bill from Blackwood for my copy of the Stirling heads,[72] which I do not intend to settle till I hear from you as if I am not mistaken I am answerable to you and not to him. Did I not take one of your copies?   .

I am very anxious to hear of your arrangements with regard to the year into which we have lately entered. Do you intend to spend the summer in London? Mr Burrell fully expects to see you again at Broomepark and I wish you could so arrange matters as to be at liberty at Midsummer. I have not seen Surtees since my return. He was in Durham a few days ago standing godfather for the young schoolmaster. Bye the bye I am not fated to be the vicar of Brantingham. Carr has accepted the living and I was the first to congratulate him which I did most sincerely. This long letter will I hope atone for my late neglect particularly as it is now near midnight and I am in no small degree put out of order by a hot room at Jack Bowlby's who has been holding a vanity fair this evening ...

22

Durham 16 Feb[ruary] 1818.

It is now more than a month since I gave a suitable reply to your objurgatory epistle and I flattered myself that you would most graciously condescend to accept my submission. But since that time I have heard nothing from you and therefore I am led to conclude that either my letter has never reached you, or the seal which I begged you to forward to me without delay has miscarried. Pray set me at rest as soon as possible after the rec[eip]t of this. I long much to have our list of subscribers printed and have been anxiously hoping to get John Nichol's list by your means. Excuse this short epistle ...

---

71 G. Baker, *The History and Antiquities of the County of Northampton*, (1822–41), contained many illustrations by Edward Blore.

72 The reference is obscure.

Have you a seal drawn of Adam Swinburne 5 garbs upon a cross garnished with boars heads dated 1317?[73] Don't forget to answer this query as the seal a very beautiful one is now out of the Treas[ury] and if you have it not I must attempt it. I shall expect to hear from you on Saturday or Sunday.

23

Durham 6 Ap[ril] 1818.

Accept my most sincere thanks for the trouble you have had with the *sigillium amoris* which arrived in perfect safety some time ago. I enclose a £5 note to settle damages as we Yorkshiremen say. I like it very much and Mr Surtees is quite delighted with it. He intends I believe to have a somewhat similar one for himself but he will give directions *viva voce*. I last week paid a visit to Mainsforth for a few days in company with Mr Burrell. The host and his guest seemed much delighted with each other, and as a general plan was formed to muster at Bamborough in the beginning of July I am very anxious to hear whether you can honour us with your presence. Mr and Mrs Surtees are to be of the party if this will be an additional inducement to you.

I see John Nichols has been firing another popgun in his last magazine.[74] I have I think given up the idea of printing the list of subscribers at present. Don't you think it will be better to wait till the end of the year as we shall in all probability have caught a few more gudgeons by that time.

I have laid the undertaking aside for a while as it is my intention to offer myself for priests' orders in September and some preparation is necessary. You have doubtless ere this have seen Frye who left this county on a wedding expedition a fortnight ago. The lady to whom he has long paid his addresses and who has hitherto been prevented from marrying him by a lucre loving father is now of age and laughs at all opposition so that Frye will be a happy man at last Mr Surtees has begun to print the second volume but I dare say

73 For this document see Greenwell & Blair, *Catalogue of the Seals* ..., no. 2362; garb is the heraldic term for a sheaf of corn.
74 The prospectus for Raine's *History of North Durham* was published by Nichols in the *Gentleman's Magazine* of April 1818.

this is [not] news to you. Hoping to hear speedily of the safe arrival of this pregnant epistle ...

24

Addressed to Edward Blore at Ripon
Durham, Tuesday [May 1820]

I shall at present spare my congratulations and merely assure you that I shall have very great pleasure in meeting you at Richmond on Saturday next. It is my intention to go by the Telegraph to Catterick Bridge from whence I can easily walk up to Richmond. I shall in all probability ar[rive ab]out two when I shall hope to find y[ou ...]arker's the King's Head.[75] We shall have time enough to see the sights in the course of the afternoon. I hope it is your intention to stay all night at Richmond ...

25

Cover: May 13 1820, *addressed to Edward Blore at Ripon.*
Durham, Saturday morning.

It was my full intention to have paid my respects to you this day at Ripon, but unfortunately poor Carr who has been for some time in a bad state of health is this morning worse than usual and as there is a probability of his not being able to attend school for a few days I am reluctantly compelled to lay aside all hopes of seeing you during your stay in the North. Be assured that Mrs Blore and yourself have my very best wishes for your happiness and welfare in the married state – and yet I cannot but wonder that you should have ventured to take such an important step without my permission. However I most freely forgive you and most sincerely assure you that I shall always have very great pleasure in hearing of the health and happiness of both Mrs Blore and yourself.

As soon as you are quietly settled in London I should like to have some arrangements made with respect to the Coldingham seals.

---

75 Michael Yarker was innkeeper at the King's Head in Richmond *c.* 1800–28, see *The Richmond Review*, (Richmond & District Civic Soc., 1985), p. 42.

Six plates only are arranged,[76] and as Nichols has been some time engaged in printing the appendix, I shall be in a short time prevented from making any further progress in consequence of not being able to refer to the plates. I almost wish you would immediately upon your return give me notice that I may send you a list of those seals which will be first wanted. With my best respects to Mrs Blore and my kind thanks for your invitation to London of which I shall I fear scarcely be able to avail myself next holidays ...

26

Durham 18 Jan[uary] 1821

I am given to understand that my silence with respect to my safe arrival in Durham has been as far as you are concerned, attended with most serious consequences. Your great anxiety for my safety has induced you to forget your favourite pork pies, salt herrings and German sausages, and you are now, if my little bird tells me rightly, reduced to a mere skeleton like poor Mrs Radclyffe's turkey. But pray take heart for I arrived in perfect safety on Saturday last after having undergone no perils either by land or water. My only disaster was this, that I was too late for the coach. I continued however to secure my place but was obliged to leave my trunk behind me which arrived in safety by the Wellington on Monday morning. It was well for my herons that they were not turkeys. Had that been the case, even though they were protected by a Sheffield whittle[77] their chance would have been by no means a good one. I regretted the absence of my friend the Black and White Lady most sincerely. Every tree and every steeple brought her to my memory but I was more particularly reminded of my loss when a boiled ham or a noble round of beef made its appearance. My fellow travellers were a middle aged man belonging to the Commissariat who swore like a trooper an elderly

---

76 In the event *North Durham* only included two separate plates of seals, following p. 374, both of early Scottish royal seals, and inscribed "Engraved by Wm. Wilkinson" and "London, Published Jany.1. 1830, by Nichols & Son, Parliament Street [Westminster]". A number of seals were illustrated in outline in the text itself.

77 A large knife, for carving, etc., or a clasp-knife. Raine's Black and White Lady was evidently a bird, see "every tree and every steeple".

Scotchman and a lad from Switzerland with all the bigotry of a most determined papist. Saturday was one of his fast days, and after he had preyed among the haddocks and other allowables I persuaded him to eat two or three spoonfuls of what I maliciously called an English omelet. The man consented and devoured so many veal cutlets much to the amusement of the Scotchman. But it is time to think of my ... with respect to the warming pan. See, here it is

[drawing of a warming pan]

This is the pan | Deny it who can | Should anyone doubt it | He knows nought about it. | It's for my friend Blore | And Sarah his spouse. | If you want to know more | Go call at their house. | 56 Welbeck Street | Cavendish Square | I know the place well | For I've often been there.

Pray give my best respects to Mrs Blore and tell her to use the pan sparingly as the weather is by no means so cold as to render its frequent use necessary. Remember me kindly to Roland Hill and Mr Ellis.[78] The B[isho]p has been confined by a severe cold and Dr Haggit only left Durham on Thursday last.[79] This accounts for the B[isho]p's break of promise. With my best thanks to Mrs Blore and yourself for your kind attention during my abode under your roof ...

<h2 style="text-align:center">27</h2>

Durham Jan[uary] 27 1821

I have this moment been commissioned by the Chapter to send you the enclosed the receipt of which must be acknowledged *immediately* either to Mr Darnell or myself.

Surtees was in Durham for a few days last week in the absence of Mrs Surtees who had gone to Hendon to look after poor Mrs Robinson, who has been for some time unwell. The last account was so very favourable that I am in daily expectation of hearing of her

78 Roland Hill (1795–1879), educationalist, inventor of the rotary printing-press and later involved with the Post Office and railways. Henry Ellis, author of *Letters Illustrative of English History* (1824), and *Introduction to Doomsday Book* (1833).
79 Francis Haggitt, canon of Durham Cathedral's tenth stall 1794–1825.

complete recovery.

I hope the warming pan arrived safe ...

P.S. I find I left the Ballads behind me. You will oblige me by not shewing the book to anyone. I am under a promise to Surtees.

28

Durham May 14 1821

Give my best respects to Dr Meyrick[80] and inform him that I have had no opportunity of hunting after the old sword which I promised to forward to him as I have only spent a day or two at home in Yorkshire since I had the pleasure of seeing him and during that time I never once recollected to look for it. I hope to find it during my approaching holidays when it shall be very much at his service.

I have met with some exceedingly curious particulars relative to the armour belonging to the monks of Holy Island at diff[eren]t periods from a very early date, with the price of each piece at the purchase. Guns are mentioned at a very early period and other tools of war occur with very antiquated names. Vide *North Durham*.[81]

Remember me very kindly to Mr Clutton. I watch the progress of the Newington Vestry Bill with great interest.[82] John Lyon resides

---

80 S. R. Meyrick (1783–1848), noted for his vast collection of arms and armour, wrote *A Critical Enquiry into Antient Armour as it existed in Europe, but particularly in England from the Norman Conquest to the Reign of King Charles II*, 3 vols, (1824).

81 See pp. 82–130 for extracts from the inventories and accounts of Durham Cathedral Priory's cell on Holy Island, including numbers of entries referring to weapons.

82 An Act of 1819 abolished the open vestry meetings which had previously dealt with parish affairs, including elections of churchwardens, overseers, etc.; all property and powers were to be transferred to a "select vestry" with limited membership and entitled to fill vacancies by co-option. In 1821, when it was proposed to rebuild the church of St Mary's, Newington, a bill was promoted to establish a select vestry in that parish. The parishioners protested loudly, raised funds to publicise their cause and eventually triumphed. See S. and B. Webb, *The Parish and the County*, (1963), p. 211. An earlier vestries act of 1818 had given the vestry the duty of deciding on the custodian and place of deposit of all parish records except the registers, possibly the reason for Raine's continuing interest in the controversy.

at Brussels. He is I understand in better plight than of late as he is now in the rec[eip]t of a yearly sum of money from a company of speculators who are trying a coal pit at Hetton.[83]

The Botany and Walter Scott – you shall have these by Andrews's first parcel. Mr Christopher's[84] will has not been proved here. He had money in the Funds[85] and it will therefore be found in London. I have delivered your message to Surtees who will act accordingly. So much for y[ou]r letter of business and now for my commissions.

The Dean and C[hapter] wish to print their Catalogue of Manuscripts[86] and have requested me to give them some notion of the number of copies which they may probably sell, exclusively of those given to members of the Body. This is a question which Mr Petrie can answer better than anyone I know of and therefore I wish you would catechise him a little upon the point and let me know his opinion quam primum. Dont forget to tell him at the same time that I think him a very worthy fellow and that nothing w[oul]d give me greater pleasure than to have it in my power to render him any service. I am truly glad [to he]ar of his undertaking.[87] Mr Surtees and [I a]re both of us very anxious to know whether you still retain your resolution of visiting the North during the summer. We start for the Highlands about the 20th June and if you could contrive to meet us at Berwick on our return matters [can] be easily settled in North Durham and elsewhere. Surtees wishes much to hear from you on this point and therefore write to me as soon as possible and tell me your plans...

---

83 John Lyons, a grandson of the 8th earl of Strathmore, owned a moiety of the manor of Hetton-le-Hole, between Durham and Sunderland, see Surtees, *History of Durham*, i,214, iv,I,109.

84 Possibly the Stockton bookseller mentioned by Raine, *Memoir of John Hodgson*, (1857), i,21.

85 Stock of the national debt often bought for investment purposes, was known as "the funds".

86 Raine arranged for the unpublished catalogue of the cathedral's medieval manuscripts, compiled by Thomas Rud (preface dated 1726), to be printed in 1825, and he appended descriptions of other collections (Hunter, Randall, Allan) acquired subsequently.

87 Henry Petrie (1768–1842), keeper of the records in the Tower of London from 1819, proposed to the Record Commissioners the publication of a corpus of materials for the *History of Britain*, and in May 1823 was appointed principal editor of this work, see *D.N.B.*, xlv,99–100.

29

[*Written on the same sheet as 28*]

Dear Mrs Blore,

I [have] been very much disappointed in not having rec[eive]d y[ou]r best thanks for the warming pan. It was by mere chance that I heard of its safe arrival in Welbeck Street. You were the very last lady in the world whom I should have suspected of ingratitude and I must beg leave to inform you that your silence with respect to my first present has prevented me from giving you any further proof of my friendship for you. I had prepared a Cotherstone cheese as high as the moon and two dozen of rabbits from Romaldkirk as a proof of my thankfulness for your kind attention to me during the Xmas holiday but under these circumstances I thought it proper to make a diff[eren]t use of them. Give your husband a good scolding when he attempts to write another letter on a Sunday morning and believe me, all jesting apart to be your sincere friend ...

30

[*Note on cover*: "no date ? after May 1821"]

Tom Shipperdson will thank you to purchase for him a Print of Christ and another of Fenelon[88] the next time you stroll out in search of Pig's Heads or Raisins and Almonds. You are commissioned to lay out four guineas upon the two, and the money shall be immediately forwarded to you the moment the deed of purchase shall arrive. He is upon the point of opening his house where he will have noone to stand in his way and you will readily conceive the manner in which it will be conducted. Divers good and weighty reasons prevented me from troubling Miller with a parcel for you. Your letter on the subject reached me the day after his departure. I feel truly glad that the Royal Seals of Scotland have been set right and I shall take especial care that other matters be duly managed before it be too late. Bye the bye, your engraving of Bishop Flambard is sadly deficient. An impression now before me gives me the following details which you have overlooked

88 Presumably the French author, 1651–1715.

[*rough drawing*] besides a running ornament which flounces his petticoats. The mitre or fillet or whatever it may be is strongly marked through a transparent varnish but it would not I fear be visible upon a cast.[89]

Miller is, I believe, expected home in a day or two with his head full of all the tithe law in London.[90] He is confident of success in his suit and Surtees who is not fond of talking upon these subjects pronounces his case to be a good one. Sharp arrived a few days ago and will shortly take possession of his post at Sunderland,[91] although it is pretty well understood that his appointment will furnish Joseph Hume with a topic of conversation in the House of Commons.[92] Remember me with all my best regards to Mrs Blore whom I have long forgiven, although the atrocity of her conduct was unpardonable. Query has she any intention of opening a shop at Gretna Green? Give my god-daughter a kiss from me, and tell her I send it. She is a child after my heart for she has some fun in her. I should be sorry to think that she had forgot me ...

31

Durham 16 Mar[ch] 1822

I thank you most sincerely for your two letters the first of which was the last in making its appearance.

I send this in a parcel to Mr Taylor who has made some glorious discoveries in the Rolls Chapel relative to Meldon.[93] His communication of a single inquisition post mortem has induced me to make up my mind on the subject. I shall be presented to the

---

89 The defects noted by Raine do not appear to have been remedied, see Surtees, *History of Durham*, I,i pl. 1 where Bishop Ranulf Flambard's seal is shewn top centre.

90 After long litigation Miller managed to set aside various *moduses* paid in lieu of tithes in his living, see G. Taylor, *Memoir of Robert Surtees*, (Surtees Soc. xxiv), p. 414n.

91 Sir Cuthbert Sharp actually took up his post as "Collector of Customs" in Sunderland in 1823 but his appointment may well have been discussed some time before that. See W. Brockie, *Sunderland Notables*, (1894).

92 Joseph Hume (1777–1855), radical politician.

93 Chancery records were at that time stored in the chapel of the Master of the Rolls in Chancery Lane, London.

Rectory on the 20th of July next and then <u>have at</u> the Governors of Greenwich Hospital.[94]

I send by the same conveyance a full reply to Mr Petrie's queries together with an original conventual seal of Durham which was blown down my chimney by one of the late high winds. It is supposed to have been blown from the tail of an old lease in the western part of the county. I shall be glad to see you along with Mrs Blore at the Parsonage at Meldon as soon as the house and glebe are recovered from the great Greenwich monster ...

32

Durham, Dec[ember] 14th 1822

Many thanks for your kind invitation. I am coming by sea with a Keel[95] of coals and a Berwick smack laden with salmon. I fear I shall scarcely be able to start till the Sunday or Monday after Christmas day so you may look for me on the Tuesday or Wednesday following. Unless indeed I shall be able to catch a stray clergyman and then I shall leave Durham on Christmas Day itself. Remember me kindly to Mrs Blore. If she should be of opinion that the salmon and coals will be too much for home consumption she is at perfect liberty to bespeak customers among her neighbours. Be ready with your gaiters to take to the streets at a moment's notice. I think upon second thoughts I shall be safer in the Mail and shall therefore give up the sea scheme, but the two ships shall be properly directed ...

---

94 The commissioners of Greenwich Hospital owned all the land in the parish of Meldon when Raine was inducted in 1822. His battles over tithes due to the rector of Meldon dragged on until August 1846, taking up a great deal of time and causing him much distress. The Law Report of August 28 1846 summarises the previous lengthy proceedings and gives the judgment of the Lord Chancellor following appeal before the House of Lords. (Cairns v. Raine 1846, volume viii p.1640.)

95 A small, flat-bottomed barge used for carrying coal from up-river sources to larger transport ships anchored out at sea.

33

Durham 24 Dec[ember] 1822

The share which it has been my duty to take in the foregoing proceedings must serve as my best apology for not having replied to your letter by return of post.

I think I shall leave Durham by Mail on Friday afternoon and shall therefore in all probability disturb your dreams on Sunday morning. I will try to comply with your request de sigillis Reg. Scot.[96]

I shall have much to do with Mr Caley and wish therefore that you would pave the way by any means in your power.[97] If you are in the habit of asking him to your house let me have an evening with him by all means quam primum. In order to smooth him down I wish you w[oul]d write a note to Mr Nichols requesting him to lay aside as much of my appendix as refers to Coldingham which I shall present as a peace offering. Meldon in great measure depends upon his assistance. Remember me to Mrs Blore ...

[Attached to this letter are the examination results of Durham School for the Christmas term. Top in the first class in both classics and maths is Raine's brother John. He was admitted sizar (aged 19) at Trinity College Cambridge in October 1822. Eventually he became Rector of Blyth, Notts (1834–74) and was one of the first members of the Surtees Society.]

34

Durham 3 Feb[ruary] 1824

You always despaired of my success with the Directors of Greenwich Hospital. I was always sanguine of success well knowing the strength of my case and my expectations have been at length realised in the most delightful manner. So long ago as last June I laid before the Board all my proofs for the establishment of my claims, and after having been kept in suspense for six months there came at last the welcome news (on New Year's eve) that my memorial had

---

96 Scottish royal seals, see above.
97 J. Caley (d. 1834), Secretary to the first Record Commission (1801–31).

been submitted to the legal advisers of the Institution and that as according to their opinion I was entitled to tythes in kind through the parish or their equivalent, the Directors had given orders to the Receiver of the Derwentwater Estates that they should no longer insist upon the Modus previously paid but should allow me to enjoy my rights. Thus I am Rector of Meldon in earnest.

Since I saw you I have done much at *North Durham* and feel anxious to know what further conversation you have had with Mr Nichols upon the subject of money matters.

Surtees has been dangerously ill – two bruised fingers hastening fast to mortification, but Sherwood arrived by chance and said nay. But jesting apart there really has been danger. Thank God all is right again now. He has made ballads upon Meldon without end and is overjoyed at the termination of the business.

I saw your manifesto the other day (you might have sent me one) and shall be glad to have a copy of your *Meditations among the Tombs*[98] and therefore forget not to put my name down.

Forget not also to present my best respects to Mrs Blore. Tell her the news and tell her also that I can now afford to marry. If therefore she knows of any lady between twenty and fifty whom she can safely recommend I am the man ...

Remember me kindly to Mr Petrie when you next see him and beg him to return the little book which I sent some time ago, as I have no note of its contents and we have almost finished printing the Catalogue of Manuscripts in which it must be entered.

---

98 The correct title was *Monumental Remains of Noble and Eminent Persons* (1824).

Part 3.

Account of her early life by Margaret Hunt

Introduction

James Raine's second daughter Margaret was born in 1831. The period covered by her memoir is roughly 1831–1840. It describes her life in Durham, first in the South Bailey, then at Crook Hall, with many long holidays in the country at Denton, five miles north-west of Darlington. Thomas Peacock (1756–1851), Raine's father-in-law, was then perpetual curate of Denton in the parish of Gainford, living in the vicarage next to the church.[1]

Margaret Raine later wrote several novels and translated the complete *Grimm's Fairy Tales*. In 1861 she married Alfred Hunt, water-colour painter and Newdigate prize winner. They lived in Durham until 1865 when they moved to London and bought Tor Villa, Campden Hill, where their large circle of friends and visitors included leading politicians as well as Tennyson, Browning and Ruskin. Hunt died in 1896 and in 1902 Margaret went to live with her daughter, Violet,[2] in Campden Hill Road where she remained until her death in 1912. It was there that she wrote her memoir. The title was originally *Life of M.R. by M.H.* A later addition to the title page in her own hand made this *Early Life of M. Raine by M.H.* The MS was typed (probably by Violet Hunt) in eight chapters with a few alterations and additions in Margaret's writing.

One or two pages of rough notes for the memoir remain, written in her distinctive scrawl, with many alterations and crossings-out. They rather confirm the view that by 1903 the early traces of senile dementia were appearing. She described herself about then as "getting dothery". This also explains some repetition towards the end of the memoir. The repetition was not exact, so all the paragraphs have been retained in the text printed here. There are occasional blanks in the memoir where a name or date has been forgotten; where possible the editor has supplied these in square

---

1   See also the introduction to part 4 below.
2   Violet Hunt (1862–1942), novelist, feminist and society hostess. Joan Hardwick, *An Immodest Violet: the Life of Violet Hunt*, (London, 1990), gives an account of Margaret Hunt's early life at Crook Hall, pp. 1–24, and refers to her novels, pp. 46–8.

brackets. The very few spelling or typing errors have been rectified. Pencil notes in Violet Hunt's writing indicated that pages 6 and 89 were missing. These figures presumably referred to pages in Mrs Hunt's original MS from which Violet was typing, the last page in the typescript being numbered 83, the reference to page 89 occurring on page 64.

Early Life of M. Raine by M.H.

[*p. 1*] Chapter I

"The little girl must be named Margaret", wrote my Uncle George Peacock when the letter announcing my birth reached him.[3] I have this letter now. My mother was his favourite sister and for that reason, probably, Margaret was his favourite name. I was born on October 14th 1831, about six in the morning.

Superstition declares that those who are born before daylight can see ghosts. I arrived before daylight and, also, before the doctor came, for my dear mother who was always most criminally unselfish would not let my father be disturbed to summon him and Mr Green was, therefore, not sent for in time. I was the third living child of James Raine, who was, at that time, second Master of Durham Grammar School under Mr Carr, and Margaret Peacock, eldest daughter of the Rev Thomas Peacock of Denton, Co. Durham, who were married on the 26th January 1828. After fog comes rain was the remark of the villagers of Denton when the engagement was made public, for my mother's youngest sister, Mary, had married Mr John Fogg about two years before.[4]

Altogether my mother and her family had much to do with weather names for, not only were these two names thus taken into it, but my father and mother became acquainted with each other owing to his visits to Dr Sherwood who lived at Snow Hall near Gainford, and my mother's dearest friend was Mary Hale, niece of the doctor's.

Denton was about twenty miles from Durham and father and

3   George Peacock (1791–1858) was a pupil of James Tate at Richmond School about the same time as James Raine, but they do not appear to have met there. See also below p. 131 n. 16.
4   John Fogg (1804–1882), Fogg Elliott after inheriting from his uncle John Walton Elliott, was well known in Durham as a philanthropist and business man; M. H. refers to him as "uncle Elliot".

his bride had to post there after the wedding, but were not allowed by the wedding [*p. 2*] guests to leave early and did not arrive at their destination, No. 20, North Bailey, until nearly eleven at night.

Father, who had a dragon of a housekeeper, had not had the courage to tell her that he was going to be married so, when he and his bride arrived she came forward to receive her master and, to her amazement, found a mistress too. She not unnaturally protested against having a mistress brought thus into the house without having had a chance of making proper preparation for her reception and scolded my father with North-country frankness. He handed his wife over to his housekeeper and forgot her, leaving her alone till bedtime while he went into his study to write.

I know very little of the first years of their married life and only one incident belonging to it seems to have been told me or to have made an impression on me and that is just a little sad. My dear mother and father were walking together in the Prebendary's walk and she, in a moment of expansion, said "You are all the world to me!" Whereupon he, who was always unable to resist a joke said, "Then here are all the world and his wife!" which hurt her feelings.

I can only recollect two things which must, of necessity, have happened in this house i.e. between October 14th 1831, when I was born, and May 1st 1834 when my father went to live at Crook Hall when I was about two and a half years old. The first of these occurred at a breakfast party given in honour of my brother's christening – he was then about three and a half years old but he, like all of us, had been privately baptized some time before – a certain old blue and gold Worcester China bowl being used on the occasion. I was present during this luncheon and, carefully bolted into my high [*p. 3*] chair, I sat by my mother's side. Fourteen or sixteen chairs were placed around the table, and all of these were occupied but one, and some of the guests began to ask who the missing guest was and why he did not appear? My father said, "It is the little Count",[5] on which someone else said, "Perhaps his wife has been angry with him and has put him on the mantle-piece to punish him and the poor fellow can't get down." This made me still more anxious to see him. I remember that, while my father was in the act of carving some bird or pie, this missing guest appeared and, to my great surprise, he was

---

5   On this popular figure on the Durham scene, see T. M. Heron, *Boruwlaski, the little Count*, (Durham, 1986).

apparently a very strange-looking little boy. He made many apologies for being so late, and went round behind my father's chair to the vacant seat – a manservant went to lift him on to it but he exclaimed, almost indignantly, "Oh no! I can get on it myself" and straightway put both hands upon the seat of it and tried to vault into his place. He tried thrice, each time unsuccessfully, and then I saw my father make a sign to the servant to help him, and he lifted him into his place.

The sight of this little creature, who was no bigger than myself and yet was allowed to sit upon the same kind of chair as grown up people sat on, and to eat what he chose to ask for while I, who was quite as tall as he was – at least I thought so, had to take what was given me whether I liked it or not and to hold my tongue unless someone asked me a question, puzzled me very much, and so did his appearance, for his face was so old. I gazed at him almost all the time and, when the few women present began to go away towards the drawingroom and my mother lifted me down from my high chair [p. 4] and led me away with her, I slipped away from her when we reached the other end of the room, under the arm of the gentleman who was holding the door open for us, made my way to "the little Count" and, putting both my hands on his knee, gazed very earnestly in his old, old face and said, interrogatively, "Man? Boy?" Of course, no one seemed to observe this, but I was quickly and quietly removed.

I saw "the little Count", as Count Borulaski was always called, once more. This time it was at Crook Hall in which my father took up his abode on May 1st 1834. On that occasion the Count was accompanied by his housekeeper or wife, and she carried him a great part of the way (i.e. when she could do it without being much observed. She confided this to our nurse). It was in my father's library that I saw him again. He was sitting at one end of the writing table with his back to the light. I myself was scarcely ever in that room and the sight of this little creature who was no bigger than I was, (he was 3ft. 3ins. In point of fact, however, he was very much older than my father – born 1739) at least I thought so, sitting there and talking as if he were quite on an equality with my father, both as regards age and everything else disturbed my sense of fitness so much that I went up to him and, putting my hands on his knees once more and once more gazing very earnestly in his face, repeated the self-same interrogation, "Man? Boy?".

According to the fashion of the period, Count Borulaski was, in his youth, passed about from country to country, and Court to Court, [*p. 5*] and his memoirs tell of parties given in his honour when knives, forks and spoons etc. were all made small to suit his size. He was made much of at the Court of Marie Theresa. On one occasion he sat on her knee and she took a diamond ring from her finger and tried to put it on his but, of course, it was much too large and would not stay on so little Marie Antoinette was told to give him one which she was wearing and took it from her own finger and placed it on his.

I am glad I saw him for not every woman can say that she has seen a man who, when a boy, sat on Marie Theresa's knee and shook hands with Marie Antoinette.

Under the heading "A Link with the Past" we occasionally see in our newspaper a notice of the death of some aged person who, in early youth, saw or knew some very distinguished person of long past times. I am "A Link with the Past" for I, living in this year 1903, have seen a man who in 1754, saw the Empress Maria Theresa and her daughter, Marie Antoinette.

Poor little Count! He was so small that his tall and not very good tempered wife or housekeeper had no difficulty in ruling him. He lived in a tiny little Greek-temple-like house which, built by Mr Bonomi, the architect, stood by the river very near the Prebend's Bridge.[6] It was quite out of place where it was, but I was almost sorry to see that it had gone when, being on a visit to Durham, I took my children to see it. This house was on what Robert Hegg calls the peninsula on which the town of Durham is built.[7] It was very small, very dark and very inconvenient and one of the rooms had a large, high and wide mantlepiece and, upon this, the Count's wife or housekeeper used [*p. 8*] to place him when he had done anything that she disapproved of, and he could not get down again until she pardoned him and went to his assistance. Some of his poor little clothes and a life-sized model of him are in the Durham Museum. [*p. 7*] "The little Count" died in Durham on 5th September 1838, in the 99th year of his age. While in Durham he lived with Mr Ebdon for some time.[8]

---

6 Despite the following sentence this house still stands, on the right bank of the river, upstream of Prebends' Bridge.
7 Apparently a misremembering of Robert Hegge, *Legend of St Cuthbert*, (1626).
8 Thomas Ebdon (1738–1811), organist of Durham Cathedral.

[*p. 8*] My only other recollection of the time we lived in the Bailey is of a day when I contrived to escape from my nurse and cousin Madge, and make my way alone into my father's library (a rather long room with a view of Elvet Church on the other side of the river). I found him sitting at his writing table. When he heard the door opening he began to remonstrate with the intruder but, as I was the one who appeared, his frown turned into a smile.

As before said, we left the Bailey house on 1st May 1834, and I never entered it again until some 18 years after my marriage, when Dora Greenwell and her mother lived in it.[9] I then asked if I might see what had been my father's library and the room which had been our dining room, and found that my recollection of both was quite exact. On the occasion when, as above related, I escaped from my nursery, I was very quickly pursued by my cousin Madge (who was then staying with my father and mother for the sake of going to school as no teaching could be obtained in Denton).

She went to a school very near my father's house, kept by Miss Fielding who was a great granddaughter of Fielding the novelist. She was very proud of this and of her high descent otherwise and it is told that one day, when one of her pupils, (a boarder) rang the bell and told the servant who came in answer to its summons to go upstairs [*p. 9*] to her room and bring down a pocket handkerchief which she had forgotten, Miss Fielding reproved her by saying "My dear, I should not have thought of bringing a servant all the way upstairs to do what I could so easily have done for myself and I am a Hapsburg!" (She was, as is well known, descended from that family.)[10]

About this time my father had a very long and dangerous illness. Typhus fever had, for some time, been prevalent in Durham and he caught it – got better and then had a relapse which was, I believe, worse than the original attack. A great many people in town died of this fever and he, when lying on his bed or sofa, could generally see the gravediggers at work in Elvet Churchyard and watch the numerous funerals. Worse still was the sound of the Church bell which seemed to be always tolling. "Oh that dreadful bell!" was, I

---

9 Dora Greenwell (1821–82), religious poet and essayist.

10 This claim has been conclusively disproved, see J. H. Round, *The Genealogist*, New series x (1894), p. 193, although Henry Fielding had used a seal with the double-headed Austrian eagle bearing a coat of arms on its front, see H. Duddon, *Henry Fielding: his Life, Times and Works*, (Oxford, 1952), i,1.

have been told, his frequent exclamation. In his weak state it got on his nerves and I believe that, for his sake they ceased to toll it, but then the mourners grieved sorely over their "marred rites".

I fancy that owing to this illness, my cousin, Madge who, of course was not able to go to school lest she should carry infection with her, was sent back to my grandfather's at Denton, in order to keep the house quieter as my father was very sensitive to noise and that I was sent with her. I also believe that, unknown to all at the moment, I stole into the library to bid him goodbye and saw him lying on the sofa looking very unlike himself. I faintly remember the journey too though, what I most recall of it is the pain and confusion I felt at the sight of the hedges hurrying past me with such rapidity. Hedges always did hurry past me in those days while I seemed to be sitting still in the carriage.

[*p. 10*] Chapter II

I do not know how long I stayed at Denton at this time but, I believe it was some months. To me it was a pleasure, for I loved being there and I dearly loved my aunt Hannah and the freedom I enjoyed when with her.

At home, owing to my father's long illness and my mother having to be so much with him, I was kept almost entirely with our faithful nurse Margaret but, at Denton, I, as my mother expressed it, "ran wild". My grandfather's household consisted of himself, my grandmother, my aunt Hannah his daughter, and cousin Madge his granddaughter. My grandfather who died in 1851 at the great age of ninety six and who would probably have lived some years longer had his daughter sent for the doctor sooner, was what is called an old man when I was born in 1831. He was then Perpetual Curate of the Chapelry of Denton which was, and perhaps still is, in the parish of Gainford. He and his brother George, or perhaps it was their father, originally came from Murragh in Cumberland, (under Skiddaw, *with interlined above by M. H.:* Saddleback).[11] They left that county to

---

11 In a pedigree of the Peacock family drawn up in 1964 by the Portcullis pursuivant, A. Colin Cole, John Peacock (1711–1798), father of Thomas, is entered as "a tailor – a good old man ... of Thornton Hall, MURRAH. of Caldbeck, Cumberland." Berrier and Murrah are small settlements 8 miles west of Penrith, east of the two northernmost Lakeland fells, Saddleback *al.* Blencathra and Skiddaw.

escape the consequences of having been involved in the "45".

I am in the dark as to all particulars with regard to their first arrival in the county – my knowledge only begins when my grandfather lived at Thornton Hall, once the seat of the Bowes family.[12] There all his children were born. It was about half a mile from Denton, and had some features which were interesting, chief among which was a cunningly concealed priest's room or hiding place during times of persecution. There is a room of the same kind [p. 11] at Beaufront Castle, Northumberland.[13] I ought to say there was for, when I stayed there it had been opened out and added to the house. It was discovered from the face of the room having no blind. The lady who had taken the Castle for a few years, having ordered her servants to put new blinds in all the rooms, was annoyed to find one room in which this had not been done. She spoke about it to the servant to whom she had given the order but she stoutly maintained that new blinds had been put in every room and begged her mistress, as an act of justice, to go round the house with her and see if this were not true. Mrs Abbot did so, and found no window without its blind. She then took the servant outside and showed her the blindless window and she, in her turn, had to own that her mistress was not complaining without cause. Mrs Abbot, however, did not stop there but ordered a manservant to bring a ladder and enter the room by the window – of course they had to break a pane to open the latch but there was no other visible entrance to it and she found that she was right. She, with the permission of the owner of the house, had a way made into this room from the inside and, thus, added a good room to the house. It was said to be haunted. I slept in it when at Beaufront but, as the North Country saying is, "Never saw anything worse than myself."

Besides the priest's room there was, at Thornton Hall, (inside the house) by the side of the stone stairs, a deep draw-well, in case besiegers should cut off the water supply, of which more anon.

[p. 12] My grandfather eked out his modest stipend of forty pounds a year as Perpetual Curate of Denton, (he proved his right to that title, by the way, by keeping his curacy for ... years) by teaching

---

12 Thornton Hall was acquired by the Bowes family in the first half of the seventeenth century, see Surtees, *History of Durham*, iii,382.
13 2 miles north-east of Hexham. The castle was largely rebuilt in 1841, see *Northumberland County History*, iv,198–9, with plates.

the village school.

I do not know if all village schoolmasters in those days taught Latin and some Greek but he did, and gathered together pupils from all the neighbourhood. John Arrowsmith, the well known [cartographer] was one of them.[14] My grandfather always got up at four in the morning and did a great deal of work before school began. He was twice married; his first wife, Ann Hodgson, bore him three sons, John, William and Thomas, and died very young in a premature confinement brought on by her seeing her little son, John, carried into the house insensible, his forehead streaming with blood. He had found the stable door accidentally open and had gone into it and, perhaps, teased the horse. He recovered from the effects of the kick but the shock killed his mother.

Grandfather lost very little time in re-marrying. His second wife, Jane Thompson, came from Houghton le Side, near Denton. She had five daughters and two sons. Two daughters, both called Jane after herself, died in infancy, thus helping to strengthen a North Country superstition which maintains that, if you give a baby a christian name which has been born by a dead brother or sister, it too will die.

Grandmother Thompson was a rigid disciplinarian and it was said by some members of her family that, while living at Thornton Hall, [p. 13] if any of her children told her a lie – a sin for which she had no pardon – she used to dip it, head downwards in the draw well. I am afraid it is true for I once ventured to ask my uncle George if she really did this and, as he did not contradict the story but looked grave and sad, I could only feel that it was so, and regret having put such a question. I had not believed this before, but wished to hear it denied. There is a story of Sir John Brown, highwayman, which my grandmother was fond of telling, which is connected with Thornton Hall. Mr Bowes, its owner, was standing one day by the entrance to his own house when by came "Sir" John Brown on horseback, struggling, as best he could, along a very bad road. The difficulties which he had encountered had ruffled his temper a little, perhaps, for, when he saw Mr Bowes, he cried mockingly, "Who knows, but Mr Bowes, in his old days, may mend his ways?" Sir John was not allowed much time to mend his own for he was captured and hanged in York.

---

14 John Arrowsmith (1790–1873), an original Fellow of the Royal Geographical Society.

My grandfather, as I said before, was a very active man, never either resting himself or allowing anyone who lived with him to rest. My dear mother's health was ruined by her getting up at three every morning to prepare breakfast for him before he began to run "his daily stage of duty". When I first remember him in 1833 or 1834, he was a tall man of 6ft. 2ins, somewhat bent by age and walking with a stick but, full of mental activity. Most of this activity was, however, pernicious or, rather, very costly and troublesome hereafter to his family, for he was fond of buying [*p. 14*] land (much of it bad land) and did so in full confidence that coal would, one day, be found beneath it and he would make a large fortune. He was, as my uncles have since told me, generally right, and he would really have made that fortune had he been rich enough to keep the land long enough, but this was not the case and it had to be sold and, besides this, he had borrowed money to help pay for it from uncle Thomas and other members of the family and had not always been able to pay the interest on this, so that he soon owed so much that his children, instead of being comparatively well off, were almost the reverse for they always had to pay off the interest on his debts and were endeavouring, as best they could, to pay off the principal and, as this amounted to [£]25,000 this was a severe strain and, of course, a great loss of money.

In the end, however, it was done and done, mainly, by the energy and business faculty of my uncle Elliot. Everyone was paid, interest and principal, except my mother who, though she married before his affairs got into a bad state, never received quite the whole of her share of the money left by her rich brother, William Thompson, who died at the comparatively early age of forty five. She doubtless would have been paid had she made a claim. He, by the way, was so well aware of my grandfather's love of speculation that he guarded the interests of grandmother and her family as much as possible by not leaving his money to her but to her children. Had he not done so all he left her would, as there was then no Married Woman's Property Act,[15] have fallen [*p. 15*] into grandfather's power and probably have been lost in some "fair seeming" speculation.

---

15 The Act of 1882 was important to Margaret Hunt. She actively supported the cause of womens' rights but more at a drawing-room level than in public demonstration. Several influential political figures were among her friends.

Some of it was lost, for my grandfather resented this will so much that he took some step which resulted in the will being thrown into Chancery and his children becoming wards in Chancery. I say all his children advisedly for, as before said, grandfather was twice married and William Thompson, very kindly and wisely, left five hundred pounds to each of grandfather's children by his first marriage to help them to learn some profession.

Grandfather's village school was very superior, in some respects, to the village schools of these days for he taught Latin, Greek and Euclid, trigonometry and land surveying, if required and gathered together pupils from all the neighbourhood.

He never was a lovable man. If he wanted anything his wife, his daughters or anyone else near flew to do his bidding. If he was kept waiting or anyone seemed long in fulfilling his behests or even seemed faintly to demur when asked to do anything she objected to, he stamped angrily on the floor. I trembled when he stamped his foot, as I called it, "at" me. I remember him stamping his foot when he was going about in 1835 and 1836 and I remember him also when he was almost entirely confined to his chair in 1847, striking the table by his side with his hand and angrily exclaiming "I keep six women to wait on me and I am not attended to!!!" During the Denton days these women were his wife, his unmarried daughter Hannah, my cousin Madge, his granddaughter, my small [*p. 16*] self and his two servants. To his mind, not one of the six was more of a servant than the others. He rose always at five and expected to find a good fire and his breakfast standing ready for him on the table. My dear mother always said that her health had been ruined by her always getting up before he did to see that his breakfast and all he wanted was ready for him. The fire was always kept on all night to make the coffee.

To give an idea of his great strength I will relate how, in 1838, when he was upwards of eighty, he walked from Denton to Crook Hall (a distance of twenty miles) to tell my father and mother that my uncle George had been appointed Dean of Ely and arrived at Crook Hall before they were up.[16] About the same time, too, he went to pay a visit to my uncle John Raine in Nottinghamshire. He had the

---

16 George Peacock was in fact nominated as dean of Ely on the death of James Wood on 23 April 1839; he held the office until his own death in 1858. He was a distinguished mathematician.

Trinity livings of Blythe and Bawtry, now divided, and grandfather, who was staying with him, wanted to see the farms upon them. When they were at one of these which was three or four or five miles from Blythe, a very heavy shower came on just as he and my uncle were about to go home. Finding that they could not wait until it was fair, the farmer offered to lend them umbrellas, but grandfather would "have none of it" and said, "Thank you, thank you, but I'm not made of either sugar or salt", (a familiar North Country saying). Of course, he got very wet but he was none the worse for that.

Grandfather must often have been very dull at home for he had no friends living near, but he talked to everyone. Grandmother and aunt Hannah must, sometimes, have been much more so for they had [p. 17] no friends living near who were educated. They loved their garden and made it very pretty with plants which seem to have perished out of the land so rarely are they now seen. They were very kind to the villagers some of whom looked to them to provide even jam in which to take their powders.

It was not easy to get anything in Denton but milk, butter, cream and flour, but you got such good milk and cream. Peter Walker, the village butcher, came once a week for orders and, if due care was not taken to provide amply on that occasion they might have to go without meat for some time, but that never happened to them. Saturday was his evening for calling and then he went to my grandmother, the Heslops and the one or two people in the village who could afford meat. On Monday morning he went to Darlington market with that meat which he had not sold in Denton and, during the rest of the week, he looked after his own fields or worked in my grandfather's fields or gardens. He was grandfather's "right-hand man" to quote the Denton saying. I adored Peter. I saw him when he "did up" grandfather's garden. He made me whistles and peeled me striped wands and talked to me while he was working. To this day I can remember my misery when I heard my grandmother and aunt Hannah discussing their house-keeping arrangements for the following week and the word saltpetre occurred several times. I bore up as well as I could but, at last, completely broke down and told them, as well as I could when crying so bitterly, that they really must get something else to eat for they should not salt Peter!

[p. 18] This is another of my recollections of about the same date. Uncle George Peacock, who was then Tutor of Trinity College, Cambridge, used to come North every year during the summer vacation to see his family, staying at each one's home in turn. Every member of his family adored him. He was very fond of me and, all my life, I have worshipped him though, for many years now, alas, I have only worshipped his memory. I think I must have been about three or three and a half when, during one of his annual visits, he one morning asked me if I would like to go out fishing with him. Of course I was delighted, and said so. He told me to get a jug or can or something to put the fish into, and a small basket through which the water would run, likewise a long stick or pole. I took these things to him and then we went into a field called "The Fyttes" which lay just below the churchyard and my grandfather's garden and fields. The cook, by the way, had offended me when I told her that I was going a-fishing by saying, as I thought very offensively, that she would "undertake to eat all the fish I caught in a very few minutes!" Uncle George guided my hand so we caught a great many, but, when it was time to go home again, he put all back into the water but three or four which he said I might take in to show my aunt. I was very proud of my morning's work for I quite thought I had caught them myself. I was most anxious to show them to the cook too, for she had mocked me. I told him so and he said, "Yes, show them to her and tell her to cook them for your dinner." This I did but she only laughed and said, "Nay, you must cook such fish as those yourself." [p. 19] So I laid the poor things on the hot plate above the oven and left the kitchen much offended. When early dinner was announced a tiny dish was set before me with four little fishes on it all dried to cinders and everyone told me that I was a very cruel child. "I could not believe that you would do such a thing" said Uncle George, "I only meant that you were to take them to her in a basin of water just as they were to show her that you had caught some. I was intending to go and put them back in the same place this afternoon." "But you said I was to take them to Mary and tell her to cook them", I said, "and I did, but she said I must do it myself so I had to do it." Uncle saw in a moment, that I had not done this from cruelty but with the idea that I was obeying him, and I was forgiven.

I think it was during this same visit of uncle George's that I was christened. It fell about in this wise. My father, who always baptized his own children privately as soon as they were born, was of opinion that all that was really important was then done so that, though we were all christened, it was done much later than is usual. My sister

Jane, indeed, walked from Crook Hall to Little Bow[17] to her christening – she was four years old. Though I was only two and a half I perfectly remember my own christening. It took place one Sunday afternoon. Aunt Hannah, cousin Madge and uncle George were all in grandfather's garden, I sitting on his shoulder as I often did while they walked about. [p. 20] They happened to see a party of villagers coming into the church yard just as a number of people were leaving church after afternoon service. Aunt Hannah or cousin Madge then said, "That child on your shoulder has never been christened." "Not christened!" exclaimed uncle, "What has her father been about? Let us have it done now. Who shall be her godfather and godmothers?" These were quickly chosen from those standing by him. He himself was my brother James's godfather, (Robert Surtees of Mainsforth was James's other godfather) the others were sponsors to Annie or Jane; uncle Elliot, cousin Madge and Miss Hunt were chosen as mine. Uncle kept me on his shoulder and carried me, thus, to church. I did not understand what was being done and, when we got home again I asked. "We have made a little Christian of you, that's all", replied uncle George, and kissed me. I am forgetting to say that uncle George donned Mr Birkbeck's surplice and performed the ceremony himself. Miss Priscilla Hunt was chosen because she was at hand, as she always was on Sundays, for grandfather and grandmother, who were very hospitable, had got into the habit of inviting her to early dinner between the services – they asked Mr Birkbeck too, and very much in the way they both often were. [Mr Birkbeck was] the curate who succeeded grandfather, and was living in 18.., a very old man, who boasted of being the 3rd incumbent of Denton since Charles II. He was supposed to be the illegitimate son of grandfather by a certain Bella Birkbeck of the parish.[18]

Miss Hunt was a lady "of a certain age" – to use the euphemism of the period – who lived at the other end of the village. She had been nursery governess for a while to Miss Noel (who married Lord

---

17 Little Bow most probably refers to the church of St Mary the Less in the South Bailey, by contrast to the larger church of St Mary-le-Bow in the North Bailey; it was perhaps a usage confined to the family, since Raine was rector.

18 Perhaps a supposition based on the fact that Joseph Birkbeck, Isabella's husband, was seventy-eight when John was born in 1798, see below p. 186 n. He was still curate of Denton in 1881, see *Clergy List 1881*, but died in 1882.

Byron)[19] and afterwards lived in the same capacity in various other families. Very few traces even of remote contact [p. 21] with the upper classes were observable in her. She was, it is true, "vastly obleeged" when anyone showed her any kindness but she had sunk to a level very little above that of the Denton villagers or, perhaps, she had never been much above it. Oh how well that name, Priscilla, fitted her! She lived at the other end of the village in a little house belonging to Dinah Dowells, who was the mistress of the village school. I think Miss Hunt had bought this house or, perhaps, she only rented it. It was very small. There was something that called itself a kitchen, a tiny parlour, and a very little bedroom upstairs. The two houses had formerly been one but were then, to some extent, divided. There were doors which led from the one to the other both upstairs and down. When I first knew Miss Hunt her little house was never used for she, who spent all her leisure time in reading newspapers which gave every gruesome detail of every bloody murder which was committed, naturally lived in continual dread of being robbed and murdered herself. Little by little, therefore, she moved into Dinah's house for safety and ate, drank and slept with her. Dinah did the rough work and Miss Hunt "such work as it was proper for a lady to put her hand to" as she expressed it. Her religion was gloomy and untrusting. She could not bear to hear anyone say "I will come with you today or tomorrow" without adding, "if I am spared". Everyone has, more or less, a subsense that this is needed but, adds it mentally – she liked it audibly expressed. Dinah had the same convictions as Miss Hunt but she was much more loving [p. 22] and trusting than her companion. No one was ever kinder to me than Dinah and yet she could do a stern and hard-hearted thing – at least so it seemed to me, though some might say that it was a bit of good practical teaching. If any boy or girl in her school told her a lie she first spoke very seriously to the child, explaining to it the sin and shame of the offence of which it had been guilty, and then she led it out to her own house (the school was a separate building in the garden at the back of this) and, having lit a candle with great solemnity, she took the child's finger and held it in the flame and, when the little creature was screaming with the torture, she would say, "Ah! You don't like the pain you are feeling in just one very

---

19 *Alias* Anne Isabella Milbanke; the Milbankes of Halnaby (N. Yorks.) had an
    interest in Denton, see Surtees, *History of Durham*, iv,1,2.

small bit of a finger but you never think of what you will have to bear when you die for, if you go on telling lies, you will then go to hell as a punishment and your whole body will be in flames, and not for a few minutes as it is now but for ever and ever." It was a cruel and rude bit of practical teaching but it can scarcely have failed to have a good effect.

[*p. 23*] We saw many strange country sights – birds mobbing owls, and strangers, who had been lured into a hay or harvest field when work was going on, mobbed by the reapers and very roughly handled if they refused to "pay their footing" in it – a custom of immemorial antiquity.

"You must pay your footing! You must pay your footing!" was the cry, even to children of our age, if we ventured into what they regarded as their dominion by right – indeed it was demanded of everyone. Worse still was it on Easter Sunday or Monday if we went without nurse or other guardian beyond our father's or grandfather's gardens or fields. The moment we passed these limits children were liable, if boys, to have their caps taken from them and, if girls, their boots and these were kept by the assailants until they were ransomed by the payment of sixpence or a shilling. Never shall I forget what I once suffered one Easter Sunday afternoon in Durham when I was with my sister and a boy named John Innes who was staying with us. He was the son of Cosmo Innes, the well known antiquary.[20] We were in what was called the Ba'field (Bathfield) close to Crook Hall, now quarried away, and I, who was then only seven, was seized by some rough Framwellgate boys who, at once, began to take off my boots. I looked to John Innes for championship, but he showed no sign of prowess so they took off one of my shoes, I meantime doing my best to resist – I could do little enough in that way and was so angry with him for standing passively waiting till [*p. 24*] they had unbuttoned my boots that I angrily exclaimed "You coward!!! Why dont you try to help me?" "It's best not to get into a row" said he and, again I informed him that he was a coward.

[*p. 25*] Chapter III

It is curious to find how memory slumbers as to certain incidents and that perhaps for years and, yet, never loses complete

---

20 1798–1874; a prolific editor of medieval Scottish documents, see *DNB*.

hold of anything that has once been in its keeping. I <u>now</u> distinctly remember something else that happened when I was two and a half years old. I had entirely forgotten it but, when I was fifteen, I had a fever and then nearly everything I had ever done and learnt, including long pieces of Shakespeare, and such long poems as Lycidas, L'Allegro, and Il Penseroso[21] came back to my mind – (it was like a foretaste of the day of judgement) and, what is more they stayed in it. This is one of the things I remembered. I seemed to see myself, as in a very vivid picture, walking as a little child of two and a half hand in hand with Miss Hunt, who had come to ask me to spend the day with her. When we passed the Heslop's house and were in the deep cutting between their garden and the field on the right which is about five or six feet above the road (being on a level with the top of the wall) a great red and white cow came galloping furiously up to the part of the wall immediately above us bellowing or, as Denton people would have said, "blairing" at us and looking as if it were about to jump straight down upon us. Miss Hunt hastily dragged me away into the middle of the road but only just in time. It did jump down but broke, at least, two of its legs by the fall. Almost immediately afterwards a cart came by and the man who was driving [*p. 26*] it left it in Miss Hunt's charge while he ran to get help for the cow. At least two of its legs were badly broken and it had to be killed. I had, as before said, entirely forgotten this but, when I remembered it during the fever, I saw the whole scene again so vividly that I began to wonder if such a thing had ever really occurred and, when I saw Miss Hunt once more, which was not until 1846 when I was fifteen, I told her of the fancy I had had during my fever and asked her if any such thing had ever really taken place. "Oh yes", she answered, "it most certainly happened but you were much too young a child when it did to remember anything about it, you were not even three years old – not much more than two – perhaps two and a half." "But I have remembered it", I exclaimed, "Have I not told you the exact spot where it took place and everything just as it really was?" "Your aunt Hannah or your cousin Madge must have told you about it sometime" she suggested, "and you think that you remember it." "Oh no", I answered, "I have asked them about it and they both said it was nothing but a delirious imagination and that they are quite certain it never did happen." "They are quite wrong! It

---

21 All three by John Milton, 1608–74.

is perfectly true!" she said, "but I am astonished at your remembering it. You were not even three years old."

I do not know when the cottages that once stood near the beck in the "Tenement" field and gave its name to it were pulled down [*p. 27*] but I remember that event though, I believe, I was then under three. They were occupied by Irish people who worked on their neighbouring farms, and had an invincible dislike to paying rent.[22] Many coercive measures were tried but in vain and, at last, the landlord (I think the Duke of Cleveland) said that, if all was not paid by a given day, they must and should go. (*Footnote:* [the Duke] wore in church a bottle green coat on [the] day after execution of Louis 17th. Mad, disgusting habits.)[23]

The day came and, what was worse, the agent came and it was not paid and they – the tenants – locked themselves in their houses and refused to go or give up the keys. The agent had men with him and they stormed the houses and soon got into them. They then began to seize the furniture and clothing of the inmates and carry it away in carts. When this was done – not, of course, without stout resistance, the Duke's agent began to pull down the cottages. Many piteous appeals were then made – many urgent remonstrances.

In one cottage was a poor woman who had just had a baby (i.e. that day or the day before) – even she was told to get up at once and go. Suddenly my dear, good, dignified grandmother appeared and she, who was usually so quiet and submissive to tyrant man, broke out in her indignation at this last order and reminded these men that they themselves had mothers. She made a great impression on them but the Duke's orders, they said, were positive and must be obeyed. She asked them, however, to leave that house to the last and sent to her home for feather beds and blankets and the poor woman and her baby were rolled in these, carried to a cart and taken to grandfather's house and put to bed, [*p. 28*] and all the other homeless men and women who had no friends able and willing to receive them at a

---

22 Famines in 1727–9 and 1740, and the severe failure of the potato crop in 1816, all contributed to the influx of Irish immigrants, see J. C. Beckett, *Short History of Ireland*, (London, 1952), pp. 99–100 and 136.

23 William Vane, 3rd earl of Darlington, succeeded his father in 1792 and was created marquis of Cleveland in 1827 and duke of Cleveland in 1833; he died in 1842. Margaret Hunt presumably intended to refer to the execution of Louis XVI on 21 Jan. 1793, rather than the death of his son, Louis XVII, which was announced in June 1795.

moment's notice were invited to spend the night in her kitchen for beds could not be found for anything like all.

I distinctly remember being taken to church for the first time when I was about two and a half or three quarters. This too was at Denton. There was some doubt, I remember, as to how I should behave but I rather liked the idea of doing such an important and grownup thing as going there, and promised to be very quiet and good, and I knew the Lord's Prayer and Creed by heart and liked their recurrence during the service on that account and enjoyed repeating them aloud when they occurred and I enjoyed the novelty of being there but, when sermon time came and I was tired and thought, from the movements of priest and clerk that service was over and everyone going home but, instead of that my grandfather got up into the pulpit and began, what I regarded as a long talk all by himself with a white surplice on – (he had had it on before of course, but our pew was, to a child of my size, a high one and I had not been able to see him until he got into the pulpit,) I felt very much tired and oppressed and, after wriggling about for what seemed to me a very long time (people did preach very long sermons in those days) I turned to him, (our pew was very near the pulpit and in a very conspicuous place) and said in a loud voice, "Grandfather!!! What is all that nonsense you are talking about up there in your white nightgown?"

[p. 29] I do not think that I was taken to church again for a long time after that, but was left at home to play with my toys and strict orders to be good. I was very good for an hour or more, after that time I always grew tired of being alone and made my way to the kitchen to the cook, who was a methodist, and went to her chapel at Summerhouse in the afternoon or evening. (She was engaged to the methodist minister, who was a shoemaker and lived in the Old Hall at Denton (now pulled down).) On the week days he plied his trade there and on Sunday evenings he preached at Summerhouse. Perhaps he was the very self same minister whose petition for grace and help was thus couched;

He, "Lord send down grace on Killerby."

Congregation, "Not forgetting Summerhouse."

He, "Lord send down grace in wagon loads."

Congregation, "Aye, and leave the end hecks off."

(the end heck is the part at the back of the cart which is removed or lowered when the load is discharged.)

When I went into the kitchen on Sunday mornings I always

found him, either kissing her or praying with her with his arm round
her waist and, of course, they did not want me there and used to tell
me to go back and play with my toys – I said that I had played with
them till "I was quite tired of them." They then said that, as they had
not been to church, they were reading the morning service and I
would disturb them if I stayed. I said that there was not any kissing in
the service when grandfather read it in church.

[*p. 79*] Jonathan Martin, who afterwards tried to set fire to York
Minster was a Methodist Minister and sometimes came to Denton
among other places.[24] John Wesley also came to preach there. He
went to grandfather's church in the morning. After the sermon he
waited in the porch for grandfather, introduced himself,
complimented him on his sensible sermon and then said, "Now I've
been to your sermon this morning I hope you will come and listen
to mine in the afternoon." Of course grandfather did. He,
grandfather always said that the sermon was a very good useful one.

[*p. 29*] I loved Denton and was very happy there and yet, even
at Denton, [*p. 30*] I had some troubles – troubles which neither my
dear, kind aunt Hannah nor my equally kind uncle John ever even
dimly understood. How few grown people ever do understand how
painful it must be to a very young child to have to walk for, what
seems to it, a very long time <u>out of its own pace</u>, dragged along
between an aunt and uncle who will insist on holding its hands and,
thus, compelling it to walk all the way in a cloud of dust far down
below them which has been raised, and goes on being raised, by its
aunt's trailing dress and its uncle's boots. I can perfectly remember
being half suffocated by this and my kind aunt and uncle, who were
up in the air so many feet above me that they had no conception
what I was suffering, urging me on and wondering what was making
me so naughty or tired. I got on much better with my uncle Robert
for he understood children better and, when I was tired and could
not walk fast enough to please my companions, would let me sit on
his shoulder and thus carried me and yet, even he could hardly
understand my mortification and despair one day when I tried to
jump over my own shadow and always found myself unable to do so.

---

24 Martin (1782–1838) succeeded in destroying the entire choir roof and the
    stalls on 1–2 Feb. 1829; he was found insane and was confined until his
    death, see G. E. Aylmer and R. Cant (eds), *A History of York Minster*,
    (Oxford, 1977), pp. 274–7.

One of the greatest sorrows of my very young life came at this time. Uncle William, his wife and his other daughters, Annie and Mary, (his London daughters) were paying a long visit to the North as, indeed, they did every year, for they always stayed [*p. 31*] there three months, dividing the time between grandfather's house at Denton, uncle Thomas's at Bishop Auckland, my father's, and uncle Elliot's in Durham. Every occupant of each of these houses dreaded their visit for, with the exception of uncle William none of them were easy to live with. [*p. 36*] Cousin Madge was their daughter too, but they had left her behind them once when on a visit, in order that she might profit by good country air a little longer and never seemed to want to have her back. She was two years and a half when they left her and she never did go back to them.

[*p. 31*] They generally ended their round of visits as they had begun it, at Denton. On this occasion uncle William had told me so much of the splendour and glories of London and of the beauty of its many great churches and palaces and how its great, wide, handsome streets were all paved with shining gold, that I longed to see it and when he, in his kind, foolish way and doubtless without the least conception how seriously I was taking it, said that I must go back with them to see it, and the King and Queen and all the other great sights of London, and this visit of mine was always spoken of as a settled thing, I quite believed that I really was invited and joyfully looked forward to the day of my departure. That the women of his family never spoke of it did not disturb me – living with my grandfather had taught me to believe that whatever the man of the family said was law. To this day I remember how bitterly and cruelly disappointed I was when the day came, and the post chaise from Darlington drove up and they all got into it and drove away, leaving me who had been led to believe I was going to accompany them in a perfect agony of grief and disappointment. It was the streets paved with gold which hurt me so – I wanted to see this gold! Glittering gold! [*p. 32*] None of them showed any feeling for me when I complained of my wrongs! Uncle was not ashamed but babbled something about "next time we come perhaps". His wife was absolutely unsympathetic, Annie and Mary were scornful and cousin Madge only said that, if anyone were ill used it was herself for not one word had any of them said about her even going back to her own home again. Poor dear kind uncle Robert – the officer who had been at Waterloo and in Paris with the Allies and had afterwards "sold out" of the 43rd regiment and come home to loiter about with a gun and be regarded as a disappointment by his family because of his idleness, was the one who addressed himself to the task of consoling me. He took me to Nanny Calvert's shop and bought me a quantity of treacle ball, more than I had ever had given me before, and as even that failed to stop the flow of my bitter tears, she said "Just you wait a bit my honey and we'll see if we can't cure that trouble", and thereupon went to her dresser and opened a drawer filled with her treasures. From this she brought out a bundle of gay patches which she, poor dear woman, had, as she told me, "been hoarding up to make herself a bed twilt", (quilt) some of which she gave me and they were such magnificent patches with tropical birds and flowers and trees, pagodas and temples, and lost in wonder and delight, I quite forgot my grief.

Every joy, however, brings pain with it for, no sooner did I get home and exhibit them than cousin Madge declared that such patches as those were far too good for any child to cut up and destroy and that she would, at once, lock them up and keep them [p. 33] safely for me "until I was old enough to value and treat them properly." "You will let me look at them sometimes?" I pleaded, after I had cried for an hour or so, and, with the word "yes", I had to be content.

This sounds a trifle but it was very serious to me at the time. Of course, when remembering little incidents which occurred in very early youth it is very difficult to fix their date with any certainty unless one has some corroborative testimony from a friend or relation who was present and, whenever I do give a date, I have this.

Having had no brother or sister with me when I was at Denton, I had been allowed to play with one or two well behaved little village children, and to bring them into grandfather's fields or gardens, and I often went into their homes – indeed, I went in to most of the houses in grandfather's parish. Everyone there was very kind to me and many a poor woman who had more than enough to do for her own "heavy handful of children" would wash my face or hands, or pinafore, or a bit of my frock if I had fallen into a ditch and made myself too dirty to be presentable, lest I should get a scolding when I went in or, as she said herself, "lest my grandmother should flyte me" (scold me). The inevitable result of this free intercourse with the villagers was that I went home to Durham using words which absolutely delighted my father as a student of his mother tongue, so old [*p. 34*] and infinitely better were they than the latinized words they considered elegant, but I shocked him by the extraordinary breadth of my accent. I spoke, indeed, exactly like a village child of that time and district. "Child" he said to me, "it is perfectly appalling to hear you speak – you must not, on any account, let anyone hear that dialect you have brought home with you! Don't open your lips in anyone's presence until you have learnt to speak properly."

A day or two afterwards he took me to church with others and, after service, he went to see Mrs Brand who was an old friend of his. "So that is the little daughter who has been away so long!" said she, "come here my dear and let me say how do you do to you." I went to her as requested and I held out my hand but, glued my lips firmly together. "Yes dear, but you must say how do you do to me too", she said and again she spoke very kindly. I said nothing, "Ah" she exclaimed, "I will try to find a way to unlock that little tongue of yours very quickly", and she went to the table and got some cake for me. "Will you have some cake?" she asked, with a touch of impatience in her voice, "say yes, please, and you shall have it." I was still silent. Upon this my father began to speak to me but she stopped him saying, "No, dear Mr Raine, let me manage this, please do. Come", she said to me. "It will cost you nothing but to say "Yes please", so why not say it?" But I held my peace and then she rather indignantly put the cake back on the tray saying "Well if you won't you won't! Little girls must be taught to do what they are told."

My father who looked much distressed, soon bade her goodbye and, when we were outside, he exclaimed "Why would you not say what Mrs Brand told you to say? Little girls should always do as they are told to do." "But I <u>was</u> doing that father!" I replied, "I was doing it hard. Much harder than I liked! You told me not to open my lips until I could speak properly, and I can't do that yet." "Ah! You were trying to do right" he said, looking very lovingly at me, "but they <u>have</u> let you run wild." "But I like to run wild!" I said. He then told me to walk quietly up and down outside Mrs Brand's house till he returned, and went back to her to explain my behaviour. The very next day Mrs Brand sent me a large cake and, also, oranges and sweetmeats. When he came back to me he said that he knew now that I [*p. 36*] had not been really naughty, but that he wanted to make me understand that I must now begin to learn to be a little lady and that I was never "on any account whatsoever" to play with any of the little Framwellgate children if any of them came near Crook Hall. Framwellgate was the long street at the very end of the town nearest to Crook Hall. There was indeed, only one field and a shrubbery between the two. (Most of that field has since been quarried away.) It (Framwellgate) was filled with people in the same station of life as the villagers of Denton but there was a very striking difference between their children and those of the homely peasants of Denton. The former were hard hearted little savages who took pleasure in torturing birds and beasts, crucifying little swallows on two pieces of stick laid crosswise, and plundering and outwitting weaker children, throwing stones and using bad language.

We children, therefore were very dull at this time for, at first, we religiously obeyed these orders and we saw very little of either my father or my mother. Besides this, we were scarcely ever all at home together, each in turn or, not in turn, going on visits of six or nine or twelve months to Denton. Besides this, again, Annie my eldest sister, went to stay with uncle John in Nottinghamshire and with uncle William in London, and was away for nine months. How we did look up to her and how she did take precedence after this! (She was called Annie because Mrs Surtees of Mainsforth was her godmother.) She had seen so much and heard so much that she looked down on all of us and spoke of us as the little children but, never thought [p. 37] of amusing us. I was clamourous for fairy tales. She was occupied with Caesar and Virgil. I could not read very well myself and I wanted fairy tales. None of the servants would tell me any because, as they expressed it, I knew all the stories as well as the cook did. That was true but I enjoyed hearing them just as much as ever.

[p. 39] Chapter IV

Crook Hall, to which my father had moved on May 1st 1834, as before said, while I was at Denton, is now a dingy, dilapidated house near the dirtiest part of the now, nearly everywhere, dirty town of Durham. It was then a pretty, old-fashioned house surrounded on all sides but one by its own three gardens and three fields. I ought, perhaps, to say that it was three houses (of very different ages and styles) run into one – the newest part being, as my father used to say, about the time of George III, the middle older and the oldest, of which nothing was left but a large and lofty room paved with "cobble stones" and no ceiling but gabled roof and rafters only, which was called the chapel – perhaps because of its three lancet windows with remains of old tracery.[25]

My father always said that he thought it was the dining room of an old baronial hall but, that a chapel did once stand there, or somewhere very near it for, in some of his researches in ancient documents, he had found a licence to use a certain part of Crook Hall as a chapel in the reign of Edward III. In my childhood no houses stood near Crook Hall but a small and not unpicturesque farm house on the slope of the hill below and a small cottage by the river where the ferryman lived.

The loneliness was terrible to me, the laws which I was told to obey oppressed me and seemed to me monstrous! I longed to get back to Denton. "Put my hat and coat on and take me to the coach and let me go back to Denton" was a request that I made incessantly. [*p. 40*] All was so different in Durham. I saw, as I thought, nice little children in the lane by our house, or in the field below it, but I was not allowed to go to play with them. I missed the children with whom I had been allowed to play. I missed aunt Hannah and my cousin Madge and my mother. She came to us in the nursery but we were not to leave the nursery and go to her. I had no one to speak to but my nurse. Luckily we had a very kind nurse and dearly we loved her.

Crook Hall and its neighbourhood were then very pretty and very picturesque, or they seemed so to me, but I believe they were. They are both very different now. There were two ponds close by it, each overhung by a fine old sycamore. A little stream from the lower pond fed a very pretty old watermill and then made its way through a rocky ravine to the river. To see the abomination of Crook Hall and its neighbourhood now is cruelly painful. The trees all around it are killed by the fumes of collieries and gasworks,[26] the little wood we loved so much is no longer there, the ponds have been drained away by quarrying for stone, mean looking little cottages have been built. No flower will blossom, no hedge grow green for lack of moisture, all is squalid, desolate and smoke blackened. When I was a child all was beautiful and delightful. I do not remember any of my first impressions of the house, but I do remember the birth of my sister, Jane (June 24th 1834) and my sufferings when I was deposed from

25 Crook Hall still stands as Margaret Hunt describes it, now, however, fully restored to good order.
26 A plan of the city of Durham, 1824, shows the gas works just a few hundred yards south of Crook Hall.

my place on the nurse's knee and in her arms in favour of, what seemed to me, to be a mere worthless (I say worthless [p. 41] because it was quite unable to talk or play) little squalling bundle of white muslin and embroidery. I can remember catching hold of nurse's dress as she was "walking it" up and down the long room which was our nursery and begging her to take me up, and standing by her when she was sitting begging to be taken on her knee. "Don't you see that I have the baby?" she used to say, "I must have the baby on my knee." "But you have two knees", I replied, "take me up on one of them." This made her laugh and say, "You are a sharp one. You'll do!"

  I felt soothed by this, somehow, though I did not know what she meant, but she did not take me up. This was, I think, our dear nurse Margaret whom we all loved. She was very kind to us but she had a lover and, when he came to see her, she left us alone sometimes much longer than my mother knew – I mean when Dorothy, the nursery maid, was away too.

On these occasions James and Annie, if they happened to be at home together (which was rarely the case as one of them was usually at Denton) were in the habit of playing all kinds of tricks – such as running about with lighted papers etc. Of course we were never left long alone for my mother had strictly forbidden the nurses to be absent from the room at the same time, but equally, of course, they did so sometimes and, one day, when she was out of the house they both went away at the same time, seeing [p. 42] their opportunity, James and Annie at once caught me and put me in a very large box nearly filled with spare linen. They then shut the lid down and sat upon it to keep me prisoner. Having me thus in safe keeping they began to settle what they should do to me. I think I had failed to obey some order they had given me. The box was nearly full and I could scarcely breathe. To add to my sufferings they then began to discuss what punishment they should inflict upon me now that they had me in their power.

"Let us cut off all her hair", suggested James. "No, they would see that and be angry. Let us brand her on the arm or leg to show that she is our slave", said Annie. "But they will see that too", said he. "Let us brand her on the sole of her foot then", was what Annie answered; "they won't notice that unless they happen to lift it up." "All right", said he, "let us get the poker". "But it is cold, quite cold" she exclaimed, "and it must be red hot." This terrified me so much that I began to scream loudly hoping to bring Nurse Margaret back. "Hold your tongue this very instant" cried one of them, "or we will brand you all over your body!" This terrified me so much that I at once obeyed, hoping and praying the while for the return of one of the nurses. Presently James said "I think it's hot enough now", and then they came and lifted [*p. 43*] up the box lid and one of them sat on me and the other pulled off my stocking or sock, and applied the poker. It hurt me but was not hot enough to do real harm, but I suffered agonies of terror, and this gave me strength enough to break from their grasp and, in spite of all the prohibitions which made my father's library sacred from us and from everyone else during the time when he usually took a nap, I made my way thither and told my story. It is needless to say that everyone was severely – very severely reprimanded even our dear nurse Margaret, whom we loved so much, came in for her share of that – I am sorry to say that I remember crying, once, because she would not let me put my finger in her eye. I did not want to hurt her but only to explore a little.

Anne the cook whom we loved, married her Absolom soon after this – it was not a marriage that my mother approved of for he was very unsteady – he was a Denton man, so my mother knew his character and told her what it was, but she was determined to have him so they had their banns published at Crossgate Church[27] and, early one Sunday morning, Anne appeared in our bedroom in the most gorgeous of wedding bonnets, and kissed us, and cried a little as she told us that we should not see her again for a very long time and so left us. My mother had no idea that she was going to leave in this way so, when she got up and found that no Anne was to be found she was amazed. Jane and I told her that she had come to bid us goodbye, but we were not believed, even though we described the very large bows of white satin ribbon [*p. 44*] on her Leghorn straw bonnet, with great exactitude, but, about mid-day, she came to explain her departure to my mother, and apologize. She had done it, she said, to avoid the pain of hearing mother's remonstrances. She died before the year was at an end in her confinement.

To return to one nursery maid, Dorothy, I must not forget the part she played in another little tale of long ago. Our dear nurse Margaret had, of course, her Sundays out and, then, Dorothy gave us our baths. I dreaded this for she always put me into the same bath

---

27 St Margaret's church, the parish-church of Crook Hall.

the baby had just had and then, as the water had sometimes grown rather cold, she added more hot water from the kettle on the fire and, very often, this carelessly calculated addition made it almost unbearably hot and it hurt me. I begged her and prayed her to put the water into the bath before she put me in, but she persisted in going on in the same way and, when Nurse Margaret was out, I used to spend a miserable day dreading the approach of night. At last I told my mother what she did and she told Dorothy that she must see that the water was in a proper state of heat before she put me in. When night came, she looked at me malignantly and, then, at the kettle which was steaming away on the fire, and then she placed my bath by the fire and began to undress me. "Put the water in the bath first, Dorothy, please do", I pleaded. She vouchsafed no answer. "Mother says that you are not to put me in the bath until you have got all the water in it and are quite sure that it is not too hot!" [p. 45] She took me up at once and planted me in the middle of the bath saying "I'll teach you not to go to your mother and complain of me." Then she seized the kettle and poured out some water – not at the side of the bath, as usual, but deliberately upon my poor little shoulder. It was very hot and scalded me, and I still bore the mark when I was a grown woman but it gradually, to a great extent, disappeared. This time my screams brought the whole household to the spot and, to my great relief, she was dismissed.

I do not remember much about the girl who came in her place except that she inflicted a still deeper wound on me – I was then and, indeed, always very fond of fairy tales and, like most children, would listen to the same stories over and over again and day after day, even when I knew every word of them by heart. Almost all of them told the adventures of kings and queens and beautiful princesses and, one day, when I was four or five years old, it occurred to me to ask the nursery maid of the time about my father. I had never thought about it before but had always assumed that, like the father of all the girls in the stories told to me, he was a king and that, when I grew up, I should be a beautiful princess and that beautiful princes would love me and giants and dragons would be slain for my sake so, one day, I asked the nurse, "What is my father?" "Well my dear, he is your father of course." "I know that, but what else is he? I mean what country is he king of?" said I, fully expecting her to reply, "He rules this land." "King!" [p. 46] she repeated! "King!! We have no kings in this house!"

I felt a little angry with her for being so stupid and just a little uneasy but I said, "Every girl's father is a king of some country! What is my father's country called?" She shook her head slowly and hopelessly and answered, "Your father is a parson, and gets up into the pulpit on Sundays and preaches – that's what he is, so you know!" and then she turned away from me and I huddled myself into a corner and cried for I don't know how long for I, who might have been born a king's daughter like everyone else that I ever heard of, was only a parson's! I suppose I had some idea what a parson was, but I had believed myself to be a princess, and she had utterly destroyed my future!

She had done me another injury of which, at first, I was not aware – she had inplanted a terror in my mind and I nearly made myself ill by thinking I should be accused of some crime falsely and, not being a royal princess and having no knight or prince to take my part and fight for me, I should be hanged or burnt at the stake. Some comfort suggested itself to me in the fact that women were never hanged, that I knew of, but a reference to the nurses deprived me even of that.

I think about this time the family, as a body, went to Hendon[28] for a month or six weeks – oh the misery of that time! No one but a little child knows the wretchedness of falling into the clutches of a blue flannelled bathing woman who assures you that a dip [p. 47] is delightful and plunges you into the water while you are screaming with terror and the uncertainty of ever coming out of it again and, of course, you are nearly choked. Worse still is the roaring of the water in your ears and the knowledge that you are to undergo this thrice. There is a path by the cliffs to Sunderland and, sometimes, it takes you quite close to the edge of the cliff and, now and then, it does, or used to do, a little more for, in one part at all events, you came to a place where two cliffs met and a triangular little bit of vacancy was traversed by the railing and, down one of these places, I fell. I had never seen the sea before at high tide and was so delighted and astonished by the rush of the incoming waves that I did not take care. A sailor, who happened to go past at the moment, came to rescue me but, of course, I was bruised and wet through. I thought it a delightful incident, afterwards. It gave me such status in nursery society.

---

28 On the coast, just south of Sunderland.

[*p. 48*] Chapter V

Seen by the light of later days Denton was a rather ugly and very dull little country village yet, even now, I, who have revisited it when a grown woman and have become aware that it had no beauty at all, still think of it as beautiful. When I was a child I thought it so delightful in every way and loved it so much that, more than once when I was at Crook Hall and had dreamed that I was at Denton with absolute vividness and happiness, and awoke and found that I was not, my disappointment and sorrow were so great that I wept bitterly and was almost inconsolable.

Denton was barely within the limits of the Palatinate or, as its inhabitants then always called it, "the Bishoprigg", i.e. the Bishoprigg of Durham, for the Tees flowed two miles to the south of it and, from the walk at the foot of my grandfather's garden ... the high hill near Richmond could be seen.

Just below my grandfather's garden too, but on a much lower level, was a long irregular-looking field called the Fyttes. I got into great trouble one day about that field for Eliza and Louisa, two very sentimental and much older cousins, came to stay with my grandfather and grandmother, and one of them asked me if I ever went into fits and I, who thought she meant the field of that name, promptly answered, "Oh yes, nearly every day of my life." "Margaret!" she exclaimed severely – very severely "How can you be so untruthful? You are a very wicked child!!! You have never even had one fit." "Fit!" I echoed in amazement, "you asked [*p. 49*] me if I ever went into fits and I thought you meant the field, and I do go into it nearly every day of my life. You may ask aunt Hannah if that is not true, if you do not believe me."

The Fyttes was a very pretty field just below the church-yard and my grandfather's garden but on a much lower level. It sloped abruptly down to the winding "beck" and, on the other side of that, just opposite, was one very fine elm tree with a low wall round it to keep the earth up to it. This, no doubt, pointed to some loyal squire or parson of the William III period who planted a lime [*recte* elm] as a compliment to a man who introduced it into this country. I went into the Fyttes very often, but I once went with a disastrous result to myself. I was then about seven years old and I was playing in the churchyard and field combined when my grandfather's cow began to run after me tossing its head, and nearly frightening me out of my senses. It was in a position, too, which enabled it to cut off every chance of escape that I had, unless I could succeed in getting over the wall before it came up to me. This wall was low on the churchyard side, but high on the other for, as before said, the Fyttes was on a very much lower level. I got on to the wall just as the cow was on me. Its horns all but touched my hands as I held the wall before dropping down, and the result was that I dropped so hurriedly that I did it badly, and grazed the wall with my right knee all the way down, turned the kneecap over and fell, a lump of agony, to the bottom. I lay there some time crying and feeling that something [*p. 50*] very bad had happened, and then I began to wonder how I was to get home. I knew that there was a stile made of slabs of stone built partly into the wall a little farther along, which led into a neighbour's garden and, in torture, I partly walked and partly crawled to it, but I was very long in doing it, and the steep, awkward steps up to this were much worse, and then I had the garden to cross and then more walking by the lane. I got home somehow. No one in grandfather's house ever took much notice of illness. They would have missed your leg if you had lost it, but I was only scolded for climbing walls and nothing was done for me though my kneecap was turned round and not only looked but felt very strange. (There was, it is true, no doctor nearer than Darlington, a distance of five miles.)

I should have been lame for life had I not luckily been going home in a week's time by way of Bishop Auckland. I suffered torture every time I moved till I got there, but when I did, my cousin Marianne, (uncle Thomas's eldest daughter) at once said, "My dear child, this can't go on! I shall send for the doctor at once", and this she did.

What makes this little event curious to me is that, for a very long time it entirely went out of my head. It went so completely that, when one of my elder cousins said to me many years afterwards, (it was in November 1858, just before my uncle George died) "Do you remember once coming to our house from Denton with your knee in such a state that you could scarcely walk [*p. 51*] – you screamed every time you moved?" (Slight exaggeration but it <u>was</u> daily getting more painful.) "It must have been someone else", I exclaimed, "<u>my</u> knee was never bad in that way." "It was you!" she persisted. "A cow had chased you, and you dropped from a wall to get away from it and turned your knee cap round." "You are quite mistaken", I said, "it was not I. That never happened to me."

She was positive and I was positive but, little by little, I remembered everything that I had done, felt and seen, down to the very texture of the curtains in the servant's bed behind which I had painfully crawled to conceal myself when I heard that the doctor (Mr George Canney) had been sent for. I had a horror of showing it or having it touched, and got between the wall and the servant's great four post bed-stead, drew the curtain before me and, being very young, thought that, as I saw nothing, no one would see anything of me. This curtain was made of beautiful old blue and white checked linen (large checks) and its threads shone in the sunshine like satin, and I sat there looking at them and waiting and fearing.

"Oh! So you didn't want to see me today", he said without seeing me, but just as he entered the room, "Well, you shall not see me unless you like, but you must let me see your knee." Whereupon he gently drew me partly out, looked at it and, almost immediately, grasped the turned knee cap forcibly with both hands and restored [p. 52] it to its place. It hurt awfully but, when he said "You would have been lame for life if this had not been done", I was reconciled, especially as the pain was over. It returned, unfortunately, as age began to tell on me, and I often feel a touch of it now.

After my positive and absolute conviction that no such accident had ever befallen me, I am sometimes almost alarmed at the vividness of my recollection of it now. It always makes me think how terrible it would be to be summoned to a Court of Justice as a witness, for no belief would be accorded there to such a gradual awakening of memory. It also gives an unpleasant foretaste of the Day of Judgement.

When I was about five (and staying at Denton) I was sent for a couple of hours each morning to be taught the rudiments of learning in a little school kept by Dinah Dowells. They were such hard, tiresome rudiments. A. stands for A. B. for B. etc; and when that was mastered, came a, b, ab, e, b, eb, i, b, ib, etc. They had such a depressing effect on me that I never taught my own children spelling of that kind at all – I made them try to remember the "look" of the words – three or four new ones being added when they had mastered those I had given before. I must say that it is a good way to teach reading and they learnt easily and quickly. I was not allowed to sit with the village children but in a very small chair by Dinah's side and, whenever she was called out of school for a few minutes, I used to seat myself [p. 53] in her chair, take up her long stick and pretend to keep school. With the long stick I used to tap the head of any child which I saw misbehaving, just as she herself always did. Sometimes she came back and caught me doing this, but she always smiled. Dinah loved me, and I dearly loved her. Her heart was warm and tenderly human, but her creed was stern and pitiless. She taught nearly all the children in the village but none of them came to school very regularly, being always kept at home if there was a chance of their earning a few pence by any little piece of work or, if a new baby brother or sister arrived which had to be nursed by them. We were all taught our "anparcys" or "andparcys" – that was how the word was pronounced, I have no idea how it was spelt. It meant the alphabet with every possible combination from A. to Z. ab. eb. ib. etc, together with the abbreviations etc; which we learnt from her to call "anparcy".[29]

We learnt from a large horn-book[30] to which we pointed with a darning needle which was passed from one to another in turn and, when we had mastered that, we were promoted to what the children called a "Ready made Easy". (Reading etc.)

There was no clock in the schoolroom, and Dinah generally asked one of the girls to go into the house to see what time it was, to which request she was taught to reply saying "Yes, Ma'am, if I am spared to do it." Owing to this I, at that time, regarded God as a dread being who was always sitting with a large pair of scissors in his hand to "slit the thin spun life."[31] If we omitted to make this proviso, she looked stern and said "Do [p. 54] you not know that you might be "called" (die) before you get back?"

She always had all the children, (either when sitting or standing) arranged round her in three semicircular rows, first the very little ones and so on, according to height, and she had by her side a long stick with which, if they were inattentive, she could administer a brisk tap to even the most distant ones – choosing by preference their heads as the point of attack. As a teacher she was as stern and pitiless as her creed but, as a woman, she had the kindest heart imaginable.

I was not so fond of Miss Hunt, though she was always very

---

29 i.e. *ampersand*, otherwise "and *per se*", commonly appended as a twenty-seventh letter to be learnt at the end of the alphabet, see J. Wright, *The English Dialect Dictionary*, i (1898), p. 50.
30 Most hornbooks had been replaced by battledores by the end of the eighteenth century. Not in Denton, apparently.
31 John Milton, *Lycidas*, line 76.

kind to me. I was a great deal with them for they kept me, whenever they could, after school was over, and they let me make little baked puddings in tea cups and tiny cakes with currants in them, and help to wash the tea things and do all the little things that children love to do. For such religious women they were "shamefully afraid of dying" by misadventure or murder. They feared fire too, and burglars, and lived in perpetual dread of swallowing pins.

When Miss Hunt made a pudding she first put four pins in a saucer on another table, and then summoned Dinah from the school to stand by and count them as she pinned up the tiny pudding in the cloth and, when Dinah made one, which was only during the holidays, Miss Hunt was expected to do the same, and they both of them always superintended the removal of these pins when the pudding was taken off the fire. They always looked "high and low" [*p. 55*] too for concealed burglars every night of their lives.

Many years afterwards when I was ... and once slept in this house after Dinah's death, I saw Miss Hunt go her rounds at bedtime and even look into a bread pot which could certainly not have held more of a burglar than his head.

They were very fond of their little garden and worked in it a great deal and, to my great delight, let me work too, – that is, let me help them a little.

There were no lucifer matches in those days or, if there were, they had not penetrated so far as Denton, and it used to be a great pleasure to me to see Dinah standing with flint, steel and tinder, trying to get a light.

Dinah, though so tender hearted and human, was rigidly stern in matters of faith. I once saw her take a little boy who had told her a lie, out of school, into her house, light a candle and deliberately hold his middle finger in the flame of the candle and, when he shrieked with pain she said "Yes, you cry like that now when only one of your fingers touches the flame, but what will you do hereafter when you are in hell and your whole body is burning and you will <u>never, never</u> be able to get out of the fire, but will just have to burn for ever and ever, for that is what will happen if you go on telling lies?"[32]

Besides her other calling, Dinah was a bit of a barber and, for the sum of four pence, used to cut the hair of anyone who sought her aid and came after school hours. She did it in the way described in

---

32 This incident is here told for a second time, see above p. 135.

Don Quixote, and I have more than once seen Mr Birkbeck, [*p. 56*] who succeeded my grandfather as Perpetual Curate, with a large white pudding basin turned upside down on his head and Dinah clipping away all the hair that came below it, Miss Hunt holding the candle during the operation. In winter of course, as he taught the school, he could only come when it was dark. Miss Hunt, on these occasions, held the candle and, once, I saw her hold it so close that she burnt his ear. He bore it more patiently than I should have done but, after seeing this, I tried to earn my own respect by not crying when hurt and when, by rare chance, I succeeded, it made me feel very grown up.

As time passed on and on I sometimes began to feel very lonely, for I was just getting beyond the age when it was considered necessary that a grown up person must always be by my side, and I had no young companions. I complained of my loneliness to my aunt and grandmother and they felt for me and said I might, now and then, ask one little well behaved girl to come and play with me and this I did but, sometimes I fear I took unto myself "power to add to this number", and I also began to go into their homes and run about as much as they did. I must say that I now regard this as one of the greatest educational advantages I ever had. They were all well brought up, well behaved and tenderly careful of my safety. I was about four and, when I went out with a little girl of my own age (at first, and then only in my grandfather's fields or close by them) afterwards a big girl always used to attach herself to me and lift me over the wet "puddles" [*p. 57*] and hold my hand when I insisted on stretching across a ditch for early sweet violets, which then grew in profusion in many of the hedges as many another flower grew then. Now most of them have disappeared, for drainage has deprived them of their necessary moisture, and the lowering of the lofty hedgerows has taken away much shade.

We gathered "posies" and called the flowers by their village names. I only wish I could remember more of those names now. All the lore connected with these flowers was freely imparted to me by my companion. She taught me also the local names for birds and, incidentally, many a strange custom and odd bit of folklore. If I wanted to pick a flower which grew on the other side of the ditch among the rank grass, my guardian girl forbade me, for I might "natter" myself if I put my hand in there (natter = adder). If I picked a scarlet poppy and wanted to smell it, it was taken from me for, if I did, I would "go blind". If I nettled my hands they rubbed them with "dockens" saying the while "Docken in, nettle out! Docken in, etc." until the pain ceased. The little white pansies which grew in the cornfields they called "stepmothers" and, if I had a little bit of torn skin by the side of my nail, they said it was a "stepmother's blessing". A certain small blue and white flower they called "God's Eye". I learnt to say "My head works" if I had a headache but struck at saying "my nose is blooding!" I am forgetting to say that ... was always called "Ladies' Bedstraw".

When I grew a little older, the girl I loved best was Mary Alderson. She was about my own age and very nice looking and well mannered. I was allowed [p. 58] to ask her to tea once or twice and to play with her when she was free to do so. After a while, however, her family left Denton and I felt her loss keenly. We gave each other parting gifts. Her's to me was a tiny little box which had been made by one of the French prisoners in the time of Napoleon's Wars, in order to obtain a supply of tobacco. Many of these prisoners were distributed about the North Country villages, and many little things of this kind were made and sold by them. It was covered with split straws of various colours arranged in a pattern and it was lined with perforated paper below, and a bit of looking glass under the lid. I kept it till I was 70 and then it was so old and worn that it was worn out. A mouse, too, had nibbled most of it away.

[p. 59] Chapter VI

My next great friend was Willie Walker. He was a little London boy with much prettier manners than any of the Denton children. His father was a clerk, in the Bank of England, or perhaps something more important, for children do not take much note of grades of rank, and his uncle was Peter Walker, my grandfather and grandmother's factotum. Willie was staying with his grandmother for a while for he was, at the time, rather delicate. I took to him at first sight, and he to me, and he very soon more than supplied the place of my dear Mary Alderson. After I got to know him I had no other friend. We met constantly, day after day, by appointment at six o'clock in the evening or earlier, at the large tree in the field called the "Tenement" of which I have already written. Neither of us ever willingly failed. I think William loved me, I loved him inexpressibly.

I went to Mr Birkbeck's school at that time, and did easy sums and reading, and learnt much from hearing the older classes repeating their lessons. I did that even at home for my father always gave Annie and James two hours teaching every morning. He gave them a piece of Latin grammar to learn, a piece of Latin verse to learn and construe, a piece of Shakespeare to "commit to memory" and, for the rest, he trusted to good memories and a fair amount of mother wit. These lessons were to be learnt during his absence, and repeated to him during his evening's walk. I had [*p. 60*] no lessons but picked up a great deal of teaching in the mornings by listening to theirs. Discovering that I was sometimes paying some attention, father, who was a stern teacher, used occasionally (when James was unable to answer one of his questions) to say "You stupid boy! Why even that young child under the table there, who has never been taught Latin at all, would answer that question if I asked her! What is the answer Midge?" Whereupon I looked up for a moment and said, with absolute confidence, as if I knew all about it, "Why it is the ablative absolute of course." In reality I knew nothing about it, and I do not imagine that anyone thought I did – I only made that answer because, just at that time when any question that was put to James was left unanswered, it generally turned out that this would not have been the case had he replied, "It is the ablative absolute."

This was in Durham – it was at Denton that I suddenly mastered the knowledge of reading at sight. It was all but done in a day, that is so far as easy words were concerned. It was some such word as sight which taught it to me and, all at once, I grasped the fact that, if the S were taken away and T substituted, the word would be *tight*, if an M, *might* etc. This done, I very soon learnt to read and, after that, I could always amuse myself. I did not always understand the little books I read. Especially was I puzzled by a Juvenile History of England which described a certain king's eyes as very bright and full of fire!

[*p. 61*] Willie read too. I loved fairy tales – he liked stories of fighting and fierce battles. I could not get him to take any interest in Mrs Radcliffe's novels.[33] When I was a little older they were a fearful joy to me and I could not tear myself away from them. James did not care for them either. Never shall I forget one evening about this time, when I who was about seven years old, went into his bedroom. He

---

33 Ann Radcliffe, 1764–1823, "was the founder of a school of romance in which terror and curiosity are aroused by events apparently supernatural, but afterwards naturally explained", *D.N.B.*, see, for example, her *Mysteries of Udolpho*.

had "been naughty" poor fellow and, as a punishment, sent to bed early. I, thinking to comfort him, stole upstairs to his room and began to recite a thrilling little bit from "The Castle of Udolpho", which narrated how the Lovely Lady Laurentina [*recte* Laurentini] ventured into a very long, dark, subterranean passage and was never more seen, (i.e. in that part of the novel). To my horror he began to scream so violently that Miss Hunt, aunt Hannah, Mr Birkbeck and cousin Madge all came running up stairs in the greatest alarm. "It is Midge!" he said as soon as he saw them, "take her away! Make her hold her tongue! She is ghosting me!" "I am not ghosting him!" I exclaimed indignantly, "he does not know the difference between ghost stories and novels. I am only telling him how the Lovely Lady Laurentina went into the subterranean passage and was never more seen." I ought to own that, until I read about the reappearance of the Lady L, that bit about her disappearance terrified me too. She might be never more seen but, to him, it was more than enough to hear of her and her very name made him begin to scream again. This time Mr Birkbeck and even poor, dear, lazy old John came upstairs in a panic, and cousin Madge was deputed to stay with him [*p. 62*] till he fell asleep.

I knew all about the Lovely Lady Laurentina because, in the spare bedroom, called by the servants the "best lodging room", there was a very large bookcase full of novels. They were delightful. Most of Sir Walter Scott's were there, and Fenimore Cooper's, Miss Edgeworth's, Miss Ferrier's, Richardson's and many others.[34] The bookcase itself was a delight to us – a delight and a wonder, for the doors of the lower part of it were so made that they could be pushed round to the back out of sight when you wanted to look for a book and, another touch, restored them to their places. Whenever we were at Denton we always steadily read through nearly every book in that room and, also, all that came weekly from the Darlington library.

When we grew older we used to beg aunt Hannah to subscribe to two libraries there when we went to Denton and she, kind soul, never failed to humour us.

We always felt a certain wonder at grandfather having so many nice books of his own. He bought all Scott's novels as they came out. So did my father, or very nearly all. What poor curate or second

---

34 Scott, 1771–1832; Cooper, 1789–1851; Maria Edgeworth, 1767–1849; Susan Ferrier, 1782–1854; Samuel Richardson, 1689–1761.

master of a grammar school would spend his spare earnings in such a way now? A guinea and a half for each novel must have made an appreciable hole in a small income. Grandfather bought Scott, Cooper and Miss Edgeworth's works even more steadily than my father, and grandfather's children drew lots for the first turn to read them, and the son or daughter who was so fortunate as to draw the lucky lot, sat up all night to enjoy his or her good [p. 63] fortune, being quite unable to put the book down till it was finished. Grandfather himself was a great reader and, no doubt, he had it first of all. He had most good things first – he regarded man as the head, roof and crown of all things and woman as a being who existed only because it was more convenient for man to have someone to wait upon him. He was indeed in the habit of saying, "I keep five women to wait on me and I am not attended to!" (His wife, his daughter, his grandchild (cousin Madge) and two servants and, in his estimation, not one of these was more of a servant to him than another.) When anyone of these so called servants was told or saw that he was going out, she no doubt rejoicing in the prospect of some rest, ran to get his shoes or boots, knelt down and put them on for him, and another got his great coat and hat and off he went, expressing no thanks and feeling no thankfulness for he regarded this only as their bounden duty and, for a time, great peace descended on that house.

He was very fond of reading newspapers and novels – so were all his family including my small self, but I did not find that it always made me happy. On the contrary, it filled me with a secret sense of unworthiness for, in most of these old novels, especially in Mrs Radcliffe's, the heroines so often fainted. I had felt my shortcoming in this respect long before, and I felt it more now – it seemed to betoken such a deeply seated want of sensibility. My only hope was that no one would remark it. Willie certainly did not, and to him my heart was given – my poor little six or seven years old heart. I still spent every hour [p. 64] with him that I could. We found nests but never robbed them. We twice saw little birds mobbing owls and could not help being sorry for the big, helpless looking owls which could do nothing but blink while so many indignities were being offered to them, and had not even sense enough to fly far away.

We did not often go far enough from my home to see owls and their assailants, our usual playing ground being the churchyard. It, like that of Haworth described by Miss Bronte, ran side by side with the clergyman's house and garden, and many a ghostly fancy came into my mind about it. I knew it was a vain and foolish imagination, but I tormented myself with the fancy that, when thick darkness fell on the land, all the occupants of all the graves arose and stood by their own graves. I knew it was a fancy, but I thought of it so much that it became very real to me and, more than once, on a dark winter's evening, in spite of cold and darkness and, what was still worse, terror, I forced myself to go to see if they were really there and, to be quite sure, went some distance, for there were no graves near the house. Then again, I firmly believed that all the people buried beneath the great oblong box-like tombstones were not laid in the earth at all but simply on it, with the large stone covering dropped over them. There were several of these stones at Denton and the cement which fastened on what I called their lids having, in some cases worn away, I used to peep inside hoping, yet fearing to see more. I am afraid that in ...

[*Violet Hunt noted the loss of a page at this point.*]

... [*p. 65*] spent in the churchyard. I snatched a fearful joy from being there. I had an idea, at that time, that I should die when very young – an idea that was shared and probably inspired by my grandmother. She was then in failing health, and used often to look at my white cheeks and say, "I think, my dear, they will most likely have to lay us both down in the ground together."

This sounds depressing but I am inclined to think that it did me a great deal of good, for it roused in me a spirit of opposition and, as I knew my delicacy was in a great measure the result of my own want of care, I reformed my ways and, after that, did not walk through streams and go on wearing my wet shoes for the rest of the day etc. I did not want to die – I had a horror of death, and of that church yard in which Nathan Parker, the sexton, seemed to bury everyone in all but the same place as someone else. I had often stood by him when he was digging graves and heard his spade crunching into bones or, as we children said "scrunching", and seen him take them up and heard him say as he flung them aside, "That's poor Jacky ...'s skull" or "Dicky ...'s thigh bone! Well, he has laid here quiet enough a long time now!" and I could not bear to think of my poor little bones being flung about in the same rough, careless way while he said "That's poor little Margaret Raine's skull or leg bone!" The mere thought of this at once made me begin to take much more care of myself and my health than I had ever done before. This means that, when I walked through a little stream without taking off my shoes and stockings, which about this time, I did at least once a day [*p. 66*] – I did not keep them on all the rest of the day leaving them to dry on my feet as best they could unless someone happened to remark them but, dutifully, went into the house and changed them.

The church yard at Denton seems to play a very large part in my recollections, but that is perhaps because it was almost the only place where, in my very early youth, I was allowed to go alone and when I chose, unless the grass was very wet. Grandfather's glebe consisted of three fields, but the first was often either a meadow, which I was not allowed to trample down, or a pasture tenanted by either one or two cows and, one or other of these was generally inclined to chase me out of it. I was allowed to go into the gardens of course, but sometimes I hurt the plants and got into disgrace, so I preferred the church yard. All my recollections of it are by no means gloomy. I and Mary Alderson played many a game of hide and seek among the tomb stones and, when I was alone, I used to go and sit in a long, low stone coffin (said to have been that of one of the Conyers family)[35] which then lay on the south side of the church, near the porch. I spent a great deal of time in this coffin. Sometimes I used to gather five or six large bunches of white flowers and, having fitted my head into the round place made for the head in the coffin, used to lie down and put my white flowers all around me to show that I was a well cared for corpse, and hope that someone would come to see how beautifully I was laid to rest, but no one ever came.

Yes, once I heard my name called in a very kind voice by one of the Heslops [*p. 67*] (their garden was very near). "Come here dear", she said, "I want you." I looked up and saw her standing by the wall, I went to her after a short wooing, and she took me round the garden and was very kind to me and gave me strawberries and cream. Our own strawberries and cream were good but her's were

---

35 For medieval coffin-lids, one apparently inscribed to Aubrey de Coynners, at Denton chapel, see Surtees, *History of Durham*, iv,I,7. The former occupant of the coffin outside has not been identified but the Conyers family of Sockburn-on-Tees, some 10 miles south-east of Denton, was of considerable standing during the medieval period: "From John the son of Galfrid, descended in a long lineal procession, gallant knights and esquires, who held Sockburn till the reign of Charles I whilst the younger branches of this ancient stately cedar shadowed both Durham and Yorkshire. All are now fallen; and not a foot of land is held by Conyers in either county", Surtees, *Ibid,* iii.245.

much better. Their garden, too, was prettier than ours. They were very good and kind to me after this and I never failed in my duty to them but once but, on that day, I behaved so ill that, even now, I am filled with shame. It fell about in this way. I was conscious that aunt Hannah and cousin Madge did not like them. They very often asked me if the Heslops ever said nasty things about them and I always said "no", for they never did but, one day, the devil entered into me and I replied in the affirmative. I forget what untruth I told them, but it made them very angry and excited and they talked a great deal on the subject and, asked many questions but I was already miserable about what I had done and would say no more. Then I stole away again to the Conyers' tomb and sat there. No wreaths for me that day – only my own unhappy thoughts. I do not know how long I sat there crying – the sky seemed to have turned black – never had I been so unhappy. I hoped I should never see anyone again, I felt I should never enjoy anything. Presently, Miss Heslop came to her garden wall and called me. I shook my head, I could not speak. "Come dear", she cried, "I want you, come." Again I shook my head. "I have got some very good strawberries and cream for you", she cried, [p. 68] "Do come!" Again I shook my head. "Are you ill?" she enquired. Yet once more I shook my head. She got over the wall and came to me, holding out the plate. I turned away from her, cried more than ever and added, "I have been very naughty, I don't deserve it!" At last I was persuaded to tell her what I had done. She looked grave and said it was very wicked to invent such a thing, and that aunt Hannah and cousin Madge would never like her again, perhaps, but that I must at once go and tell them the truth – that I had invented this. "They will be very angry with me – I don't think I dare do that", said I. "God will be much more angry with you if you don't!" was her reply, so I went.

I made my painful confession and then, after scolding me a little, they forgave me and I went back to the Conyers' tomb and, very soon, poor dear Miss Heslop came to me with the strawberries but I could not eat them after what I had done. She had to take them back again and I sat where I was, more ashamed and unhappy than I had ever been in my life.

When at last I took my red eyes and sad heart home again, cousin Madge said, "Where do you think I have been?" I shook my head. I did not want to know – I did not care about anything. [p. 69]

"I went to the Heslops to make sure that you had been to tell them the truth, and they gave me that plate of strawberries and cream that you would not have. It was made of the cream of an Alderney cow and I never in my whole life tasted anything so good."

[p. 70] Chapter VII

In spite of this last incident life was still, though not for some little while, happy to me at Denton. Doubtless sin and suffering were to be found there but I knew little of them. To me it was a place of blessed freedom where everyone was good and kind. They were good and kind at my real home, but my father was too busy to see much of us, and my mother so often ill. I was at first strictly ordered to "keep myself to myself". This Denton saying being interpreted, means that I was not to make the acquaintance of anyone, and I was never to go beyond grandfather's two or three gardens, three fields and the churchyard but, as weeks and months went by, I began to pine for companionship, and was occasionally permitted to invite a certain very well brought up little village girl into the garden but we were forbidden to go beyond the prescribed limits.

The churchyard at Denton, like that in Miss Bronte's home at Haworth, ran parallel with the vicarage gardens and house and as weeks and months went by, I began to pine for companionship and was occasionally permitted to invite a certain well brought up little village girl, Mary Alderson by name to come and play with me. We played in the gardens and churchyard. No graves were ever dug near Grandfather's house or garden. This was, we thought, a very pretty garden, with interchange of flower beds and orchard and vegetable ground. Many a flower grew happily in it which has either perished out of the land altogether, ceased to be cultivated, or never blessed my eyes with a sight of it since, [p. 71] and proud my grandmother was of all of them, and tender too as any mother when she handled them.

At the bottom of the garden but on a much lower level was a large picturesque field with a shallow winding stream running through it. Also a very old elm tree, probably planted in the reign of "Dutch William", for he it was who brought elms to England. This tree was on the slope of a hill and possessed, what seems to me, the great distinction of having a low wall round it to keep the earth about its roots. The field itself was called the Fyttes, a name which once, but not until I was seven or eight years old, got me into trouble.[36] A very sentimental cousin of mine, five or six years older than myself, much addicted to the reading of romantic novels such as Mrs Radcliffe's, in which the heroine faints on every possible occasion, said to me one day, "Margaret, do you ever go into fits?" To which I replied, "Oh yes, nearly every day of my life", and, to my amazement, she said severely, "Margaret, you are not speaking the truth. You are a very wicked child!" She had meant to ask me if I ever fainted. I tried to make her explain how it could be wicked to go into a field of that name and then she saw that I had misunderstood her question and all was put right again.

I was very happy at Denton and thought every field and lane and hedgeside divinely beautiful. It was an unspeakable joy to me to watch the slow peeping forth from the imprisoning earth of each flower in field or garden and delightful sometimes to find one which I had never seen before. Gradually, however, I began to find [p. 73] it irksome to be shut up within such narrow confines, and we strayed away into more distant fields and even into, what seemed to us, to be strange and remote places. Fences were no barriers to us – there was always some point in them at which one could either slip or force our way through, – walls we could climb as well as any boy and drop from. We feared nothing and no one but a fierce gander and a *resurrection of men*,[37] of whom we had heard stories which terrified us, but before we set out on one of these stolen expeditions we invariably cautioned each other, and almost always in the same words. "Now mind, if any strange man comes up to you and offers you a glass with brown-looking liquid in it you are not, on any account whatsoever, to drink any of it, but to call and warn me if I am not close by you, and run away from him yourself as fast as ever your legs will carry you!" And, this said, we wandered away sometimes for miles and, as the Denton saying was, "never saw anything worse than ourselves." On the contrary, we were often hospitably entertained and treated with the greatest kindness both by the cottagers whom we knew, and by those whom we had never seen before. How happy we were! How happy we ought to have been for, on looking back on long past days, I do not for a moment think that my recollections of them are gilded by time.

---

36 The incident that follows has already been recounted, see above p.150.
37 Body-snatchers were sometimes known as "resurrection men".

[*p. 81*] Of the sin that was to be found at Denton we knew little or nothing – of the suffering we had occasional glimpses. Miss Hunt once took me into a room where a young girl was lying dead and there were many who, in Denton parlance, were "well aware of what illness they were going to die." Only once, however, do I remember being brought into direct contact with such illness myself. This was when I saw an old and very poor woman who had stretched out her hand to lift the latch of the Heslops' gate, (usually open) but could neither lift it up nor draw back her hand. She asked me to put her hand back by her side. "Lift it off for me", she said, "please do." "Can't you lift it off the latch yourself?" I asked in much surprise. "No my dear, no. I can put my hand out but I can't draw it back. Lift it off for me please." I did so but was terrified – it was so cold and seemed so helpless. I kept hold of it though and gently laid it by her side. She did not live very long after this.

It seems unkind to say so but, at that period I loved Denton much more than Durham. This was partly because I knew it so much better and had been so much more there and because, when there, we had liberty.

[*p. 73*] Chapter VIII

When I did go to Durham it seemed very dull after Denton and its happy freedom. We, that is Jane and I, (for the two others were nearly always doing lessons) were not allowed to go beyond our own three gardens and three fields and, when in doors, lived for the most part in our nursery playing our little games and clamouring for stories.

Even the narrow limits assigned to us, however, permitted a great deal of dangerous play, for we climbed the trees and ran along high walls and did everything that suggested itself to us. Our greatest danger, however, was our brother who, being a very delicate boy and the only one, (who lived) was very much indulged. We were told every day by my mother that on no account whatsoever was he to be contradicted for, if he got into a passion, which he usually did on such occasions, he might break a blood vessel and die and, in any case, it would be bad for him.

We played with him, therefore, when we were at home together but by no means on terms of equality, for he was fifteen months older than I and much stronger and he always put out his full strength against us when we were playing at fighting or quarrelling, and then he hurt us.

I only remember contradicting him once and that was when we were playing at being soldiers and each had a fortress. Mine was the stable and his the hayloft above it. Jane helped me to hold the stable against him. We had bolted both doors so he could not come in by either of them. He knew that, and lay in wait with a stick [*p. 74*] which he called his sword, to attack us if we ventured to approach the little sliding shutter in the door, which was the only window, but we kept carefully out of the way of the thrusts he made through this. He summoned me to this opening to parley with him. I was aware of this stick and would not go. Then he went to the granary and told me to come to the place by the manger (over which there was an opening from the floor of his fortress for filling the manger with hay) and confer with him from thence. I suspected danger and approached this very carefully. As soon as I was within his range he dropped one of the little collection of bricks he had taken from a neighbouring wall. I avoided this and he got another, and again I got out of the way. He persisted but so did I, and then he lost patience and went off to the house by the round-about garden way to complain of us to my mother. We got out into the lane by the other door and ran to mother ourselves, arriving just in time to hear him say in a very injured voice, "Mother, Midge and Jane <u>have</u> been so unkind!! They wouldn't let me drop bricks down upon them!!!" At that time mother was so accustomed to grant his every wish and take his part against everyone that she at once said very indignantly "Oh you naughty children! How can you be so unkind to your poor brother when you know how ill he has just been?" And then she saw what she was saying and she and all three of us laughed and were reconciled.

Mother, however, when not ill as she only too often was, was always busy, and we children were left very much to ourselves, so we began [*p. 75*] to try to resume the free life of Denton with the result that Miss Hunt was engaged to come and look after us. Then began a time of utter misery. We had not particularly dreaded her arrival but we soon found out that Miss Hunt, in a position of trust in Durham, was a very different person from Miss Hunt at Denton. She was strictness itself – the change from the happy liberty we had enjoyed to her governance was intolerable. She had more fads and fears too than anyone I had ever known and she was so low church that she made our lives wretched. Her idea of God seemed to be that he was always lying in wait to snatch life or happiness from everyone who disregarded any little law or superstition; for instance, if you said, "I will go to ... tomorrow", without adding, "if I am spared" you would not be spared etc.

She was afraid of damp too for us and did her best to make us delicate by forbidding us, when we were alone, to go into any of the gardens but the front one which had a flagged walk in the middle of the wide gravel path from the front door to the garden gate and we were not allowed even to set our feet on the gravel-walk of which this was the centre. As for "stepping on any of the other paths" that was, "on no account whatsoever", to be done because of the said damp. This was, of course, torture to us, but father always took us a long walk in the evening and, after a while, this restriction was to some extent relaxed in consequence of my going to him one evening and saying, "Father, when you were a little boy did they never let you walk anywhere but on one little short bit of path in a small shut in garden, as Miss Hunt [p. 76] makes us do?"

She had a very bad way of teaching us, terrifying us so much by her severity of manner that she generally drove all that we had just learnt completely out of our heads. I did not then like lessons. She gave me – a child of six or seven – poems to learn which did not in the least interest me. "Edwin and Emma"[38] and, what I called, "The Curfew tolls" (Gray's Elegy). I hated "Edwin and Emma" and "she shivered, sighed and died", and was, indeed, glad that she did die, and that there was an end of her. I got into sad disgrace one day for not being able to repeat my daily portion of it. (Miss Hunt's harsh words and manner affected me so much I could not remember it in the least) and, when my father came home before our early dinner, he must have spoken to her about her severity for, after this, she was rather kinder, but she could not overcome her faults of manner.

She had a small income of her own, having played the part of nursery governess in several families before she came to us and carefully invested most of her salary. Of course my father paid her for looking after us but she was always parsimonious and that, I think by preference. She was not only economical as regarded herself but did her utmost to be for him too, spending much time in making sponge bags out of old newspapers and, also, little cases for slate and "wine" pencils, stitching at these with infinite care and patience. She had

---

38 By David Malloch, later Mallet, (1705–65), who published three volumes of poetry in 1759, see his *Annotated Ballads and Songs*, (Edinburgh, 1857).

"her own trouble" (as they say in the North) with us children I fear, and a dull time, except when we were naughty and she had sent each of us into a corner with our faces [p.77] to the wall, she comforted herself, however, by reading every detail of every bloody murder which took place. She "snatched a fearful joy" from the perusal of every gruesome detail and read the newspapers again and again until a new crime was committed and her mind was filled with that. She told us all about these murders too and let us read accounts of them in the papers. Father and mother discovered that she did this for, although she said that we were not to let anyone know that she had even talked of such things to us, we must have betrayed our interest in them somehow.

This, and perhaps other reasons of which we were not cognizant, caused my father to put an end to her rule over us. Oh! How rejoiced we were when we heard that she was going! How much more glad when she actually departed! We leapt, we danced, we cheered – not in the house for we were too much afraid that if we made what they called an unbearable noise we should supply our father and mother with a strong reason for bringing her back – but, in the most distant of father's three fields. We had taken the dinner bell with us and two other bells used for fixing on the shutters at night to warn the family of the approach of burglars, and we used our voices with a heart felt sense of rejoicing. The noise we made must have been heard even across the river. The farmer who lived nearest Crook Hall came to see what was the matter. "We are rejoicing because our enemy has departed! She has gone! and we hope that she will never, never, never come back [p. 78] again." "I have often thought she was a bit hard on you when I saw you out walking with her", said he. And we said "Hear! Hear!" and went on with our rejoicing. At last father came to put an end to the noise which penetrated even to his distant ears. He must have known what made us so full of delight, but he said, "Children, what is the meaning of this disturbance?" "We are rejoicing!" we answered, "our enemy has fallen!! She has fallen and we are glad." He told us that the noise we were making was "unseemly" and must be stopped, but he appreciated the biblical allusion.

[p. 38] I was once taken to him with a long story of my naughtiness and obstinate refusal to learn my lesson. "What is the reason of your being so naughty?" he asked, when we were left alone, "Why don't you learn your lessons?" "I do learn them", I answered, "but when Miss Hunt is so cross she frightens every word of them out of my head." "If you have learnt that lesson properly you can repeat it now" he said, "so let me hear it." Thereupon I did repeat the verses and without a mistake. Then he said, "How long would Miss Hunt have kept you in the corner?" "All the afternoon", I answered, "all the whole long afternoon until my legs were so tired that I could scarcely stand." "You may come out of the corner but you must go and beg her pardon", said he. "Must I really?" I asked, for I felt that this was an injustice. "You really must." When I went back to the nursery therefore I said all that I could bring myself to say, which was, "Miss Hunt, father says that I am to beg your pardon", and she was, at once, so kind that I was very much ashamed of myself.

[*p. 78*] After Miss Hunt's departure we were tolerably good for some time but, gradually, we began to wander beyond the limits assigned to us and go into more and more distant fields. We did this partly from love of variety and partly because our own fields were not half so interesting as those which lay beyond them, being too level and dull. The field we loved best was one we called the broomfield. It was indeed much the most picturesque field in the neighbourhood and more broom grew in it than anywhere else near and more real flowers. At that time, indeed, very rare flowers grew close to Durham itself but collieries were then much fewer in number and much further away. [...]

[*p. 80*] In 1840 I was invited to spend a month with the Hodgsons at Hartburn for I had had an illness and needed a change. Mr Hodgson was the author of "*The History of Northumberland*"[39] and a very great friend of my father's. Hartburn, which is still a very beautiful place, was then bewitchingly so. The Hodgson family consisted of Mr Hodgson, who was kindness itself – his wife, two sons and two daughters, but three of these were married and had "fligged and flown" from the family nest. Only one daughter remained in it. The vicarage is a very handsome house built for a man of much larger means than Mr Hodgson possessed and the river and wood were ... [*the text breaks off at this point*].

---

39 Newcastle, 1827–58. John Hodgson (1779–1845) was vicar of Hartburn, 7 miles west of Morpeth (Northumb.), from 1833 until his death; this parish adjoined Raine's parish of Meldon. Raine published a two-volume *Memoir of the Rev. John Hodgson* in 1857; see also *Archaeologia Aeliana*, 3rd ser. 10 (1913), 127–8.

Part 4.

The letters of Thomas Peacock concerning the will of Mrs Elizabeth Birkbeck, widow of John Birkbeck, British Consul at Nice.

Introduction

In the memoir of her childhood Margaret Raine painted a grim picture of her maternal grandfather, Thomas Peacock, in his old age. These letters show that he had been a kind and conscientious parish priest earlier in his life.

Born in 1756, Peacock attended Bowes School where he became an usher in 1771. Following ordination in London, he was offered the curacy of Denton in the parish of Gainford in 1780. Two years later he became involved in the episode covered by these letters which dragged on for over ten years. In 1781 he married Anne Hodgson of Denton but she died in 1788. In 1789 he married Jane Thompson of nearby Houghton-le-Side. Among the seven children of this marriage were Margaret who married James Raine, and George who became Dean of Ely.

Little is known of the Birkbeck family except for what can be gleaned from these letters and the parish registers. John Birkbeck, whose death in Nice begins this affair, was the oldest of six children living in or near Denton, three of whom, Beaker, Joseph and Lilles (Lillo), were still alive in the 1780's.

The letters cover the period from March 1782 to May 1792. Peacock retained copies written in his own hand following the death of John Birkbeck, obviously realising that he might become involved in legal matters. Those copies are printed here. The letters from John Birkbeck (1–8) are addressed "to the Revd. Mr Peacock at Denton near Barnard Castle in the County of Durham by way of London par Turin and Milan." When Nathaniel Green took over as Consul on Birkbeck's death his letters were sent by way of Paris.

Robert Slade was the lawyer named as co-executor with Green in Mrs Birkbeck's will. On his death in 1787 Birkbeck left everything to his wife. She died in January 1788 and it is her will, with its effect on the remaining members of the Birkbeck family, which is the main subject of the correspondence.

All the letters headed "Denton" are from Thomas Peacock. Letters 1–8 are from John Birkbeck in Nice, the remainder from Nice are from Nathaniel Green. The letters from Robert Slade to Peacock and Green are headed "Doctors Commons, London".

A few alterations have been necessary to regularise spelling, and over-zealous use of capital letters has been eliminated. Otherwise the letters are printed *in extenso*. Opening and closing formalities have been omitted.

1

[John Birkbeck to Thomas Peacock]
Nice the 18 March 1782

Some time ago I was favoured with a letter from you, wherein you represented to me the unhappy state of my poor brother Joseph. I answered your letter immediately desiring the favour of you to dispose of a Bill of £20 which I therein remitted you for his use in the best manner that your Christian charity suggested to you, and to favour me with an account of your reception of my bill,[1] and of course, the manner in which it was applied for his relief, but I having not been favoured with your answer altho' I see by my banker's accounts on whom it was drawn, that the bill has been paid, I must own that it surprises me a little, and makes me fear that your letter to me has miscarried, for I naturally imagined that a gentleman who has taken the pains to express himself in so Christianlike a manner as you have done in your letter, cannot have been wanting in so essential a point, a line from you will tranquilise me in this point, and let me know how my poor brother does, in expectation of which I have the honour etc. ...

2

[John Birkbeck to Thomas Peacock]
Nice the 13 October 1782

I received the favour of your letter of the 9th September yesterday only, the post is so long a coming by the way of

---

1 Bills, bills of exchange, or drafts served the same purpose as modern cheques and money orders.

Germany,[2] and I thank you for your goodness in interesting yourself in the manner you do for my poor brother. I wish that it suited me to do more for him, but during this present war it does not. I am indispensably obliged to make a certain figure suitable to my situation, which I can barely sustain. However I send you here inclosed my draft on Messrs Gosling's for 10 guineas which must serve him for a year at least and I cannot say but that I think it strange that he has never given me a line under his own hand as he knows how to write. I am just recovering from a long fit of illness which renders me weak and my hand not so firm as usual ...

3

[John Birkbeck to Thomas Peacock]
Nice the 15 Sept[embe]r 1783

Annexed hereto I send you my bill for 10 guineas on Messrs Goslings which you will have the goodness to apply as usual to my brother's necessities and I beg you to advise me of your receipt of it accompanied with a line from my brother which will greatly oblige.

4

[John Birkbeck to Thomas Peacock]
Nice 17 Sept[embe]r 1784

I duly received your favour of the 18 of August giving me an account of my poor brother's bad state of health which I am very sorry for. I wish it were in my power to relieve him more than I do. I am not in debt to my brothers and sisters, for as soon almost as I was able to subsist myself I sold my patrimony and divided the produce amongst them since which I have only had my own industry to subsist me. Annexed I have sent you a bill of exchange for eleven pounds for the next year and I expect that when you are so kind as to acknowledge the receipt of it – that my poor brother will join a few lines in your letter. I wish all manner of happiness to you and your family and I have the honour ...

2   In June 1799 Spain had joined France in the war against England.

5

[John Birkbeck to Thomas Peacock]
Nice, the 20th August 1785

I received your truly kind and good letter yesterday, and I take the earliest opportunity to thank you for it. I only wish that I had been acquainted with the contents of it sooner.

I know that my poor brother's conduct has not been the most regular, "But he that is without sin, let him cast the first stone." I pity him and will relieve him as much as in my power. It is true, in my situation where I am obliged to make a sort of figure for the honour of the nation I represent and am forced to make a greater expense than I should otherwise choose, my appointments not being large, however I thank God I can spare something for the distress of an unfortunate brother. I therefore remit you herewith my bill on Messrs Goslings of London for twenty pounds which you will please to receive cash for, and after paying what expenses may have occasioned you, I beg you will employ the rest as you may judge the most proper for his relief and subsistence. As I have all manner of reason to hope from your letter that it will be employed in a proper manner I beg my love to my brother, and I wish for an opportunity to show how much I think myself, dear sir ...

6

[John Birkbeck to Thomas Peacock]
Nice the 5 October 1785

Annexed you have my bill on Messrs Goslings for eleven guineas, ten of which you will give or lay out for my brother and I desire you accept of one for your troubles.

I beg you will desire my brother to write me a full account what brothers and sisters I have left alive and how they live, also what children they have and in what station those children are in. In short tell him that I expect that he will write me a full and particular account which you will be so kind to inclose me in a letter, and it will much oblige ...

7

[John Birkbeck to Thomas Peacock]
Nice 24 October 1786

Annexed is my bill of exchange for eleven guineas ten of which are for the use of my brother Joseph and one of which I beg you to accept for your trouble. I beg a line on receipt of it in which letter I hope my brother will write me a few words. I wish you all many happy new years ...

8

[John Birkbeck to Thomas Peacock]
Nice 26 Dec[embe]r 1786

I received your kind letter and annexed you have a bill of five guineas which after retaining five shillings for your trouble I beg you to apply to the necessities of my brother Joseph's wife. It is so cold I can scarcely hold my pen ...

9

[Nathaniel Green to Thomas Peacock]
Nice Aug[us]t 2nd 1787

Your agreeable commands of the 9th of March, arrived at Nice in due course and were carefully forwarded to me in Germany where I then was and could not entirely quit till the beginning of last month or arrive in this place till within these six days. You will therefore I hope allow this account to serve for my apology for having so long delayed an answer.

I have now seen Mrs Birkbeck and communicated to her your letter. The sentiments of benevolent regard this lady expresses for the relations of her late worthy husband, make it easy for me to conceive the degree of admiration and esteem with which you tell me Sir she inspired the whole family.

Mrs Birkbeck informs me that she has also received a letter from you, to which she would willingly have given an answer ere now but for the variety of inquietudes and occupations which together with her affliction have absorbed all her attention for these six months past in addition to all which she has suffered for some time a painful inflammation in her eyes which however it is hoped may go off as the season becomes more moderate.

Mr Birkbeck left a will made in all due form, and though within a few months of his death was however before any appearance or even distant thoughts of sickness. By this will, Mrs Birkbeck becomes sole and universal legatee of her late husband and consequently enters into full and indisputable possession of all the effects of every kind whatsoever belonging to him. The disconsolate widow charges me to assure you of her respectful regard and wishes you may rest assured and assure also the brothers or other near relations of the deceased, that she feels a tender affection for all those who were dear to him and shall at all times be ready and desirous to assist and comfort them and particularly by participating to them in case of their being in want, such portions as she can spare of the small remains of her own and Mr Birkbeck's united fortunes, which by his generous indifference to gain was continually subject to diminution but rarely made any acquisition. I hope the above information will be satisfactory and I shall think myself happy if it serves to persuade you of the respect, consideration and esteem with which I profess myself ...

10

[Thomas Peacock to Mrs Birkbeck]
Denton, 24th Sept[embe]r 1787

Though I had not the honour to be personally acquainted with your late worthy husband, yet I was favoured with his correspondence for many years, and was the happy conveyancer of many very substantial kindnesses from him to his relations in this county. The account of his death distressed them all very much, and I was solicited by them to make enquiries into his affairs, and after you who, they were much afraid, had been called away before him. The arrival of Mr Green's very kind and polite letter has been doubly satisfactory, as it informed them you are still in being, and that he had left his affairs entirely subject to your control, a circumstance extremely pleasing, as you always possessed the highest share of their esteem, and as you kindly flattered them you intend to continue your affectionate notices towards them all. They are extremely sorry to hear of your indisposition, but hope you will recover from it in a little time. They likewise join me in their kind love and respects to you, and beg leave to condole with you most sincerely on the loss of your husband, a loss which you must feel in the severest manner. The only comfort which can be derived from the severe affliction is that he died in a good old age and full of honour.

Mr Birkbeck has left behind him here two brothers and a sister who are all neighbours of mine, and whose situations humanity induces me to submit to your consideration. Beaker, the eldest, is about 74 years of age and very healthy for his years, but he has many difficulties to struggle with on account of the four grandchildren, all young, which were left to his care by one of his sons who died in the prime of life. To provide for and educate these tender orphans he has no other resource but the united endeavours of himself and his wife, and the charge is much too heavy for his debilitated strength. For nine long years Joseph has been unable to do anything of consequence towards his own support, or that of a most dutiful wife who is lately dead, having been all that time a wretched cripple tottering on the brink of the grave which must be a most welcome retreat to old age worn out with incessant pain. Lillo the sister is upward of seventy years of age, a period of life when little can be done to procure it a comfortable support. To alleviate the distress of his brethren your late most worthy husband was ever ready to lend his assistance, having generously supported Joseph by a liberal annuity of from fourteen to twenty pounds a year for seven years past, generally about ten guineas annually, and also humanely contributed, within these last two years, to relieve the distress of the other two by most kind benefactions. The many favours you have already done the family, the extreme respect your goodness has raised in them and your most humane offer to relieve their distress make it quite unnecessary for me to do anything more than to recommend their situations to your notice.

I must beg you to accept of my best acknowledgements for your politeness in remembering me and my warmest assurances of being at all times happy in receiving your commands in any matter I can possibly serve you. I must also trespass so far on your patience as to beg you will make my sincere acknowledgements to Mr Green for his readiness and attention in executing the request I took the liberty to make of him. If at any time I can serve him or you you cannot conceive how happy it would make ...

11

[Nathaniel Green to Thomas Peacock]
Nice Jan[uar]y 21st 1788

On the 13th August last I had the pleasure to answer your much
esteemed letter of the 9th March and to give you all the information
which I thought could be of importance to the family you are so
laudably concerned for. I have always ever since had the interests and
rights of that family in view and have frequently conversed with the
widow Mrs Birkbeck on their subject. She has always assured me of her
kind intentions and good will towards them and has lately told me
that she had given orders for remitting them a small sum of money.
As the good lady has been for a long time extremely infirm and
subject to frequent attacks of the nerves which seem to render her life
precarious I have been very anxious for her making a will and have
continually exerted my best endeavours to induce her to set about
that important business without any loss of time as I well know that
without such a disposition in due form all the hopes of your friends
would be totally frustrated, as they could never claim anything under
any title or pretence whatever of heirship. All my arguments and
persuasions were however insufficient till three days ago finding her,
to all appearances in imminent danger I got a most respectable
gentleman in whom she has much confidence to accompany me to
her bedside and in his presence as he is the Chief Magistrate in this
city I exhorted her to settle her affairs. She acquiesced in the most
cordial manner and I immediately called a Notary who before several
of her most intimate and confidential friends rogated her will in due
form. Her disease has ever since been abating and she may probably
recover and draw on still for some time but I hope she will never wish
to change in any essential point the dispositions she has already made
for I am happy to tell you they are such as the brothers of the late Mr
Birkbeck will have abundant reason to be satisfied with.

You may rest assured Sir that I shall be continually attentive to
prevent any prejudice happening to the interests of the two brothers
and as she has honoured me with some considerable degree of
confidence I hope I shall be able to succeed though one cannot
always foresee what changes may happen in the mind of a person of
such an age and state of health. Circumstances may happen to
require that I should know better than I do the names of the brothers
Birkbeck, the state and condition of their families, their residence etc,

I wish therefore Sir that you would take the trouble to give me as speedily as possible all such information as you think may be useful.

Mrs B's legacys in this country are only trifles to four of her old friends. I am not in the list and for many good reasons am very glad of it ...

12

[Nathaniel Green to Thomas Peacock]
Nice Jan[uar]y 28th 1788

You will please to reflect on the contents of this letter before you communicate them to the persons concerned.

On the 21st currt. I wrote you a few lines to inform you of the situation of Mrs Birkbeck, the relict of your late friend my predecessor, and that after many difficulties I had at length succeeded to persuade her to make a will. It is now proper that I acquaint you that on the 24th she departed this life and that I have, as was incumbent upon me in consequence of her own particular desire, as well as of my station, charged myself with the management and execution of all business occurring from this event, and I beg you will in my name assure all parties of my diligence and attention to secure them every possible benefit and advantage they can wish and expect. Mrs Birkbeck made her will just six days before her decease and appointed myself and Mr Robert Slade, Proctor in Doctors Commons[3] her executors. She has bequeathed the chief part of what she possessed to the younger brother of her late husband saying that he has a large family and is lame, and she believed the name to be Joseph. Item two legacies of £20 each to two of her friends. Item some household furniture (of no great value) to another friend and a harpsichord to the Prefectorial Judge here.

All of the rest of the residue is to be equally shared and divided between the two brothers, and their respective children. What this

---

3   Doctors' Commons was an association, formed in 1511 and dissolved in 1857, of doctors of civil law practising in the ecclesiastical courts and sharing a "common table", occupying buildings that also housed the ecclesiastical courts and the court of Admiralty, see W. Holdsworth, *A History of English Law*, xii (London, 1938), pp. 46–51; descriptions by Charles Dickens occur in *David Copperfield*, chapters 23 and 33.

residue will amount to cannot yet be known as it depends upon the value of the effects in the house and the recovery of a debt due from a gentleman in France; it may be in the whole, five or six, or even eight hundred pounds. The legacy to the younger Mr Birkbeck consists of about twelve hundred pounds, in the hands of a merchant here, and about seven hundred pounds which has been just now invested in the long annuities at London.

These Sir are the dispositions which Mrs Birkbeck from all she knew or could recollect of the state and circumstance of her late husband's family, thought equitable and prudent. Want of more exact information or weakness of memory may have been the cause of involuntary error in the distribution of her favours, the fear of which made me request you in my last letter, to give some account of the persons who could have any hopes or pretensions, and is also the reason why I have begun the present with a caution to read it with attention before you communicate it, supposing it probable that the influence which your sacred character and the confidence of friendship must necessarily give you over the hearts of all concerned, may enable you to correct in some measure such defects as may have happened from the circumstances above mentioned.

I have been told just now that Mr Birkbeck had a sister who is probably unprovided for, if that should be the case I think it would be very reasonable and even equitable that those who are benefitted to her prejudice by reason of the forgetfulness or ignorance of the testatrix in regard to her, should contribute something towards her comfortable support, and in proportion (as for instance so much per cent) of their shares, and this perhaps you might persuade them to agree and oblige themselves to, before they know the extent of their good fortune, and so the real intentions of the late Mr and Mrs Birkbeck, to comfort the whole family will be justly, equitably, and completely fulfilled.

I flatter myself Sir that you will not disapprove of my offering you these observations, and as you are now by your knowledge of the circumstances and state of the parties concerned, a compleat judge of what may be proper and prudent to be done in the affair I shall not presume to trouble you with any further remarks of mine but shall pursue with diligence the business I have undertaken and continue to advise the heirs from time to time of what concerns them, either by the channel of your correspondence or any other they may think fit to indicate ...

13

[Thomas Peacock to Nathaniel Green]
Denton 7th Feb[ruar]y 1788

I have been duly favoured with your very kind and obliging letter, and return you my best acknowledgements, accompanied with the warmest thanks and prayers of all the late Mr Birkbeck's relations in this neighbourhood for your generous attention to their interests and for the kind concern you show for their success.

When I first came to this place, about 8 years ago, I found one of Mr Birkbeck's brothers a very honest and industrious man had unfortunately got a hurt in his leg which deprived him of procuring a comfortable support for himself and his aged partner. Humanity induced me though a stranger to Mr Birkbeck to state his deplorable situation to him and he generously supported him and shewed me such marks of polite attention as must for ever endear his memory to me. His brother's infirmities continuing your worthy predecessor continued his bounty to him till his dying day, and extended it still further to another brother and sister whose situations requiring his assistance did not come under his notice till a few months before his decease. This was the origin of my acquaintance and correspondence with the late Mr Birkbeck.

As soon as Mr Birkbeck's death was known in England his sorrowful brothers applied to me to procure for them any information I possibly could regarding his affairs. They were personally acquainted with his worthy widow and had the highest esteem and regard for her. Humanity had been a constant spur to his generous conduct towards them all. But though I had corresponded so long with Mr Birkbeck, he had never said in any of his letters to me whether she was living or not and every other intercourse between the parties had been totally shut up for 20 years excepting in one or two instances in which that important detail had never been mentioned. In consequence of their application I took the liberty to address you and the very singular attention you have paid to my request makes me think myself extremely happy in being honoured with your correspondence.

Your first letter to me so perfectly satisfied me that all further enquiries were immediately given up; but as you were so kind as to intimate that Mrs Birkbeck would not forget her husband's relations, I took the liberty, on the strength of your letter, to recommend to her two brothers-in-law and a sister as fit objects for her compassion. In doing this I had no other hope but that of procuring a slight benefaction at convenient intervals to soothe the anxiety which old age must feel when unable to struggle with want and disease. I will not distress your feelings by descanting on their situations; it is to your generous friendship they are indebted for the cheering hope that one day they may be placed above want.

As my hopes of advantage to the family were so weak, I was not sufficiently particular in stating to you its various members and branches. A small sketch is here annexed which I will be happy to extend at any time as far as you may be pleased to direct. Though the brothers are poor they are rich in gratitude and I feel the most exalted satisfaction in doing them every good office I possibly can.

The family, of which John Birkbeck Esq was the oldest, originally consisted of three other sons, Beaker, Alexander and Joseph, and two daughters Elizabeth and Lillo. Beaker is now living at Staindrop, a market town and parish in this county 4 miles from this place. He has had two sons and three daughters, Thomas the eldest son is now living in London, John the other son is dead as are all of his sisters, but there are many children which have proceeded from them some of which are living at Staindrop. Alexander is dead but has left a son and two daughters who have also numerous offspring. Joseph is living in this town but without any children. Elizabeth was married to Henry White but is now dead; she has left three sons and a daughter here who have numerous families. Lillo was married to Thomas Moses but is now a widow near a place called Hamsterley about 6 miles from us. She has three sons and three daughters who have many children. If this account be not sufficiently explicit I hope you will be so obliging as favour me with your commands and it shall be made as particular as you desire it to be.

The remittance you so obligingly speak of never came to hand. I wish to leave it to your judgement whether any enquiry should be made about it. In this and every other matter respecting the family I shall be happy to receive your kind advice; and if you will be so obliging as favour me with continuance of your correspondence when you judge a few lines necessary you will very highly oblige a grateful family ...

14

[Thomas Peacock to Robert Slade]
Denton Feb[ruar]y 18 1788

Four days ago I received a letter from Nathaniel Green Esq Consul at Nice, a copy of which I have hereunto annexed. In consequence of this letter I called together the two brothers and sister of the late Mr Birkbeck and signified to them that a considerable sum of money was left to the family and recommended their entering into engagements to have such a distribution made as that every part of the family might feel the good effects of the humane bequest I had been advised of. For eight years past I have been connected with them and have enjoyed considerable share of their confidence. This induced them to hearken to my advice and to request me to undertake the management of their affairs offering to furnish me with such powers for the purpose as I might desire. Upon consulting with my attorney I find a copy of the will must be had before any legal conveyances can be drawn which copy I hope you will be so obliging as to furnish me with. Or, if you will be so kind as undertake to prepare a conveyance for the signature of the parties it will be much more acceptable to us all. To enable you to do this, if you will be so kind as to undertake it, I have hereunto annexed a state of the family and the nature of the powers they wish to put into my hands. In the mean time I beg it may be understood that your kind directions will always be duly attended to and if my waiting upon you should be thought necessary it shall be done. It is further to be noted that no step will at any time be taken but such as will meet the approbation of the executors in the fullest manner.

The family of which John Birkbeck Esq was the eldest brother, originally consisted of three other brothers, Beaker, Alexander and Joseph and two daughters Elizabeth and Lilles. Beaker is now living at Staindrop, a market town in the county. His wife is living, and he has had two sons and three daughters who are all dead, except Thomas the eldest son, and have left many children behind them. Alexander is dead but has left a son and two daughters who also have numerous offspring. Joseph (the principal legatee) is living in the town but has neither wife nor child. Elizabeth was married to Henry White but they are both dead and have left a large family. Lilles was married to Thomas Moses but is now a widow at a place called South Side near Hamsterley in this county and has 6 children and many grandchildren. The above named are all in very obscure situations.

The powers they wish to put into my hands are a legal authority to settle and transact all business whatsoever with the executors of the late Mr Birkbeck, and to make such a distribution of the effects I may receive on the accounts as may appear reasonable to the executors and myself, with clauses to be repaid expenses, indemnified from law suits or any other proviso we may judge proper.

These Sir are the steps already taken agreeable to the humane wishes of Mr Green. I shall write to him immediately and acquaint him with this letter to you, and desire him to give you and me such additional directions as he may judge proper. In the mean time, I shall be happy to hear from you by the first post and will have the greatest pleasure at all times in receiving your commands ...

15

[Thomas Peacock to Nathaniel Green]
Denton 18th Feb[ruar]y 1788

I have received your very kind letter of the 28th ult. containing an account of the late Mrs Birkbeck's death and your most humane and equitable advice respecting her relations. The two brothers and sister have been with me and have agreed to give over to me full powers to manage the whole affair for them and to make such a distribution of the effects committed to your care among them and the representatives of the deceased brother and sister as the two executors and myself may judge reasonable and to add such provisos and clauses to the assignment as we might think necessary. On consulting my attorney I found a copy of the will would be wanted before any legal conveyance could be made. I therefore wrote to Mr Slade on the subject and have taken the liberty (which I hope you will excuse) to send him a copy of your last and benevolent letter to me and to desire him either to furnish me with a copy of Mrs Birkbeck's will or else provide a proper conveyance of the effects for the execution of the parties, offering at the same time to attend him in London if necessary, or follow any other plan he might point out.

I thought with you that it would be improper to name to the family the purport of the will until proper obligations had been entered into to fulfil what Mrs Birkbeck's ignorance and my inattention prevented her from doing. Fortunately, Joseph has neither wife nor child so I flatter myself this important end may be accomplished. They all seem remarkably tractable and ready to follow the counsel I have given them, and I shall use my utmost endeavours to prevent any evil-minded person from persuading them so as to hinder their good intentions being brought into effect.

I hope, Sir, you will approve of the steps I have taken and will obligingly continue to give me such directions as you wish to have followed as I do assure you, as long as I am concerned, no one step of consequence shall be taken without its having obtained your approbation. You will see by the state of the family which I have had the honour to transmit to you in my letter of the 7th inst. how unfortunate the issue would be to many if the present dispositions should be no way modified. I shall be unremittingly anxious till that be accomplished and shall then wait with the utmost tranquillity for the settling of the affairs in your hands and to receive any commands you may honour me with.

I have only to repeat to you the thanks of all the family for your goodness to them ...

16

[Robert Slade to Thomas Peacock]
Doctors Commons 21 Feb[ruary] 1788

I am favoured with your letter of the 18th inst. and have to regret that my present pressing avocations, just at the conclusion of the term prevent me from observing so fully as I should wish on the humane and meritorious part you have taken to serve the relations of my late friend Mr Birkbeck. Suffice it therefore for the present to say that I entirely approve your plan and that on receipt of the will from Nice you will hear further from me ...

17

[Thomas Peacock to Robert Slade]
Denton 3 March 1788

I hope that you will be kind enough to excuse this additional trouble I am now giving you in consideration of the motives that have induced me to write to you a second time. Since my last to you of the 18th ult. which you kindly answered on the 21st, some evil disposed persons have persuaded Lilles Moses, sister to the late Mr Birkbeck, to stir up much uneasiness in the family respecting the bequests of her late good master in Nice and flattering her with the idea that as she had the largest family she was justly entitled to the greatest share of her sister's effects. In consequence of which she has declared her aversion to come to any terms of agreement whatever, and is taking such steps as must eventually defeat the good and humane intention of Mrs Birkbeck's executors and the wishes of the family, unless prevented very soon. Beaker seems ready as yet to follow my advice, and I have sufficient influence over Joseph to bring him to follow my directions in every thing unless the continuance of his sister's provocations which are directed against him, entirely disappoint my good wishes for them all. By unveiling the secret to the sister I could easily prevent the progress of the imprudence, but this I think would be acting dishonourably towards the rest. While I pity her misguided zeal I tremble for the consequences of it, and as I am embarked in the cause of humanity I wish unremittingly to bring it about, though the sole recompense on my part is foreseen anxiety and trouble.

Far be it from me to wish to dictate you anything, but I hope you will excuse my submitting it to you whether a written obligation, though deficient in some respects of legal exactitude had not better be executed by such of the parties as cause it. Perhaps I can yet prevail upon them all, before the will be produced in court. While I suggest this I must beg you will observe that my ignorance of the niceties of the law may have induced me to propose an improper thing and therefore I presume you will permit a good intention to be an apology for dear sir, ...

18

[Robert Slade to Thomas Peacock]
Doctors Commons 8th March 1788

I send you enclosed a copy of the translation of Mrs Birkbeck's will and as the drawing up of such an agreement as you propose is out of the line of my profession I recommend you to get it done by your attorney and to have it signed by as many of the parties as will come into it. I have, I own, my fears that you will have great difficulty in carrying your humane intentions into execution.

A gentleman of the name of Sir Thomas, or William Appleby, was with me yesterday on behalf of Thomas the nephew who is it seems in service and who, concerning himself to have been neglected by his other relations, will not come into any agreement, and take anything but what he is entitled to under the will. I take him to be the son of Beaker and as such, interested in the residue. I have lately received a letter from Mr Green mentioning that the merchants at Nice who owe the £1200 refuse paying it till they are indemnified from a bond they entered into on Mrs Birkbeck's taking administration to her husband. While matters are thus circumstanced I shall not prove the will but keep it in my custody, nor am I sure that I will prove it at all unless the affairs of the deceased are likely to be settled without involving me in much trouble.

19

[Thomas Peacock to Robert Slade]
Denton 19th March 1788

I was duly favoured with your kind letter, covering a translated copy of Mrs Birkbeck's will, and immediately directed such an agreement to be prepared as I had named to you, but an event has since taken place which has entirely defeated the whole project and left the matter where I first took it up.

You mention an application that was made to you by a Sir Wm. Appleby of the City of Durham. Sir William wrote a letter to one of his friends in the country giving an account of his waiting upon you, of his having seen the will, of my offering to serve the family, and insinuating such matter and giving such advice to the parties as made many of them imagine that I only wanted to make a property of them. This letter was handed from one to another and at last to me, and the clamour and suspicion which it produced obliged me in my own defence to open the whole affair together with my instructions from Mr Green and your letters approving of his advice. Had it not been for this untoward circumstance I flatter myself the humane and benevolent scheme would have been happily completed.

I forbear to remark on the contents of my dignified countryman's letter. As it was shewed to me in the confidence of friendship I cannot with propriety descant upon it. And yet, to throw some light on this very singular and paradoxical business, I cannot help observing that Sir William's eccentrical disposition is extremely well known in the neighbourhood of Durham. But though I have been disappointed in the prosecution of this plan I have still good hopes of benefitting the family if I can only keep them within the bounds of moderation and prevent them from flying out into invective against the dispositions in the will. Joseph Birkbeck my neighbour has most solemnly assured me that he will be implicitly guided by my advice in extending his bounties towards all his relations, and has so pressingly requested me to continue my good offices with you in settling the business that I cannot properly refuse my assistance.

In his name, therefore, I must beg you will go forward with proving the will in such a way as you judge best. If you will undertake to manage affairs their obligation to you will be great indeed. But if you feel it inconvenient to yourself to do them that honour any advice or assistance you may be pleased to impart will be most gratefully acknowledged. You mention the demand of Messrs Le Clercs respecting Mr Birkbeck's will. Perhaps you will be so obliging as to send me a copy of that will and at the same time such other information you may judge proper ...

20

[Thomas Peacock to Robert Slade]
Denton June 10th 1788

The information you kindly gave me by Mr Parrington was so perfectly satisfactory to me that I did not think of troubling you again on the subject till the matters were altogether ready for settling. But I have been induced to write to you again in order to state some matters to you which have fallen out, and upon which, I am persuaded a line from you would be very acceptable.

The age and situation of the parties you already know. Joseph, at my request, has promised to give £300 to his sister and other relations as soon as the money can be got, and more as he sees occasion. To enable him to make a comfortable establishment and to relieve his sister and other relations, I have already advanced him near £100. At present he wishes to do more for his friends but it does not suit me to advance the money, nor would I wish to borrow it unless I were certified how long it would be wanted. They of course are anxious to see matters settled, and often press me to hasten the business. My wish is to do everything I possibly can to make the matter easy to Mr Green and you; but perhaps you will not think it too much trouble to give me a few lines on the subject containing such information and advice as you may judge proper.

21

[Robert Slade to Thomas Peacock]
Doctors Commons 26 June 1788

I have deferred answering your letter of the 10th instant in expectation of being favoured with a second call from Mr Sanderson. In regard to the affairs of the late Mrs Birkbeck they seem to be a good deal involved, having received advice lately from Mr Green that Messrs Le Clerc and Co. of Nice, persisting in their refusal to pay the money left in their hands, he has been obliged to commence a suit against them. The account with the owners of the Mahon privateer remains also unsettled, and I have lately received a letter from Mr John Birkbeck of East Rainton, giving me notice not to part with any of the property until he, and all the other claimants have authorized me so to do. I have answered him that no distribution will be made till the usual time, viz twelve months after the deceased's death, and if he apprehends he has any claim (which I think he has not) there is ample time to make it good. He complains loudly of your conduct in the business, to which I have given him what I conceive to be a proper answer; I shall write to Mr Green next Friday and send a requisition to him as one of the executors of the deceased's will ...

22

[Robert Slade to Thomas Peacock]
Doctors Commons 5 August 1788

I have just received the enclosed letter from Mr Green by whose desire I take the liberty of handing it over to you for your perusal and in order that you may put it under cover and then forward it to Mr John Birkbeck at East Rainton to whom it is addressed. Mr Green writes me word that Messrs Le Clerc and Co. have obtained a decree in their favour which authorises them to retain the money in their hands until such time as they are exonerated from the Bond in which they joined on Mrs Birkbeck's taking administration to her husband's will, for that I shall be obliged to institute a suit in order, if possible, to obtain the delivery of such bond.

23

[Nathaniel Green to John Birkbeck (nephew of Joseph Birkbeck)]
Nice 20 July 1788

A few days ago I received your letter of the 16th June and I hope by my answer to convince you that I am and have been desirous to render all the service in my power to every one of the relations of my predecessor the late Mr J. Birkbeck whose intention it most certainly always was that his subsistence should come at last to his own family. But in what manner he wished it to be divided was not, nor could not be known to anyone here except his wife, to whom he gave full power to make what distribution she pleased by making her the sole and universal legatee. Perhaps she promised him to dispose of it in favour of his family but this is only a supposition, and she was certainly at full liberty to give what she possessed to whom she pleased.

On my arrival here I found her very infirm (near 70 years of age) and much embarrassed about settling her affairs in which respect she sometimes asked my advice, but with all great reserve and caution for she was much inclined to be suspicious and was particularly anxious to hide the true state of her fortune from me for certain reasons of her own. I was informed that there were brothers of the late Mr Birkbeck in England, and I saw there was great danger of all the benefit that had been intended them, because, first, there were people who would persuade Mrs Birkbeck to lay out all her money in a life annuity and offered her 12%, next she might die without making a will and then her own relations would claim all as heirs at law. She herself confirmed to me the idea I had formed of the situation of her late husband's brothers, professed her intention of making them her heirs, declaring that she had not any relations who could possibly want or to whom she would ever leave anything. I therefore used all my endeavours to prevent her laying out all her money for annuities and at the same time to persuade her to make a will. Her own humour and caprices, besides her infirmities, and the contrary advices of some other persons who had interested views threw many difficulties in my way, until at length in the month of January last she was taken so ill that there appeared to be little or no hope of her recovery. I then resolved to exert myself to the utmost to secure something at least for the benefit of the Birkbeck family and in the presence of several of her friends I exorted her to make a will. She consented to do it immediately, and in a few hours the work was completed with all the formality and solemnity possible, the Chief Magistrate of the city who was her particular friend and several other persons of note also her friends being present. She dictated to me and I to the notary.

Several of the witnesses understood English, but yet I took care to repeat to her every article in French and have her confirmation in each language. I first enquired what she would do for her own relations. She said positively she would not leave them anything then dictated the first legacy, in the terms, and with the name and description as you see in the will. She was a long time before she could resolve to dispose of the rest and residue and we all began to fear that all our labour would prove in vain and that she would never finish what she had begun, after much trouble she gave the residue to her late husband's two brothers and their children. Though in many instances she gave proof of her memory and judgement being perfectly clear at the time, she did not then recollect, if ever she knew the true state of the family. It was not possible then to seek for any better information nor were there any hopes of obtaining any in time, and I was well satisfied in having succeeded so far in my desire of doing some service to those who I thought wanted it.

I knew the excellent character of the Rev and Mrs Peacock, and his humane concern for the family. I therefore immediately informed him of the will being made in their favour but did not tell him the particulars. He answered me with an exact account of all the different branches of the family but it was too late to make any change. The old lady was dead and I had wrote him a second letter with an account of all the legacys. I had heard by accident that Mr Birkbeck had a sister, I thought that perhaps she or some other relation might merit attention and therefore proposed to Mr Peacock to keep my letter secret till he could try to persuade those who were most benefitted by the will to participate with those who had been forgotten or unknown. He would certainly have succeeded to procure from the principal legatee some allowance for you and the rest if the mistaken zeal of some of your friends and your own impatience had not raised a clamour against him and prevented his operations in your favour.

You see Sir that the wrong which has been done you, was done through unavoidable ignorance here, and unhappily though innocent, I was the instrument. So soon as I perceived that such a misfortune was possible I endeavoured to repair the evil and asked the assistance of Mr Peacock whom I knew to be just, equitable and humane; it evidently appears that he was so, and also your best and most important friend. I hope that his christianlike and charitable temper will lead him to forgive all that is past and that he may still befriend you. I therefore advise you as a friend to make him the best reparation you can for the complaints you have made against him and beg he will consider them as mistakes arising from misinformation and ill understood advice, and so endeavour to procure a reconciliation between him and you, your uncle, etc. etc. This is the only possible way for you and your sister etc. to obtain any benefit, for you cannot by any means set up any claim at law and the counsellor who you tell me gave you an opinion concerning the will did not know, or did not observe, that your uncle was dead a year before and having left all to his wife she had power to give it to whom she pleased, consequently your family has no right to dispute her will. I sincerely wish you peace and harmony with all your friends and relations, as well as every other blessing ...

24

[Thomas Peacock to Robert Slade]
Denton 12 August 1788

I was duly favoured with your letter of the 26th June and thank you for the information it contained. I should have answered it before now if I had not expected a call from Mr Sanderson at this place. He sent me word that he wanted to see me, and would be with me soon, but did not come till last Thursday. He begged me to give his compliments to you, and inform you that he was disappointed of seeing you again by the impatience of his companions who obliged him to leave town in great haste. On Friday morning I received your second letter covering one to Mr John Birkbeck of East Rainton which I have forwarded to him. When you write to Mr Green, I beg you will inform him that I am duly sensible of his polite attention to me and am much obliged by the last instance of it.

You already know the steps I have taken to serve the Birkbeck family in general, which were rendered ineffectual by the officiousness of the person who complains of my conduct. After my first attempt was defeated I prevailed upon my neighbour [Joseph Birkbeck] to promise his friends £300 as soon as money came to his hands and more when he saw it necessary, £40 of which he designed to give to John Birkbeck of East Rainton, and he also intended to have left him a greater share of his effects than any other of his nephews, which intention he communicated to him. This was not all. About the middle of June he came to his uncle and begged him to assist him in getting a cow to give milk for his family who were distressed for want of it. His uncle with my approbation agreed to it and I lent Joseph ten guineas which he gave to his nephew for that purpose. I am told the cow is still unbought, and it is said in the family the money is intended to carry on a suit at law against the giver of it.

The recompence I have met with you know, but though I feel as a man, I will be ready on his application to me, to endeavour to reconcile him to his uncle, which I fear will not easily be effected. I hope he will be influenced by Mr Green's most excellent advice, and endeavour to atone for the mischief he has spread in the family. I am very sorry indeed that the bequests in the will are not more general. Had I been fortunate enough to particularise matters when I first solicited Mr Green's assistance perhaps they would have been. But I still hope if he and his other friends will be quiet I shall be able to procure from my neighbour such a disposition as may leave them no grounds for complaints. At all events my best offices shall not be wanting in order to effect it. I don't know what can influence him and his associates to take such imprudent steps unless it be the counsels of designing men.

Joseph has lately taken a second wife which I hear they are

angry about.⁴ It was a thing not approved of though he had many
reasons for so doing. He had a perpetual running sore which required
great attention to keep it clean, his sight was much impaired one eye
being entirely lost, and he had other infirmities which may be
expected at 68 years of age. He has married a woman who nurses him
well, is a good wife in every respect, and a most steady friend to all
his relations. He has settled upon her ten pounds a year for life, and
also two rooms to live in, which at this place are worth no more than
ten shillings per annum each. If all things can be managed properly I
see no great loss they will sustain by this marriage for it is not
probable there will be any issue by it. If they persist in their
impudence I will not say but that my neighbour may leave her more
than either she expects or he intends to do at present.

The interested people here, Joseph and Beaker, have the most
perfect reliance on Mr Green and you, and are happy in having you
to manage for them. Thank you in their names for your care and
attention to their affairs, and I beg you will continue to take such
steps as the complexion of the business may require, and when
anything worth communicating occurs I shall be glad to hear from
you ...

25

[Robert Slade to Thomas Peacock]
Doctors Commons Nov[ember] 14 1788

I deferred answering your favor of the 4th instant in
consequence of my being in daily expectation of hearing from Mr
Green in regard to the suit against Messrs Le Clerc and Co. for the
recovery of the property left in their hands by the late Mrs Birkbeck
and in which two sentences have been given against him for want of
the delivery of the bond in which they joined with her when she
took administration to Mr Birkbeck. I am now applying to the court
here in order to obtain the delivery of this bond upon our taking
administration of the effects inadministered of the late Mr Birkbeck

4   In 1788 Joseph married Hannah Hogarth of Romaldkirk; she died in June
    1793, and in September of the same year, at the age of 73, he married
    Isabel Lumley, aged 32. In October 1798 the Denton registers record the
    birth of John, first son of Joseph Birkbeck by his wife Isabel.

with his will annexed and giving fresh security. This done, I shall forward the bond to Mr Green and trust that he will succeed in his third attempt against these gentlemen. I received Mr Green's bond from him by yesterday's post and have his direction to apply to Mr Wm Smith as his security. If you have advanced any sum of money to the legatees I shall be ready to reimburse it to your order payable at ten days after sight, on receiving an acknowledgement signed by the legatee for so much on account of his legacy. I shall not sell out the money in the funds till all matters are fulfilled and in the mean time shall give the estate credit for the interest to be received ...

26

[Thomas Peacock to Robert Slade]
Denton 22 Nov[ember] 1788

I am requested by Joseph Birkbeck and his brother Beaker to return you their best thanks for your kind offer of the 14th instant of repaying me the money I had advanced them in order to make old age comfortable in consequence of the legacies left them by their sister. It was my wish to delay calling upon you for the disbursement I had made for some time longer, but they were so pressing to repay me and some other contingencies also happening to me I have been induced this day to draw upon you for £100 to the order of John Mowbray ten days after sight, and have left the bill and receipts, Joseph's receipt for £130 and Beaker's for £10 in his hands and suppose both will be presented to you in the course of four posts.

I do not observe from your letter any mention made of Beaker's receiving any money at this time, but old age hangs so heavy upon him that he wished much to have a little before his death if it could be got. I fear much he will never live to sign another receipt as he totters upon the brink of the grave. Joseph's kindness to many of his relations, added to some difficulties he was under when the money was left, and the expences of stocking him a small farm, and fitting up a cottage for his comfortable reception have made his calls upon me more than I wished them to be. With the value now drawn for they will be able to hold out till you have finished what has been to you a troublesome business. Their obligation to you they wish to acknowledge ...

27

[Thomas Peacock to Robert Slade]
Denton 1st May 1789

I have had Beaker Birkbeck with me to enquire when his claims
are to be finally settled. He is very uneasy about the matter and seems
rather to hearken to the suggestions of some about him who scruple
not to insinuate things which can only arise in base or ignorant
minds. I have taken some pains to satisfy him, and assured him that
every dispatch possible had been used both by Mr Green and you to
serve the family, and I durst venture to say you would both continue
to do all you possibly could to finish the business in the most
honourable manner. As it is some time since I heard from you and as
I am ignorant about the affair with the Le Clercs, I must beg you will
let me hear from you, and I should be much obliged to you if you
will communicate all the information you can on the subject ...

28

[Robert Slade to Thomas Peacock]
Doctors Commons 2nd May 1789

I have this day paid your last draft for £100 in favor of George
Culley and on the account of Joseph Birkbeck. Your plan of
indemnifications to be inserted in the will appears to me to be very
proper. The last letter from Mr Green states the difficulties that still
exist in bringing Messrs Le Clerc and Denny to account and that the
same are to be enforced to an arbitration in regard to interest. He also
makes mention of three sequesters to be done away. I mean
forthwith to advertise in the Gazette for all claimants to come in, and
have desired Mr Green to do the same at Nice. I have intimated to
him the intention of the heirs to present him with a piece of plate
and that probably ... in his next whether he approves the plan or
means to make a charge. He certainly saved the ... for the heirs and
has sustained all the ... and quarrels about the property which must
have given him infinite trouble besides attending to the taking of an
inventory and making sale of the effects which in that country is a
very tedious business. I have fixed the value of the intended
compliment at £30 and upwards. Please in your next to give me a

line on this head in order that I may be enabled to write to Mr Green fully thereon ...

29

[Robert Slade to Thomas Peacock]
Doctors Commons 2nd June 1789

I yesterday received a letter from Mr Green containing remittances to the amount of two hundred pounds which will be due in the course of this month and he tells me "that he shall now invite the parties concerned in the two sequesters to bring forward their claims, and that he shall endeavour to settle the interest account with Le Clerc who still holds out." I shall write to him by this night's post and inform him, agreeably to the contents of your last favor that Joseph Birkbeck wishes to charge himself exclusively with the payment of such commission as he, Mr Green shall think proper to demand or accept as a compliment. As matters now stand, I shall have no objection if Joseph Birkbeck wishes it, to pay him the produce of the short annuity sold £715.5.5. which is specifically bequeathed to him deducting therefrom the money he has already received which is £200 I believe, and the payment of a stamp for his receipt. In this case you will please to favor me with a line as I will then forward you a proper stamp, on the return of which, I shall be ready to accept Joseph Birkbeck's draft as heretofore for the balance. I await your answer ...

30

[Robert Slade to Thomas Peacock]
Doctors Commons 4th July 1789

The pressing avocations of the term have prevented me until this day looking into the accounts of my executorship, and preparing the necessary receipts for Mr Joseph Birkbeck's signature, and settling with him in regard to the produce of the short annuity which he is entitled to under Mrs Birkbeck's will. The sums he has already drawn for amount together to £350 as stated in your letter. I wrote from memory on the 2nd of last month when I mentioned the sum already advanced to have been £200 only, and relied on your accuracy and a further investigation of the accounts for the correction of any error in the supposition I then made. The account stands thus, viz

22 November 1788 To bill of this date for £260, ten pounds of which was for account of Beaker Birkbeck	£250
4th Feb 1789 to ditto of this date	£100
4th April 1789 to ditto of this date	£100
to stamp for receipt	£8
July To bill of this date	£257.5.5.
Net produce of short annuity	£715.5.5.

You may therefore draw upon me for this sum of £257.5.5 and on production of Mr Birkbeck's receipt witnessed by yourself I will do honor to the draft by my acceptance of it. I have heard nothing new since my last from Mr Green ...

31

[Robert Slade to Thomas Peacock]
Doctors Commons 27 Oct[ober] 1789

I am just returned from a journey into Yorkshire and have not before had any communication of your favor of the 18th ult. owing to its arrival just after I left town, or I should have answered it sooner. You have on the other side a copy of a letter from Mr Green which came to hand during my absence. Also a copy of another letter received from him this day. Please to communicate them to the Birkbeck family. I hope from their contents that matters are likely to be brought very shortly to a conclusion which will give great pleasure to ...

32

[Copy of letter, Nathaniel Green to Robert Slade]
Nice Sept[ember] 7th 1789

I received yours of the 2nd June but have deferred until now making you any answer because I wished and intended at the same time to make you a remittance on the executorship accounts, but with all the diligence I could use I am not able yet to find any good bills unless from distant places, which I found would be attended with great loss, for I have corresponded on the subject with Genoa, Leghorn and even Venice and had also good hopes of doing something by way of Paris, but the troubles[5] which arose there stopped me as I was beginning to procure effects there. I have too much money by me and am impatient to send it to you, which I hope to begin to do early in next month which is the season for bills to become more plenty in this place.

I am not yet any further advanced settling the disputed accounts but am endeavouring to induce those who have sequestered, to bring the affair before the tribunal here, but as the principals are in distant places, the business goes on slow. My next, which I hope will be soon, shall enclose some good bills ...

33

[Copy of letter, Nathaniel Green to Robert Slade]
Nice October 10th 1789

Confirming my last of Sept.7th, I have pleasure to remit you herewith £300 in the following bills viz

Elizabeth Pocock on Baillie, Pocock and Co at 30 days date	£100
Rebecca Pocock on the same at 30 days	£100
My own bill on Richard Muilman and Co at 3 days sight	£100
	£300

for which you will please give me credit in our executorship accounts and favor me with a letter of advice. I hope soon to find some more bills and make you further remittances and I shall be very glad to see the end of the whole business ...

34

[Robert Slade to Thomas Peacock]
Doctors Commons 2nd Feb[ruary] 1790

I have to inform you, agreeably to the request in your last letter of the 12th Dec, that yesterday's post brought me a letter from Mr

---

5   The outbreak of the French Revolution.

Green enclosing two bills value together £300 which will come due in the course of a few days. I send you on the other side a copy of the letter so far as it relates to the Birkbeck business, which with this you will please to communicate to them. I have acknowledged the receipt of Mr Green's letter and contents and requested him to bring the matter to a conclusion as soon as possible ...

35

[Copy of letter, Nathaniel Green to Robert Slade]
Nice January 20th 1790

I received in due course your favor of the 4th ulto. and herewith I have the pleasure to remit you the sum of £300 sterling viz Lady Rivers on Joseph Allen for £200 and Mrs Jane Matthews on Messrs Goslings for £100 at 3 days sight. You will please to do the needful and credit my executorship account as before.

I employ a great deal of my leisure time in the examination of my old papers which are strangely confused and of great antiquity some of them being 40 years old. I am impatient to finish this odious business. All papers that are worth preserving I shall send you as also several trifling articles and diamond buckles unless the claimant at Marseilles complies presently with the sums I at first demanded ...

36

[Thomas Peacock to Robert Slade]
Denton 16th March 1790

I have to acknowledge receipt of your kind favor of the 2nd Feb. and to inform you that I have communicated its contents to the parties concerned. It is my particular wish to make matters as easy as possible for Mr Green and you, and to prevent the claimants from being uneasy. Though I am not always able to accomplish my purpose I cannot say but I succeed in it as well as I could expect.

When you paid Joseph Birkbeck the balance of one of the legacies last July I did all I could to persuade him to send what money he did not want and dispose of the remainder when ready in the Public Fund as you advised, but I did not succeed in my attempt.

Some money he did send but he would not dispose of the whole till lately, when he bought a small estate contrary to my advice, and by doing so has involved himself in some difficulties. When I consider the temper of the man and the purchase he has made which is not too dear, I can only blame him for doing it at an unreasonable period, before he had money to pay for it. The whole purchase before it is completed will cost him between £700 and £800, £150 of which are already paid, and he has some more money which he can command, but there will still be a defect of £500 or £550. It was my particular wish to urge you no more on the subject of disbursements till matters were fully completed, but as things have taken a turn contrary to my expectation I must beg you will be so kind as inform me if you are willing to advance any more money and how much. The bargain should be completed early in April and I wish to know what sum suits you to part with as I must provide what may fall short against that time ...

37

[Thomas Peacock to Robert Slade]
Denton 7th April 1790

On the 16th March I took the liberty to trouble you with a few lines respecting the Birkbeck affair, informing you that Joseph Birkbeck had made a purchase which was to be completed in this month, and that for the purpose of settling the affair money would be wanted, requesting you to say what sums you would be willing to advance out of his estate in your hands for that purpose. To this letter I have not yet been favoured with an answer which has given me some uneasiness as the day for completing the business is at hand. I shall be much obliged to you if you will send me a line by the first post respecting these particulars.

38

[Robert Slade to Thomas Peacock]
Doctors Commons 13th April 1790

I have not had it in my power to inspect my accounts till this day, in order to see whether the sum wanted by Joseph Birkbeck could be advanced to him. He has not to be sure paid either you or myself a compliment by acting contrary to our advice, but be this as it may, I am desirous of accommodating him to the utmost of my power and shall therefore be ready to relieve him from any difficulties in which you say his purchase has involved him, by declaring myself ready to accept his draft for the greatest sum you mention him to stand in need of, viz £550.

Thomas Birkbeck was with me yesterday with a request of a further advance which I made him accordingly, altho it appears on casting up the account today that he has already received more than what is due to him out of the monies that have hitherto come to hand. The sums paid him amount to £175.10. When I receive any post advices from Mr Green they shall be communicated to you ...

39

[Thomas Peacock to Robert Slade]
Denton 17th April 1790

Your very kind favour of the 13th inst has been duly received by me, and Joseph Birkbeck desires me in his name to make due acknowledgement to you for the offer of assistance you have made him and for the information you have given him respecting his nephew. In consequence of your obliging consent I have this day drawn upon you for £550 in favour of Mr John Mowbray at 15 days after sight and accompanied the bill with a receipt from J[oseph] B[irkbeck] in the usual form.

I wish Thomas Birkbeck lay out his money prudently. The purchase Joseph has made is a good one, and will bring the value paid for it at any opportunity. He has done some things I do not approve, but he has not wasted much money. He has been persuaded to lend some small sums into suspicious hands, on account of favours formerly received, though I opposed the money being lent on the score of common prudence. His losses however will be trivial, and he has now found out by experiences the uncertainty of pretended friends. I dare say he will be wiser for the future ...

40

[Thomas Peacock to Robert Slade]
Denton 12 June 1790

Some time ago Beaker Birkbeck applied to me to request me to advance him a little money as his wife was much indisposed, and he had lent most of the £50 he had before got from you upon a good security and was unwilling to call it in. To supply his wants I gave him ten guineas which, at that time he thought sufficient, but his wife growing weaker and having now been confined to her bed for four months, he has desired me to solicit you to supply him with more money to defray his increased expenses, and to be ready for any emergency. I have agreed to use my interest with you to advance him £50 more, which will make the sum £100 received by him. I have no doubt of your complying with this request and I shall take the liberty to draw upon you for that sum if I do not hear from you to the contrary, in the course of a week, sending you a receipt from him with the bill. He is a remarkable economist and has done wonders for a long time, being unable to work and having to support a sick wife and three grandchildren, out of the interest of a small sum of money he has lent and the money I lately advanced him. When any further matter arises respecting the family a line from you would oblige ...

41

[Robert Slade to Thomas Peacock]
Doctors Commons 9th July 1790

I have this day paid your draft for £50 on account of Beaker Birkbeck and for the information of the parties send you an extract of a letter lately received from Mr Green, which will show the present situation of the affairs in which they are interested ...

42

[Copy of letter, Nathaniel Green to Robert Slade]
Nice June 6th 1790

Your last mentions your wish to see a final settlement of our account with the heirs of Birkbeck, and I beg leave to assure you that I am fully as desirous of the same as anyone can be, for I cannot describe to you the trouble I have had and have still to go through in the affair, so that very many times I wish I could have escaped the charge. I just now thought to have made a good progress, by sending you a case with the diamond buckles, some books, two portraits and some trinkets etc. For though Mr Wilkie of Marseilles has not relinquished his claim upon the buckles, I think it is useless to keep them here any longer. When preparing the expedition the news arrived of the disputes with Spain[6] and it was no longer safe to send anything by sea.

Please do let me know what part of the papers and documents of the accounts etc. should be sent to you. The inventory, estimates and auction account fills about 240 pages small folio. I think an extract might be made by the same notary abridging all formalities and yet be authentic, which would reduce it to half the bulk and be more intelligible, as the language and form are all of this country. I have spent a great deal of time this last winter in examining even with assistance a prodigious quantity of old papers. There is a much greater quantity which is still untouched which I shall attack at every leisure hour. I have found in an old letter from Messrs. Goslings, dated 23 July 1782 a bill of exchange: Heselrige on Stavely and Turner, for £100 dated Cairo March 31st 1777 at 30 days sight, in favour of George Baldwin, and by him endorsed to Birkbeck, by him to Messrs Goslings and returned by them, seeing no probability of payment, but without protests. I have not yet met with any note in book or account concerning this bill, so have preserved it and will send it to you if you think it worth while.

I have had some notice of an opposition to one of the sequesters, so hope that question will soon be agitated. I shall set about liquidating the accounts as far as I can go, and by the time I may receive your answer to this, shall be ready to permit you all that can be parted with and send you at the same time by land if necessary the papers and effects of value and of small bulk, which I shall rejoice to get rid of! ...

---

6   In 1790 a clash between the English and Spanish over Nootka Sound in British Columbia brought both countries to the brink of war. Spain only gave way when France withdrew her support.

43

[Thomas Peacock to Robert Slade]
Denton 24 Sept[ember] 1790

I communicated the contents of your last letter to the Birkbeck family who beg me to thank you and Mr Green for your attention to their interest. They are very desirous to see matters finally settled, but as I am fully persuaded you do all you can to expedite the business, I will wait the issue with patience and endeavour to prevent their being rendered uneasy by ignorant or designing men.

Joseph once more wishes you to accommodate him with a little money if you can conveniently do it. He manages the greatest part of his purchase which, with several needful repairs and some trifling sums he has lent to old friends and benefactors, has brought him to rather a low ebb. As the present call is not founded on any extravagance I the more readily submit it to you, £50 or £100, as you can spare it, will be all he wishes to trouble you for at present ...

44

[Robert Slade, signed by his clerk, to Thomas Peacock]
Doctors Commons 29 Sept[ember] 1790

Your favor of the 24th inst. came duly to hand and shall be delivered to Mr Slade on return from Paris where he is gone on business and from whence he is not expected home till the latter end of the next or the beginning of the following month ...

45

[Robert Slade to Thomas Peacock]
Doctors Commons 12 Nov[ember] 1790

I am but lately returned from my expedition to Paris or you should have had an earlier answer to your last letter, the receipt of which was acknowledged by Mr Kiernan in my absence. You have on the other side a copy of so much of the last dispatches from Mr Green as relate to the affairs of the late Mrs Birkbeck, and which you will please to communicate to the family. Captain Trewfitt has arrived and has brought me a sword and some old seals, but the case containing the several articles specified in Mr Green's letter is not yet landed. I shall get them sold at the best advantage as soon as possible as they come into my hands. Mr Joseph Birkbeck may in the mean time draw on me as heretofore for the larger sum mentioned in your letter, namely £100 with which you are desirous he should be accommodated ...

46

[Copy of letter, Nathaniel Green to Robert Slade]
Nice Aug[ust] 28th 1790

Herewith I have the pleasure to hand you bill of lading on the ship Salerno, Capt. Trewfitt, of a larger case marked RS NOL containing sundry articles belonging to the estate of the late Mrs Birkbeck and reserved unsold after closing the sale by auction as you will see by referring to the concluding act of the notary Rossetti at the close of the said public sale also some other articles not made mention of in said concluding act the whole being as follows viz:
No 42 a stock buckle set with diamonds valued £500
    43 a pair of shoe buckles ditto £1668
    255 a tippet Martins' tails £18
    257 two cloak trimmings and a lining £40
    398 sundry old coins and medals
    27 a silver repeating watch £60
    14 a blood stone jasper snuff box set in gold £80
    145 Voltaires works complete 69 volumes £210
        Prints maps etc. £53.10
        All the other unsold books £38.10
Articles not mentioned by the notary.
    Two portraits in gilt frames Mr and Mrs Birkbeck
    Sundry silver coins English and foreign and a bit of gold.
    A white agate seal set in gold, three old seals with wood handles
        delivered to Capt. Trewfitt in a paper apart.
Articles disposed of since the auction.
    253 Fur trimmings for cloaks, half stockings, thread, sold for
        £70.10
    256 Two tippets and a muff ordinary, 24 ermine tails the tippets
        and muff thrown away the tails in the box with the trimmings
        £12

Total value of the effects estimated and not sold at auction £2550.10 of which total amount of £2550.10 Piedmontese currency. I am still accountable for £70.10 goods sold since the auction as above which completes the account of all the moveables left by Mrs Birkbeck, all the house furniture having been bequeathed to Mr Veillon and the harpsichord to Mr Bottini the prefect.

As I did not foresee that I should so soon have the means of sending anything by ship I sent about a fortnight ago by Mr Gould Francis Leckie who was going to London a packet addressed to you containing authentic copies of the inventory and the estimate which packet by the time you receive this will probably be at the bank of Sir Robt Harris and Co. where Mr Leckie promised me he would have it and I told him you would send for it. From these two documents you will see a full and legal account of all the monies and effects with a specification of the value of every article. You may if you please have also the account of the sale as taken by the notary on the spot. Messrs Barr and Morillo of Mahon have at length made their claim for the balance of their account and contest the sequester of Collet which seemed by Birkbeck's books to be at most £3000 but the claim now made is for more than £5000. I have given them an answer with a true statement and expect their reply nevertheless I herewith make you a small remittance of £20 in a bill of Chas. Tinling on Cox Cox and Greenwood of London at 30 days sight for which you will please to do the needful and when encashed place to my credit in "Executorship" account ...

47

[Thomas Peacock to Robert Slade]
Denton 16th Nov[ember] 1790

I have been favoured with your letter of the 12th instant and am desired by Joseph Birkbeck and his brother to thank you and Mr Green for the continuance of your care in the management of the affairs of their family. They now flatter themselves with a speedy conclusion of the trouble you have had, and the final arrangement of their concern, the happy issue of which must be attributed to the great attention bestowed on them both by Mr Green and you. It is their wish that you should receive proper recompence for all your labours, but being unable to estimate the returns they ought to make you, they desire you would both make such charges as you think reasonable when the final account is made out. Joseph Birkbeck begs me to say that he wishes to receive the pictures of his brother and sister. If they are not very valuable I cannot help applauding his wish as it conveys an idea of respect, but if they will fetch a considerable sum, perhaps the future emolument to the family ought to be preferred. It does not appear to me that they can be sold for very much money. If you are of the same opinion I beg leave to recommend their being sent hither and such a charge made upon them to the effects as you suppose they deserve.

I have drawn upon you for £100 this day, agreeable to your kind permission, in favour of Mr Mowbray. I am afraid I gave you some reason in my last to be offended by implying an idea of neglect. It was not my intention to convey that idea to you though upon perusing the copy of my letter I see it was done. I meant to signify a wish to save you trouble, which I shall be happy to do at any opportunity. This error I beg you will excuse ...

48

[Thomas Peacock to Robert Slade]
Denton 22nd Feb[ruar]y 1791

I will be very much obliged to you if you will let me know how the affairs of the Birkbeck family are going on and what prospect there is of getting them terminated. The parties interested wish much to hear from you on the subject and to have your opinion when you think a final settlement will take place. I wrote on a former occasion about Mr and Mrs Birkbeck's pictures being sent here, if you approved of it, and my neighbour could wish to know your determination about them ...

49

[Robert Slade to Thomas Peacock]
Doctors Commons 25th Feb[ruary] 1791

The pressing business of the term has prevented me writing you fully on the business of my accountship and as the term does not end till next week, I must request your indulgence and that of the parties interested till the following week, when you may expect to hear further from me. I have to inform you in the meantime that I have sold the diamond buckles to M. Jeffries and Jones jewellers to the king for the sum of £81.18 for which they have given me a note payable in two months, as they assured me they had given a value beyond ready money the diamonds being of an inferior sort not fit for the English buckles. I have got a case made for the pictures and beg to hear how you will have them conveyed. There is some fur skin fit for a cloak which I have offered to sale to an eminent furrier in the City and he puts so small a value on it, not a guinea, that I think Mr Birkbeck had best have it for his wife. It will make a comfortable winter cloak. Also a little snuff box set in gold and silver repeating watch valued at three guineas but which will be a very good thing in the country telling the hour in the night. These I recommend Mr Birkbeck to take at their value. Let me know his determination ...

50

[Thomas Peacock to Robert Slade]
Denton 28th Feb[ruar]y 1791

Yesterday I received your very kind favour of the 25th inst and have communicated its contents to my neighbour Joseph Birkbeck. In his name I thank you for the trouble you have taken about the buckles and the other effects of the family. The pictures I am inclined to think had better be sent by sea to Stockton, consigned to the care of Mr James Wilkinson, wharfinger there. If you will be so kind as get them conveyed to Bell Wharf, Dowgate, my brother-in-law Mr Thompson clerk to Mr Young will take due care to forward them to me for Joseph Birkbeck who thanks you for your kind advice about the furs, snuff box and watch which he will be glad to take in the way you mention. I presume it would be best to send them by the coach to Darlington, directed to me, to be left at the Post House there, and I can get them from that place any day I chose.

I have no doubt of your readiness to expedite matters as much as possible and I shall be happy to assist you in any way I possibly can, either by attending upon you in Town, or doing any other service I can perform. Mr Joseph Birkbeck is in a very precarious state of health, and I ardently wish to see the business wound up during his life time, for many good reasons. I do not make the above observations either to imply the least censure upon your conduct or to convey a wish to hurry you in the midst of more important business ...

51

[Thomas Peacock to Robert Slade]
Denton 30th March 1791

I am extremely sorry to give you additional trouble about the Birkbeck affairs, but I hope you will forgive my requesting you to inform me whether you think it will be necessary for me to come up to Town about that business and if so, when it would suit you that I should wait upon you. I by no means think myself a competent judge, but I am apprehensive that our voluminous transactions will require a personal interview to arrange them perfectly. I before told you and now repeat that I wish to suit your convenience in every way, as the whole of your conduct has satisfied me that you will not allow unnecessary delay in the way of an ultimate conclusion a matter I most sincerely wish to see accomplished. The reason of my giving you this trouble is that knowing your sentiments on the above articles I may be able to be properly prepared to take every necessary step to accommodate you and serve that family ...

52

[Robert Slade to Thomas Peacock]
Doctors Commons 5th April 1791

Thomas Birkbeck and his nephew Thomas, son of Esther who is as I understand lately come to London are now in my office and are looking over the case of books etc. which I have received from Nice and I have likewise shown them the two pictures of Mr and Mrs Birkbeck, the watch, snuff box and pieces of coin, all of which, particularly the pictures they have examined with great pleasure, which makes me rather satisfied at their not having been sent off before. I have procured a case to be made for the pictures which are very carefully secured and with the watch, seal, snuff box and coins, as likewise the furs, will be delivered on Post Day at the White Horse Inn in Cripplegate in order to be forwarded by the waggon which sets out on Friday to your address in Darlington. This method, I find on enquiring of your brother in law is cheaper than sending the case by sea, and much safer. The note of Mssrs Jeffries and Jones for the diamonds £81.18 became due on Saturday last and has been received by my bankers.

I shall endeavour to make up the account as far as I have hitherto received remittances, and send it to you before the case will come to your hands. It does not appear to me at present that there is any necessity for you to trouble yourself to come to town. Should I at any time conceive such a journey necessary I will apprize you of it. Thomas Birkbeck and his nephew having each expressed a desire to have one of the pieces as a keepsake I have delivered them each one, the whole of them having been valued by Messrs Jeffries and Jones at £1.1.0. I thought it would be more satisfactory to the parties not to have them sold. I think it will be best to have the prints and other things of small value divided. The books consisting chiefly of the edition of Voltaire's works I mean to get appraised and sold. Hoping to hear from you when the case is come to hand ...

April 5th 1791
Mr Joseph Birkbeck dr to the estate of Mrs Birkbeck

To 2 pictures in gilt frames of Mr Birkbeck £2.2.0.
to a silver repeating watch £3.3.0.
to a seal set in gold £1.1.0.
to a blood stone jasper snuff box set in gold £3.18.0.
to furs, tippets and cloak trimmings £1.1.0.
to 19 pieces of silver and metal coins 16.3.
                    Total £12.1.3.

53

[Robert Slade to Thomas Peacock]
Doctors Commons 26th April 1791

I wrote to you on the 5th inst noticing my having forwarded a case containing the portraits of Mr and Mrs Birkbeck, the snuff box, furs etc. and trust that it has ere this, with its contents, come safe to the hands of Mr Joseph Birkbeck. I have employed a considerable part of the present week in looking into and settling the accounts relative to my executorship and which the Easter holidays have very fortunately afforded me licence to inspect, without being subject to the interruptions usually occurring at other times.

The total amount of my receipts is £2762.17.5. The payments £77.5.6. The proportion due to Joseph Birkbeck is as follows: first a specific legacy of the money remaining in the hands of Messrs Gosling the bankers and which they had invested in the short annuities £715.5.5. Secondly a further specific legacy of the money in the hands of Messrs Le Clerc and Co. estimated in the will at £1200, and one third of the residues amounting to £256.15.6. or thereabouts. I have already advanced as follows: viz to Joseph Birkbeck £1365.5.5. to Beaker Birkbeck £100 and to Thomas Birkbeck £195.

Mr Green observes that Mr Wilkie of Marseilles still persists in making a claim for the diamond buckles which have been sold and with the produce of which I have charged myself in the account. He likewise informs me that the sum of 3805 Piedmontese livres appears by the books of the late Mr Birkbeck to be due to the owners of the ship St Antonio, and for this sum I am personally responsible, having given an undertaking in the Admiralty Court here to that effect at the time she was condemned as prize – Messrs Barr and Morillo of Mahon claim 5000 P. livres and upwards are due to them and contest a sequester made by Mr Collet of Leghorn on said sum.

Mr Green further informs me that the inventory estimate and auction of the deceased's property making in its original form 240 small folio pages has been attended with infinite trouble – a copy written close on 42 sheets of paper has, it seems been delivered by Mr Green to the care of a gentleman of the name of Leckie who was coming to England and promised to have it at the Banking House of Sir Robert Harris in St James's St where I have applied but without any tidings of it. Mr Green has amongst other papers sent me a bill dated 31 March 1777 and drawn by Sr Hesilrige on Stavely and Turner for £100. It is endorsed by George Baldwin from whom Mr Birkbeck probably received it but as it was returned protested and found among some old papers there is every reason to suppose that Mr Birkbeck had not advanced any money upon it, or if he did, that he considered it as a bad debt and that no benefit will ever arise from it to his estate. Finding however on enquiry that Mr Baldwin is now

His Majesty's Consul at Grand Cairo I have written to him on the subject and shall hope to receive his answer.

Mr Green as I have already informed you expects a handsome compliment for the trouble he has had in managing the deceased's affairs, but he has not hitherto given any intimation as to the sum. I will therefore venture to do it for him, and being now concerned in three other executorships all of them less troublesome than that of Mrs Birkbeck, I will tell you what has been done in them, and then make a proposal for the consideration of Mr Joseph Birkbeck out of whose share the gratuity to Mr Green and myself ought to come, seeing that he inherits upwards of £1700 more than the other legatees. In the first of the three executorships the testator has given me £100 and his children have just now, on my winding up the concerns, requested my acceptance of a piece of plate value 30gns as a testimony of their approbation of my conduct. In the second the testator has given me a £100 legacy and his affairs will all be settled within the twelvemonth, and in the third the testator has bequeathed me a legacy of £50. There are two other executors in this last trust, and the deceased's property being all in the Funds, the interest is received half-yearly by one of my co-executors and I have no trouble in it. I propose therefore that Mr Green and myself should be complimented with £50 each and should Mr Green be of opinion that more ought to have been done for him Mr Joseph Birkbeck will probably have no objection to send him a piece of plate as a further token of his gratitude. It is certain that he and the family owe the whole of their good fortune to Mr Green by his getting Mrs Birkbeck to make the will and secondly by his faithful management of the estate. Be pleased to submit this proposal to Mr Joseph Birkbeck and if he approves of it and will give an order to that effect, directing so much to be deducted from his share, I will immediately accept his draft for £550 and that of Beaker for £150, and pay Thomas £50 which will leave only a few pounds in my hands to answer further contingencies.

I will also prepare a receipt to be signed by the parties on proper stamps viz that for Joseph's signature on a £22 stamp that for Beaker on a £4 stamp all of which you will readily conceive must be deducted from their particular shares. I will also cause a proper release and indemnification to be prepared, as well against latent debts, and the claims before mentioned, as against the indemnification given by myself in the Admiralty Court. Mr Green tells me that he has still a demand on Le Clerc and Co. which he thinks may produce from 300–600 Piedmontese livres worth about 9d each. I shall await your answer ...

P.S. 29 April. Since writing the foregoing your letter of the 25th inst. acknowledging receipt of the coins came to hand.

54

[Robert Slade to Thomas Peacock]
Doctors Commons 10 Aug[ust] 1791

I have taken the first opportunity of the vacation to make a copy of the account of my executorship especially to your request and you receive the same enclosed, together with a discharge and a £22 stamp, to be signed by Mr Joseph Birkbeck. You will likewise, after he has perused the account get him to sign the same in the presence of a witness and afterwards return it to me, keeping a copy if he sees fit. I likewise send an Indemnification to be signed by Mr Birkbeck and yourself as his security, agreeably to what has heretofore passed between us. All this is done upon a presumption that the account is right. If otherwise I shall be ready to rectify it.

The works of Voltaire in French, 69 volumes, still remain in hand, having applied to several booksellers without finding a purchaser. It seems that most of the persons who mean to have the work are already provided with it. The only offer I have had made is from a M. de Boffe a foreign bookseller who says he will give me three shillings a volume. He assures me that he shall be under great difficulty in getting volumes unbound finished so as to match those that are bound, and he observes that the foreign binder has injured the work by cutting too much off the edges. I mean to apply to my private friends and try to get four shillings a volume and, not succeeding in this, I will take them at 3/6 myself, unless you can meet with some person in your part of the kingdom that will give a better price. It is the last edition large octavo printed in Germany. The other books shall be divided into three parts and two of them sent to you for Joseph and Beaker Birkbeck. The remaining third shall be delivered in Town to Thomas Birkbeck ...

55

[Thomas Peacock to Robert Slade]
Denton 18 Aug[ust] 1791

Inclosed you will receive Joseph Birkbeck's receipts, your account, and the bond of indemnity all duly executed. It would have given the parties much satisfaction to have seen the Account Mr Green mentions, or an account of his receipts and payments up to this time. This matter I by no means desire for my own satisfaction; I can perfectly rely on both Mr Green and you, and the whole tenor of your conduct in the business has convinced me that you have uniformly regarded the benefit of the family you undertook to serve. But old people are suspicious of ill designs and evil disposed persons are not wanting to fan the fires of discontent when there is not so much the shadow of a cause for it. However, I felt so unwilling to increase what has already been too much trouble to you both that I have prevailed on my friends to rest satisfied that everything has been done in the best manner possible both by Mr Green and you.

Should any accounts respecting the business come to your hands at a later date, I rely on you sending them to me as I also do on your completing the accounts with respect to the balance on hand or any other sum that may be received at a proper time. The volumes of Voltaire's works you mentioned would not sell here, and, besides, I think you offer a fair price for them. When convenient you may send the other books etc to this place ...

56

[Robert Slade to Thomas Peacock]
Doctors Commons 2nd Nov[ember] 1791

I am just returned to town from the West Riding of Yorkshire where I have been to spend the vacation with my friends. Your letters of the 20th Sept and 29th are both laid before me and I will shortly answer them to your satisfaction as far as I can again look into the accounts. I do not find any directions in regard to that part of my letter which related to the sale of Voltaire's works, nor do I find the discharge of indemnity. If these matters have been attended to, the letter is not before me, and should you have given no direction, or sent the discharge, please to write me thereon ...

57

[Robert Slade to Thomas Peacock]
Doctors Commons 3rd Nov[ember] 1791

I wrote you in haste yesterday in the absence of my principal clerk who had put your letter of 19 August into the bundle of papers relative to the Birkbeck Trust, instead of leaving it on the file of letters unanswered. It appears by that letter that you have given the necessary directions in regard to Voltaire's works and sent the release of indemnification. I write this to prevent you the trouble of sending an answer and hope to be able to forward you the account in the course of next week ...

P.S. I am much surprised to find that our old friends can suffer any suspicions to be created in their minds by any evil disposed persons. If however their counsellors will point out anything in which they think the laws can give further satisfaction, it shall be complied with. I know that the relatives of the late testatrix owe everything to the friendship of my co-executor and I flatter myself that they owe thanks rather than suspicions to our joint exertions and integrity.

58

[Robert Slade to Thomas Peacock]
Doctors Commons 18 Feb[ruary] 1792

Having received no answer from Mr Green to my letter, I am still at an uncertainty whether there will, or not, be any further claims on him or myself on account of our executorship, and as the small balance in my hands was left for the purpose of answering contingencies, I could have wished it had been suffered to remain till I had heard from Mr Green; but as you say that Mr Joseph Birkbeck wishes to be accommodated with an hundred pounds in part of said balance, I am ready to oblige him with that sum if he thinks proper to draw upon me as heretofore. If I have not looked further into the accounts it has been for want of time, the business of the term which does not end until the first of next month, occupying the whole of my attention. I will write again to Mr Green by Tuesday's mail, and in case he has no objection the accounts shall be finally made up in the course of next vacation ...

59

[Robert Slade to Thomas Peacock]
Doctors Commons 15th June 1792

I delayed answering your last letter in hopes of receiving an answer from Mr Green which is at length come, as you will perceive by the extract on the other side which explains the footing upon which he means to put the payment to be made to him. I shall therefore account to him for the fifty pounds charged as paid to him in part of the commission he claims a right to receive. I send you enclosed an account to be signed by Beaker Birkbeck and shall be ready on the return of it, witnessed by yourself and some other person to accept his draft for £7.3.0. the balance. I have delivered a share of the prints etc. to his son Thomas and have had Joseph's share packed up to be sent to him. You perceive therefore that there is nothing now remaining in my hands of the deceased's estate, save about thirty pounds due to Joseph Birkbeck which must wait the further advices of Mr Green as his demand may exceed it. Under these circumstances there can not be any occasion for you to come to town on this business. If called to town for other purposes I shall be glad to see you. It seems I have paid too high for Voltaire's works, but the parties are welcome to it ...

[Enclosed – extract from a letter from Mr N Green dated Nice 30 May 1792]

"Thus my dear sir your letter being at first laid aside, which I confess it ought not to have been, it is no great wonder that it was afterwards in a manner forgotten as indeed was all correspondence but that of the day or the current time. I am greatly obliged to you for your kind care about securing a gratuity for me but there is no need to make any reserve for any thing of that sort. I once before wrote on the same subject that I expect to be paid for my trouble by some way and therefore I shall charge commission for the goods sold by auction and commission on all monies remitted which altogether will amount to more than £50. I am only sorry that I cannot yet completely close the accounts which I much wish to do as well as you and the heirs. I have at length terminated the dispute on the sequester of Collet of Genoa on the money of Barr and Morillo of Mahon and have paid it off. There now remains the other claim for the sale of another prize and the claimant is in Spain or Gibralter all the concerned are captious and litigious but I shall now enter into a conference and correspondence on the subject and if I cannot obtain the security of indemnification to full satisfaction I shall obtain a judicial discharge and deposit the money and then send you the general account and balance which may yet amount to £150 for I ought yet to receive somewhat more from Le Clerc and Co. which they would dispute at law and I would settle by arbitration. I desired Mr Wilkie of Marseilles to advise the heirs of Mr Shaw of my having sent you the diamond buckles and I suppose he has but I hear of no claim however it is necessary to clear up that account. The vols of Voltaire were bound before I saw them. I could not get half-a-crown a vol. for the whole so there can be no great loss of sending them home ..."

Translated from the Italian

Will of Mrs Eliza Maria Jones Widow Birkbeck

In the name of our Lord Jesus Christ Amen; the year after his nativity one thousand seven hundred and eighty eight in the nineteenth of the month of January in the afternoon at Nice know all men by this present Public Instrument; that appeared personally in the presence of us Royal Notary and of the undersigned witnesses Mrs Eliza Maria Jones daughter of the late Mr Ries, born at Kivendrabeck[7] in England, widow of Mr John Birkbeck British Consul for these many years past an inhabitant of this city who being now sound in all her senses and faculties of the soul, although detained in bed by bodily infirmity has resolved to dispose of her property and future estate in the following manner. The said Lady Testatrix bequeaths nothing to the Hospital of Charity in this city nor to that of Saint Maurice and Lazarus in the capital city of Tur[i]n altho' interrogated by me and persuaded so to do by me the undernamed Royal Notary in the

---

7 This English place name obviously defeated the notary and/or the translator. It has not been possible to trace Mrs Birkbeck's place of birth.

presence of the witnesses also undersigned. The said Testatrix Mrs Eliza Maria Jones Widow Birkbeck appoints for Testamentary Executors to the end that they may cause to be punctually fulfilled what shall be devised in this her will and realize the funds belonging to her the said Lady Testatrix Messrs <u>Robert Slade</u>, Doctor of Civil Law in the City of London and <u>Nathaniel Green</u> Consul in this city for his Britannic Majesty confirming in the same both jointly and severally all requisite power and authority for the performance of the above.

The said Lady Testatrix bequeaths to the younger brother of her deceased husband, Mr John Birkbeck, who is lame of one leg and has a large family whom the said Lady Testatrix believes to be <u>named Joseph</u> resident in the County of Durham, in England, the sum in ready money belonging to the said Lady Testatrix now in the hands of Messrs <u>Locker</u>[8] and company amounting to <u>Twelve hundred pounds</u> sterling as also <u>that other sum</u> in like manner the property of the said Lady Testatrix now in the hands of <u>Messrs Gosling and Co</u> bankers in London or which by order of the said Lady Testatrix may have laid out and vested in the Public Funds of the said City of London or of England.

The said Lady Testatrix does further bequeath to the most illustrious Senator and Prefect of this City and Province Mr John Anthony Bottini the harpsichord or spinet together with all the music books that she has in her present dwelling and which shall be found in the same after her death. The said Lady Testatrix does likewise bequeath to Baron Le Clerc twenty Louis dors of France in specie of the last coinage, as also twenty similar Louis dors to Mr Molins of the city of Marseilles, and finally the said Lady Testatrix Widow Birkbeck bequeaths to Mr Gabriel Isaac Veillon, Danish Consul in this City all the goods, and large wooden furniture her property which shall be found after her decease in the dwelling house of the said Lady Testatrix or elsewhere and all this as an acknowledgement for the good offices and affection which the said gentleman legatees have respectively done and shewn to her the said Lady Testatrix.

The sums and effects bequeathed as above to the four legatees above mentioned to be to them respectively paid and delivered immediately after the demise of the said Lady Testatrix by the

---

8   For "Locker" read "Le Clerc".

aforementioned British Consul <u>Mr Nathaniel Green</u>, and one of the aforesaid testamentary executors.

Lastly as to all her other <u>goods and chattels</u>, rights, demands, pretensions and debts owing to her, wheresoever they may be found in the hands of whatsoever persons she the said Lady Testatrix Mrs Eliza Maria Jones Widow Birkbeck hath appointed and with her own mouth named her general and special Heirs, the <u>Elder Brother of the said Mr Birkbeck</u> her late husband whose name the said Lady Testatrix does not know, as also the aforesaid <u>Mr Joseph his younger Brother</u> and <u>their respective children</u> begotten in lawful wedlock <u>all for equal parts and shares</u> and so in <u>Capite</u> and not in <u>Stirpe</u> the said Lady Testatrix now declaring to recollect that the name of the said elder brother of the said deceased Mr Birkbeck, coheir as above mentioned is <u>Beker</u>.

And this the said Lady Testatrix desires may be her last will and final disposition which she wishes may avail by way of testament and not being valid as such that it may avail by way of Codicil Donation in case of death was any other act of last will whatsoever by which it may of right be most valid, the said Lady Testatrix requiring me the Royal Notary undersigned to receive and pass this present act of her last will and the undersigned witnesses to be witnesses of the truth thereof all being known to her, the said testatrix and they knowing her, which I have done and passed read and published in the place as above mentioned in the presence of Messrs David Altari son of the late Mr James of the City of Nimes, John James Vial son of the late Mr Peter of the City of Geneva, Frances Vierne son of another Mr Francis late of the said City of Nimes, John Gabriel Ruchels, son of Mr Peter of the City of Bex in Switzerland, David Vierne son of the aforesaid Mr Francis of the City of Nimes deceased, John Wolfgang Du Moulin, son of the late Mr John Anthony of Switzerland and Mr John Bodington son of the late Mr George of the City of London in England, and all now resident here, witnesses required present and subscribed which the said Lady Testatrix has not done as not being able to subscribe in any manner nor even to sign with a mark through excessive illness according as she has declared in presence as aforementioned.

Three livres are due for the registering. The said Lady Testatrix declared that a note of the present act has been to her delivered by the undersigned Royal Notary pursuant to the regulation of the chamber. Having all the witnesses aforesaid assisted at the publication of this present will with one candle in hand, whereby the said room is sufficiently illumined it being seven o'clock in the afternoon according to the French computation of time and this a late hour. John Bodington witness. D.Alary witness. Francis Vierne witness. David Vierne witness. J.W. Du Moulin witness and I Joseph Rossetti Royal Notary as appears in the original minute.

The above written instrument received by me Joseph Rossetti Royal Notary by Perpetual Grant of the 17th May 1774 I have extracted from its original, with which having been collated it agrees registered the first of January 1788 in the first book of Nice fol. 323 as per the receipt of the Registrar Mr Carlo Galli in testimony whereof I have manually and notarially subscribed Nice the 7th of February 1780.

(*signed*) Joseph Rossetti, Royal Notary.

[*Then follows in English*]
We Nathaniel Green his Britannic Majesty's Consul at Nice and its dependencies do hereby certify that the Sieur Guiseppi Rossetti is a Notary Publick duly authorized and appointed in this City and that the above is his usual form and signature courts and thereout. In witness whereof we hereunto set our hand and seal of office, at Nice, the eleventh day of February, one thousand seven hundred and eighty eight.

[*seal*]   [*signed*] Nathl. Green
Faithfully translated from the Italian original hereunto annexed and with the same carefully collated, London the 3rd of March 1788,
which I attest
T Vernet, Not.Pub.

Index of Persons and Places

45, 51, 55, 57, 59–63, 65, 67–71, 81, 84, 86, 94; Old Hall 1, 13
Oxford university 5, 37

Page, Hannah, mother of Harry and Martha 56–7; Harry 54, 57–9; Jacky, bastard son of Martha 57; Martha 57
Paris 141, 171, 199, 205
Parker, Nathan, sexton at Denton 160
Parrington, Mr. 188
Peacham, H., author of *Compleat Gentleman*, 30
Peacock, Revd Thomas [TP], James Raine's father-in-law, Margaret Hunt's grandfather 121–2, 127–8, 130–4, 138–42, 150–1, 155, 158- 9, 161, 163, 171–218; Anne, née Hodgson, of Denton, TP's first wife 129, 171; George, TP's brother 127; George, TP's son 122, 129, 131–4, 151, 171; Hannah, TP's daughter 127, 131–2, 134, 137, 140, 145, 150, 155, 158–9, 162; Jane, née Thompson, of Houghton- le-Side, TP's second wife 127, 129–32, 138, 142, 150, 155, 159- 60, 163, 171, 191; John, TP's father 127; John, TP's son 129, 140; Madge, TP's grand-daughter 126–7, 131, 134, 137, 141–2, 145, 158–9, 162; Margaret, TP's daughter, wife of James Raine, see Raine; Mary, TP's daughter, see Fogg; Robert, TP's son 140–1; Thomas, TP's son 129–30, 141, 151, his daugher Marianne 151; William, TP's son 129, 141, his daughters Annie and Mary 141
Peat & Son, of Thirsk 42n.
Pennington (Lancs.) 68
Penson, Peter, minor canon of Durham 96
Percy, Thomas, editor of *Reliques* 41
Petrie, Henry, editor of *History of Britain* 115, 118, 120
Phillpotts, Henry, canon of Durham, bishop of Exeter 86, 88, 94- 5, his wife 85
Piercebridge (Map no. 41) 34, 40
Piper-well-syke (between Winston and Caldwell) 19
Pittington (Map no. 12) 70–1, 92, 96
Pocock, Elizabeth 199; Rebecca 199; Pocock & Co., see Baillie, Pocock & Co.
Powell, schoolmaster at Hutton 41

Raby castle 1, 19, 55, 65, 73, 106
Radcliffe family, of Dilston 62
Radcliffe, Mrs Ann, novelist 157, 159, 164
Radclyffe, Mrs 112
Raine, James (1791–1858) [JR], 1–124, 126–7, 131, 133, 141–5, 147–9, 157, 158–9, 163, 167–9, 171; Anne, née Moore, JR's mother 1, 3, 28–9, 31–2, 34, 53; Annie, JR's daughter 134, 144, 146, 157; Anthony, JR's brother 64; Edmund, JR's grandfather 1, 10–1, 28, 56; Edward, JR's great-grandfather 10; James (1760–1839), JR's father 1, 10–1, 14, 26, 28–31, 34, 38, 49; James (1830–96), JR's son 3, 6, 77–81, 123, 134, 146–7, 157, 165–6; Jane, JR's daughter 133–4, 145–7, 165–6; John, JR's brother 26, 119, 131, 144; Margaret, née Williamson, JR's grandmother 10–1, 13–6, 54; Margaret, née Peacock, JR's wife 4, 122–4, 126–7, 130–1, 144–8, 163, 165–6, 168, 171; Margaret, JR's daughter, see Hunt; Margaret, JR's aunt, "Girlington Peggy", later Sayer, 11–3, her step-daughter Ruth, see Brown; Mary, JR's aunt 11–3, ? 29; William, JR's uncle 11, ? 29; William, JR's brother 17, 42, 45, 48, 144. For other members of JR's family, see Allison, Dixon, Harwood, Hunt, Moore, Peacock, Thompson
Raine, of Forcett, James, 48; his sons James and William 48
Raine, of Hartforth, Matthew 36; his sons Jonathan and Dr Matthew 36
Ramsay, Allan, poet 23 and n.17, 24 n.18, 33n.
Ramshaw (Map no. 22) 53
Randall, Mr. 12
Ravensworth (Map no. 60) 35, 68, 75
Reed, Willy 8, 11, 84–7, 93
Remington (Northumb.) 56
Richardson, Samuel, novelist 158
Richmond (Map no. 56) 26, 28, 34, 39, 44, 69, 98, 111; archdeaconry 75; court 27; King's Head inn 111 n.75; market 1; St Martin's priory 19 n.11; school 1, 17, 51, 78; town-chest 98
Richmondshire 35, 98
Rickman, Thomas, architect 83
Ripon, 111, manuscripts 3
Rivers, Lady 200

MAP

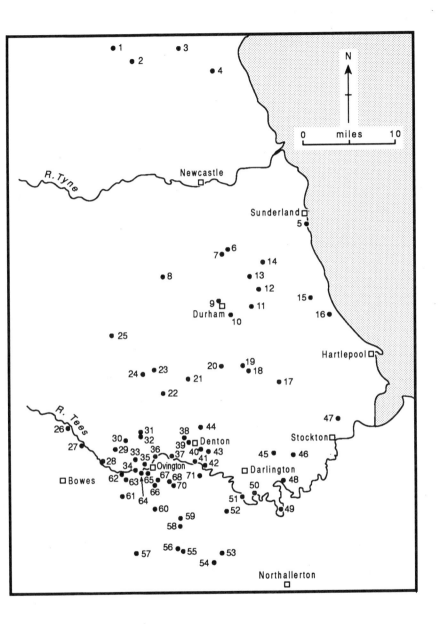

N

0   miles   10

1
2
3
4

R. Tyne

Newcastle

Sunderland
5

6
7
14
8
13
12
9
11
Durham
10
15
16

25

Hartlepool

24 23 20 19 18
21 22 17

R. Tees

47

26 31 38 44 Stockton
30 32 39 40 Denton
27 33 36 37 41 43
29 35   42
28 34 65 67 68 71 Darlington 45 46
Bowes 62 63 66 70 48
  61 64 50 51 49 52
  60 59
  58
  57 56 55 53
  54

Northallerton

SURTEES SOCIETY
Established in the year 1834
In honour of the late Robert Surtees of Mainsforth, Esquire, the author of *The History of the County Palatine of Durham*, and in accordance with his pursuits and plans.

RULES OF THE SOCIETY
Agreed upon in 1849; revised 1863, 1925, 1954, 1967 and 1991

1. The Society shall be called the SURTEES SOCIETY (hereinafter referred to as the Society).

2. The object of the Society shall be the advancement of public education in the region that constituted the ancient kingdom of Northumbria, especially by the transcription, editing, translating and publication of original historical documents. The word 'region' as defined covers those parts of England and Scotland between the Humber and the Firth of Forth on the east, and between the Mersey and the Clyde on the west.

3. Members of the Society shall be persons or institutions, who are either members of the Council of the Society, or who have been elected to the Society at a meeting of the Council following written application to the Secretary, and whose subscriptions are not in arrears.

4. The rate of the annual subscription shall be determined from time to time by the Council of the Society and shall be payable in advance on the 1st day of January in every year.

5. The management of the affairs of the Society shall be vested in a Council consisting of the president, treasurer, secretary, and a number of at least seven and not exceeding twenty-four vice-presidents to be nominated by the Council for election at the general meeting. Vacancies occurring between general meetings may be filled by the Council until the next general meeting. Meetings of the Council shall be convened by the Secretary as needed, or on a requisition to do so signed by at least four members of the Council. A quorum for the conduct of business to require at least one-third of the members of the Council to be present.

6. Each subscribing member shall be entitled to one copy of every work published by the Society following that member's

election to membership. Any work published prior to a member's election may be supplied to that member on such terms as the Council may from time to time determine.

7. Persons and institutions that are not members of the Society may be supplied with the publications of the Society on such terms as the Council may determine.

8. The funds of the Society, including the vouchers or securities for any investments, shall be kept at a Bank to be selected by the Council in the name of the Society. Such investments shall only be dealt with by an authority signed by the Secretary and by the Treasurer.

9. The accounts of the receipts and expenditures of the Society, and of its assets and liabilities, for each period of twelve months ended 30th September shall be audited by an Auditor or Auditors to be appointed by the Society.

10. An annual general meeting of the members shall be held in Durham on the second Thursday in December, to receive the Council's report; to receive the Treasurer's financial statement and to elect an auditor or auditors; to elect any persons nominated by the Council as either president, treasurer, secretary or vice-president; and to transact the general business of the Society, but leaving for final decision by the Council the form, content and number of copies of each publication to be printed and the selection of a printer. Members shall be informed of the time and place of the general meeting on application to the Secretary.

11. The editor of each publication shall be entitled to receive five copies of that publication without payment.

12. The Secretary shall keep a minute-book wherein shall be recorded the transactions as well at meetings of the Council as at general meetings of the Society.

13. The rules shall only be amended at a General Meeting called for that purpose giving at least 21 days notice of the proposed amendment. No amendment shall be made to the constitution that would cause the Society to cease to be a Charity at Law. Any amendment to the constitution must receive the assent of not less than two-thirds of those present and voting. Any amendment to Clause 2 or Clause 14 or this Clause shall require the prior approval

of the Charity Commissioners for England and Wales.

14. The Society may be dissolved by a resolution passed by a two-thirds majority of those present and voting at a General Meeting. In the event of dissolution any property remaining after the satisfaction of all debts and liabilities shall be given or transferred to such other charitable institution or institutions having objects similar to the objects of this Society as the Charity Commissioners or other authority having charitable jurisdiction may determine.

Volumes still available are marked *; they may be ordered from the Secretary of the Society. It should be noted that volumes 2, 32, 38, 112 and 142 are reprints bound in a somewhat different style from the original.

1. *Reginaldi monachi Dunelmensis libellus de admirandis beati Cuthberti virtutibus.* Ed. J. Raine.

*2. Wills and inventories of the northern counties of England, from the eleventh century downwards. (Chiefly from the Registry of Durham). Vol. i. Ed. J. Raine. See 38, 112, 142.

3. Towneley mysteries. Ed. J. Gordon. Pref. J. Hunter.

4. *Testamenta Eboracensia;* or wills registered at York ... from the year 1300 downwards. Vol. i. Ed. J. Raine. See 30, 45, 53, 79, 106.

5. *Sanctuarium Dunelmense et sanctuarium Beverlacense.* Ed. J. Raine. Pref. T. Chevallier.

6. Priory of Finchale. The charters of endowment, inventories, and account rolls. Ed. J. Raine.

7. *Catalogi veteres librorum ecclesiae Dunelm.* Catalogues of the library of Durham cathedral ... of the abbey of Hulne and of the mss. preserved in the library of Bishop Cosin at Durham. Ed. B. Botfield.

8. *Miscellanea biographica: Oswinus, rex Northumbriae; Cuthbertus, episcopus Lindisfarnensis; Eata, episcopus Haugustaldensis.* Pref. J. Raine.

9. *Historiae Dunelmensis scriptores tres: Gaufridus de Coldingham, Robertus de Graystanes, et Willielmus de Chambre.* Ed. J. Raine.

10. *Rituale ecclesiae Dunelmensis.* Ed. J. Stevenson. See 140.

11. Chronicle of the war between the English and the Scots in 1173 and 1174, by Jordon Fantosme. Ed. & trans. F. Michel.

12. Priory of Coldingham. The correspondence, inventories, account rolls, and law proceedings. Ed. J. Raine.

13. *Liber vitae ecclesiae Dunelmensis; necnon obituaria duo ejusdem ecclesiae.* Ed. J. Stevenson. See 136.

14. Correspondence of Robert Bowes, of Aske, esquire, the ambassador of Queen Elizabeth in the court of Scotland. Ed. J. Stevenson.

15. Description or breife declaration of all the ancient monuments, rites, and customes belonginge or beinge within the monastical church of Durham before the suppression; written in 1593. Ed. J. Raine. Cf. 107.

16.   Anglo-Saxon and early English psalter ... from manuscripts in the British Museum. Vol. i. Ed. J. Stevenson. See 19.

17.   Correspondence of Dr. Matthew Hutton, archbishop of York; with a selection from the letters, etc., of Sir Timothy Hutton, knt., his son, and Matthew Hutton, esq., his grandson. Ed. J. Raine.

18.   Durham household book; or, the accounts of the bursar of the monastery of Durham from Pentecost 1530 to Pentecost 1534. Ed. J. Raine.

19.   Anglo-Saxon and early English psalter. Vol. ii. See 16.

20.   *Libellus de vita et miraculis S. Godrici, heremitae de Finchale, auctore Reginaldo monacho Dunelmensi.* Ed. J. Stevenson.

21.   Depositions and other ecclesiastical proceedings from the courts of Durham, ... 1311 to the reign of Elizabeth. Ed. J. Raine.

22.   Injunctions and other ecclesiastical proceedings of Richard Barnes, bishop of Durham, from 1575 to 1587. Ed. J. Raine.

23.   Latin hymns of the Anglo-Saxon church, with an inter-linear Anglo-Saxon gloss. Ed. J. Stevenson.

24.   A memoir of Robert Surtees, esq., F. S. A., author of the *History of the county palatine of Durham*, by George Taylor. A new edition, with additions, by J. Raine.

25.   Boldon buke: a survey of the possessions of the see of Durham, ... 1183. Ed. W. Greenwell.

26.   Wills and inventories from the registry of the archdeaconry of Richmond. Ed. J. Raine, jun.

27.   Pontifical of Egbert, archbishop of York, A.D. 732–766. Ed. W. Greenwell.

28.   Lindisfarne and Rushworth gospels. [Vol. i: Matthew]. Ed. J. Stevenson. See 39, 43, 48

29.   Inventories and account rolls of the Benedictine houses or cells of Jarrow and Monk-Wearmouth. Ed. J. Raine.

30.   *Testamenta Eboracensia*: a selection of wills from the registry at York. Vol. ii. Ed. J. Raine. See 4, 45, 53, 79, 106.

31.   Obituary roll of William Ebchester and John Burnby, priors of Durham, with notices of similar records preserved at Durham, from the year 1233 downwards, letters of fraternity, etc. Ed. J. Raine.

*32.   Bishop Hatfield's survey ... of the possessions of the see of Durham. Ed. W. Greenwell.

33. Rural economy in Yorkshire in 1641; being the farming and account books of Henry Best, of Elmswell, in the East Riding. Ed. C. B. Robinson *al.* Norcliffe.
34. Acts of the high commission court within the diocese of Durham. Ed. W. H. D. Longstaffe.
35. Fabric rolls of York minster. Ed. J. Raine.
36. Visitation of the county of Yorke, ... 1665 – 1666, by William Dugdale. Ed. R. Davies.
37. *Miscellanea* [Vol. i]: Letters of Dean Granville; Account of the siege of Pontefract by Nathan Drake; Rokeby correspondence. Ed. G. Ornsby; W. H. D. Longstaffe; J. Raine. See 47.
*38. Wills and inventories from the registry at Durham. Vol. ii. Ed. W. Greenwell. See 2, 112, 142.
39. Lindisfarne and Rushworth gospels. [Vol. ii: Mark]. Ed. G. Waring. See 28, 43, 48.
40. Depositions from the castle of York, relating to offences committed in the northern counties in the seventeenth century. Ed. J. Raine.
41. Heraldic visitation of the northern counties in 1530, by Thomas Tonge. Ed. W. H. D. Longstaffe.
42. Memorials of the abbey of St. Mary of Fountains. Vol. i. Ed. J. R. Walbran. See 67, 130.
43. Lindisfarne and Rushworth gospels. [Vol. iii: Luke]. Ed. G. Waring. See 28, 39, 48.
44. Priory of Hexham. Vol. i: its chroniclers, endowments, and annals. Ed. J. Raine. See 46.
45. *Testamenta Eboracensia*: a selection of wills from the registry at York. Vol. iii. Ed. J. Raine. See 4, 30, 53, 79, 106.
46. Priory of Hexham. Vol. ii: its title deeds, black book, etc. See 44.
47. Remains of Denis Granville, D. D., dean and archdeacon of Durham. Vol. ii. Ed. G. Ornsby. See 37.
48. Lindisfarne and Rushworth Gospels. [Vol. iv: John]. Ed. G. Waring. See 28, 39, 43.
49. Survey of the county of York, taken by John de Kirkby. Ed. R. H. Skaife.
50. Memoirs of the life of Mr. Ambrose Barnes, late merchant and sometimes alderman of Newcastle upon Tyne. Ed. W. H. D. Longstaffe.
51. *Symeonis Dunelmensis opera et collectanea.* Vol. i. Ed. J. H. Hinde.

52.   Correspondence of John Cosin, D. D., lord bishop of Durham. Vol. i. Ed. G. Ornsby. See 55.

53.   *Testamenta Eboracensia*: a selection of wills from the registry at York. Vol. iv. Ed. J. Raine. See 4, 30, 45, 79, 106.

54.   Diary of Abraham de la Pryme, the Yorkshire antiquary. Ed. C. Jackson.

55.   Correspondence of John Cosin ... Vol. ii. See 52.

56.   Register, or rolls, of Walter Gray, lord archbishop of York. Ed. J. Raine.

57.   Register of the guild of Corpus Christi in the city of York; ... account of the hospital of St. Thomas of Canterbury without Micklegate-bar. Ed. R. H. Skaife.

58.   *Feodarium prioratus Dunelmensis*. Ed. W. Greenwell.

59.   *Missale ad usum insignis ecclesiae Eboracensis*. Vol. i. Ed. W. G. Henderson. See 60.

60.   *Missale* ... Vol. ii. See 59.

61.   *Liber pontificalis Chr. Bainbridge archiepiscopi Eboracensis*. Ed. W. G. Henderson.

62.   Autobiography of Mrs. Alice Thornton, of East Newton, co. York. Ed. C. Jackson.

63.   *Manuale et processionale ad usum insignis ecclesiae Eboracensis*. Ed. W. G. Henderson.

64.   Acts of the chapter of the collegiate church of SS. Peter and Wilfrid, Ripon, 1452 – 1506. Ed. J. T. Fowler. Cf. 74, 78, 81, 115.

65.   Yorkshire diaries and autobiographies in the seventeenth and eighteenth centuries. Ed. C. Jackson. See 77.

66.   *Chartularium abbathiae de Novo Monasterio*. Ed. J. T. Fowler.

67.   Memorials of the abbey of St. Mary of Fountains. Vol. ii. Ed. J. R. Walbran & J. Raine. See 42, 130.

68.   Selections from the household books of the Lord William Howard of Naworth Castle. Ed. G. Ornsby.

69.   *Cartularium abbathiae de Whiteby*. Vol. i. Ed. J. C. Atkinson. See 72.

70.   *Dialogi Laurentii Dunelmensis monachi ac prioris*. Ed. J. Raine.

71.   *Breviarum ad usum insignis ecclesiae Eboracensis*. Vol. i. Ed. S. W. Lawley. See 75.

72.   *Cartularium abbathiae de Whiteby*. Vol. ii. See 69.

73.   Family memoirs of the Rev. William Stukeley, M. D., ... correspondence of William Stukeley, Roger and Samuel Gale, etc. Ed. W. C. Lukis. See 76, 80.

74. Memorials of the church of SS. Peter and Wilfrid, Ripon. Vol. i. Ed. J. T. Fowler. See 78, 81, 115; cf. 64.

75. *Breviarum ad usum insignis ecclesiae Eboracensis.* Vol. ii. See 71.

76. Family memoirs of the Rev. William Stukeley ... Vol. ii. See 73, 80.

77. Yorkshire diaries and autobiographies ... Vol. ii. Ed. C. Jackson & S. Margerison. Cf. 65.

78. Memorials of the church of SS. Peter and Wilfrid, Ripon. Vol. ii. See 74, 81, 115; cf. 64.

79. *Testamenta Eboracensia*: a selection of wills from the registry at York. Vol. v. Ed. J. Raine. See 4, 30, 45, 53, 106.

80. Family memoirs of the Rev. William Stukeley ... Vol. iii. See 73, 76.

81. Memorials of the church of SS. Peter and Wilfrid, Ripon. Vol. iii. See 74, 78, 115; cf. 64.

82. *Halmota prioratus Dunelmensis.* Containing extracts ..., 1296–1384. Ed. W. H. Longstaffe and J. Booth.

83. *Cartularium abbathiae de Rievalle.* Ed. J. C. Atkinson.

84. Churchwardens' accounts of Pittington and other parishes in the diocese of Durham, 1580 – 1700. Ed. J. Barmby.

85. A volume of English miscellanies illustrating the history and language of the northern counties of England, [1417–1533]. Ed. J. Raine.

86. *Cartularium prioratus de Gyseburne.* Vol. i. Ed. W. Brown. See 89.

87. Life of St. Cuthbert in English verse, *c.*A.D. 1450. Ed. J. T. Fowler.

88. Three early assize rolls for the county of Northumberland, s. XIII. Ed. W. Page.

89. *Cartularium prioratus de Gyesburne.* Vol. ii. See 86.

90. Chartulary of Brinkburn priory. Ed. W. Page.

91. Certificates of the commissioners appointed to survey the chantries, guilds, hospitals, etc., in the county of York. Vol. i. Ed. W. Page. See 92.

92. Certificates of the commissioners ... Vol. ii. See 91.

93. Extracts from the records of the merchant adventurers of Newcastle-upon-Tyne. Vol. i. Ed. J. R. Boyle & F. W. Dendy. See 101.

94. *Pedes finium Ebor. regnante Johanne.* Ed. W. Brown.

95. Memorials of St. Giles's, Durham, being grassmen's accounts and other parish records, together with documents relating to the hospitals of Kepier and St. Mary Magdalene. Ed. J. Barmby.

96. Register of the freemen of the city of York. Vol. i: 1272–1558. Ed. F. Collins. See 102.

97. Inventories of church goods for the counties of York, Durham, and Northumberland. Ed. W. Page.

98. Memorials of Beverley minster: the chapter act-book, 1286–1347, ... Vol. i. Ed. A. F. Leach. See 108.

99. Extracts from the account rolls of the abbey of Durham. Vol. i. Ed. J. T. Fowler. See 100, 103.

100. Extracts from the account rolls of the abbey of Durham. Vol. ii. See 99, 103.

101. Extracts from the records of the merchant adventurers of Newcastle-upon-Tyne. Vol. ii. Ed. F. W. Dendy. See 93.

102. Register of the freemen of the city of York. Vol. ii: 1559–1769. See 96.

103. Extracts from the account rolls of the abbey of Durham. Vol. iii. See 99, 100.

104. Wills and administrations from the Knaresborough court rolls. Vol. i. Ed. F. Collins. See 110.

105. Extracts from the records of the company of hostmen of Newcastle-upon-Tyne. Ed. F. W. Dendy.

106. *Testamenta Eboracensia*: a selection of wills from the registry at York. Vol. vi. Ed. J. W. Clay. See 4, 30, 45, 53, 79.

*107. Rites of Durham. Ed. J. T. Fowler. Cf. 15.

108. Memorials of Beverley minster. The chapter act-book ... Vol. ii. See 98.

109. Register of Walter Giffard, lord archbishop of York, 1266–1279. Ed. W. Brown.

110. Wills and administrations from the Knaresborough court rolls. Vol. ii, with index to original wills, etc., at Somerset House. See 104.

111. Records of the committees for compounding, etc., with delinquent royalists in Durham and Northumberland, 1643–1660. Ed. R. Welford.

*112. Wills and inventories from the registry at Durham. Vol. iii. Ed. J. C. Hodgson. See 2, 38, 142.

113. Records of the northern convocation. Ed. G. W. Kitchin.

114.   Register of William Wickwane, lord archbishop of York, 1279–1285. Ed. W. Brown.
115.   Memorials of the church of SS. Peter and Wilfrid, Ripon. Vol. iv: Ingilby ms. Ed. J. T. Fowler. See 74, 78, 81; cf. 64.
116.   North country wills ... Vol. i. 1383–1558. Ed. J. W. Clay. See 121.
117.   Percy chartulary. Ed. M. T. Martin.
118.   Six north country diaries. Ed. J. C. Hodgson.
119.   Richard d'Aungerville, of Bury. Fragments of his register, and other documents. Ed. G. W. Kitchin.
120.   York memorandum book. Vol. i: 1376–1419. Ed. M. Sellers. See 125, 186.
121.   North country wills ... Vol. ii: 1558–1604. See 116.
*122. Visitations of the North. Vol. i. Ed. F. W. Dendy. See 133, 144, 146.
123.   Register of John le Romeyn, lord archbishop of York, 1286–1296. Vol. i. Ed. W. Brown. See 128.
*124. North country diaries. Vol. ii. See 118.
125.   York memorandum book. Vol. ii: 1388–1493. See 120, 186.
126.   Register of the priory of St. Bees. Ed. J. Wilson.
127.   *Miscellanea* [Vol. ii]: Two thirteenth-century Durham assize rolls; North country deeds; York visitations, 1407[–1452]. Ed. K. C. Bayley; W. Brown; A. Hamilton Thompson.
*128. Registers of John le Romeyn, archbishop of York (1286–1296), pt. ii; and of Henry of Newark, archbishop of York (1297–1299). Ed. W. Brown. See 123.
129   York mercers and merchant adventurers, 1356–1917. Ed. M. Sellers.
130.   Memorials of the abbey of St. Mary of Fountains. Vol. iii: bursars' books, 1456–1459; memorandum book of Thomas Swynton, 1446–1458. Ed. J. T. Fowler. See 42, 67.
131.   Northumbrian documents ... comprising the register of the estates of Roman Catholics in Northumberland (1717–87); correspondence of Miles Stapylton (d. 1685). Ed. J. C. Hodgson.
132.   *Horae Eboracenses*. Ed. C. Wordsworth.
*133. Visitations of the North. Vol. ii. Ed. F. W. Dendy. See 122, 144, 146.
134.   Percy bailiff's rolls of the fifteenth century. Ed. J. C. Hodgson.
135.   Durham protestations, or the returns made to the House of Commons in 1641–2 for the maintenance of the Protestant religion ... Ed. H. M. Wood.

136. *Liber vitae ecclesiae Dunelmensis.* A collotype facsimile ... Vol. i.
      Ed. A. Hamilton Thompson. See 13.
137. Early deeds relating to Newcastle upon Tyne. Ed. A. M. Oliver.
*138. Register of Thomas Corbridge, archbishop of York (1300–1304).
      Vol. i. Ed. W. Brown. See 141.
139. *Fasti Dunelmenses.* Ed. D. S. Boutflower.
140. *Rituale ecclesiae Dunelmensis.* The Durham collectar. Ed.
      U. Lindelöf, with A. Hamilton Thompson. Cf. 10.
141. Register of Thomas of Corbridge ... Vol. ii. Transcr. W. Brown.
      Ed. A. Hamilton Thompson. See 138.
*142. Wills and inventories from the registry at Durham. Vol. iv. Ed.
      H. M. Wood. See 2, 38, 112.
143. Statutes of the cathedral church of Durham. Ed. A. Hamilton
      Thompson with J. Meade Falkner.
144. Visitations of the north. Vol. iii. Ed. C. H. Hunter Blair. See 122,
      133, 146.
145. Register of William Greenfield, lord archbishop of York,
      1306–15. Vol. i. Transcr. W. Brown. Ed. A. Hamilton Thompson.
      See 149, 151–153.
146. Visitations of the north. iv. Ed. C. H. Hunter Blair. See 122,
      133, 144.
147. Register of Richard Fox, bishop of Durham (1494–1501). Ed.
      M. P. Howden.
148. Chronicle of St. Mary's abbey, York. Ed. H. H. E. Craster &
      M. E. Thornton.
*149. Register of William Greenfield ... Vol. ii. See 145, 151–153.
*150. The Surtees Society 1834–1934. Including a catalogue of its
      publications ... and a list of the members. By A. Hamilton
      Thompson.
*151. Register of William Greenfield ... Vol. iii. See 145, 149, 152,
      153.
*152. Register of William Greenfield ... Vol. iv. See 145, 149, 151,
      153.
*153. Register of William Greenfield ... Vol. v. See 145, 149, 151, 152.
154. Poems of John of Hoveden. Ed. F. J. E. Raby.
155. Durham annals and documents of the thirteenth century. Ed.
      F. Barlow.
156. Autobiographies and letters of Thomas Comber, sometime
      precentor of York and dean of Durham. Vol. i. Ed. C. E. Whiting.
      See 157.

157. Autobiographies and letters of Thomas Comber ... Vol. ii. See 156.

158–159. Northumbrian pleas from *De Banco* rolls 1–37 (1–8 Edward I). Ed. A. Hamilton Thompson.

160. Durham civic memorials [1602–1666]. Ed. C. E. Whiting.

*161. Registers of Cuthbert Tunstall, bishop of Durham (1530–1559), and of James Pilkington, bishop of Durham (1561–1576). Ed. G. Hinde.

*162. Records of Antony Bek, bishop and patriarch (1283–1311). Ed. C. M. Fraser.

163. Estate accounts of the earls of Northumberland, 1562–1637. Ed. M. E. James.

164. Register of Thomas Langley, bishop of Durham, 1406–37. Vol. i. Ed. R. L. Storey. See 166, 169, 170, 177, 182.

*165. Letters of Spencer Cowper, dean of Durham (1746–1774). Ed. E. Hughes.

166. Register of Thomas Langley ... Vol. ii. See 164, 169, 170, 177, 182.

*167. Lawbook of the Crowley Ironworks. Ed. M. W. Flinn.

*168. Naworth estate and household accounts, 1648–1660. Ed. C. R. Hudleston.

*169. Register of Thomas Langley ... Vol. iii. See 164, 166, 170, 177, 182.

170. Register of Thomas Langley ... Vol. iv. See 164, 166, 169, 177, 182.

171. Diaries and correspondence of James Losh. Vol. i: Diary, 1811–1823. Ed. E. Hughes. See 174.

172. Clifford letters of the sixteenth century. Ed. A. G. Dickens.

*173. Durham recusants' estates, 1717–1778. Part i. Ed. C. R. Hudleston. See 175.

174. Diaries and correspondence of James Losh. Vol. ii: Diary, 1824–1833; letters to Charles, 2nd earl Grey, and Henry Brougham. See 171.

*175. *Miscellanea* Vol. iii: Durham recusants' estates, Part ii; Durham entries on the recusants' roll, 1636–1637. Ed. C. R. Hudleston; A. M. C. Forster. See 173.

176. Ancient petitions relating to Northumberland. Ed. C. M. Fraser. Cf. 194.

177. Register of Thomas Langley ... Vol. v. See 164, 166, 169, 170, 182.

*178.   Correspondence of Sir James Clavering. Ed. H. T. Dickinson.

179.   Durham episcopal charters, 1071–1152. Ed. H. S. Offler.

*180.   Disbursements book (1691–1709) of Sir Thomas Haggerston. Ed. A. M. C. Forster.

*181.   Records of the company of shipwrights of Newcastle upon Tyne, 1622–1967. Vol. i. Ed. D. J. Rowe. See 184.

*182.   Register of Thomas Langley ... Vol. vi. See 164, 166, 169, 170, 177.

*183.   Parliamentary surveys of the bishopric of Durham. Vol. i. Ed. D. A. Kirby. See 185.

*184.   Records of the company of shipwrights of Newcastle upon Tyne, 1622–1967. Vol. ii. See 181.

*185.   Parliamentary surveys of the bishopric of Durham. Vol. ii. See 183.

*186.   York Memorandum Book [B/Y]. Vol. iii. Ed. J. W. Percy. See 120, 125.

*187.   Royal visitation of 1559: act book for the Northern province. Ed. C. J. Kitching.

*188.   Lonsdale Documents [1797–1804]. Ed. E. Playne & G. de Boer.

*189.   Commercial papers of Sir Christopher Lowther, 1611–1644. Ed. D. R. Hainsworth.

*190.   Meditations of Lady Elizabeth Delaval, 1662–1671. Ed. D. G. Greene.

*191.   Lowther family estate papers, 1617–1675. Ed. C. B. Phillips.

*192.   York City chamberlains' account rolls, 1396–1500. Ed. R. B. Dobson.

*193.   A seventeenth century flora of Cumbria. Ed. E. J. Whittaker.

*194.   Northern petitions ... in the fourteenth century. Ed. C. M. Fraser. Cf. 176.

*195.   Diary of John Young, Sunderland chemist and Methodist lay preacher, 1841–1843. Ed. G. E. Milburn.

*196.   Songs from the manuscript collection of John Bell [d. 1864]. Ed. D. I. Harker with F. Rutherford.

*197.   Letters of Henry Liddell to William Cotesworth [1708–17]. Ed. J. M. Ellis.

*198.   Durham cathedral priory rentals I: bursar's rentals. Ed. R. A. Lomas & A. J. Piper.

*199.   Durham quarter sessions rolls 1471 – 1625. Ed. C. M. Fraser with K. Emsley.

*200.   Raine miscellany. Ed. A. Marsden.